MW00676189

Love your Muslim neighbour

Understanding Islam in today's world

© Day One Publications 2006

First published as *To Love A Muslim* by Grace Publications, 1988 ISBN 0 946462 15 1

Revised August 2005

ISBN 1-84625-009-9

9 781846 250095 >

All Scripture quotations, unless otherwise indicated, are taken from
the **New King James Version**®. Copyright © 1982 by Thomas Nelson, Inc.
Used by permission. All rights reserved.
All references from the Qur'an are taken from N.J. Dawood's translation
(*The Koran*, Penguin Classics) unless otherwise stated.
Internet sites quoted were accessed between 1 and 15 August 2004, unless otherwise stated.
British Library Cataloguing in Publication Data available

Published by Day One Publications
Ryelands Road, Leominster, HR6 8NZ
☎ 01568 613 740 FAX 01568 611 473
email—sales@dayone.co.uk
web site—www.dayone.co.uk
North American—e-mail—sales@dayonebookstore.com
North American—web site—www.dayonebookstore.com

All rights reserved
No part of this publication may be reproduced, or stored in a retrieval system, or
transmitted, in any form or by any means, mechanical, electronic, photocopying,
recording or otherwise, without the prior permission of Day One Publications.

Designed by Steve Devane and printed by Gutenberg Press, Malta

Contents

Contents

Contents

Contents

Back in 1986 I was invited to give lectures under the title 'Facing the Muslim: Are We?' through the auspices of the SW District of the Metropolitan Association of Strict Baptist Churches (now known as the Association of Grace Baptist Churches (South East)). Afterwards a request was made that the lectures be reproduced as a book, and *To Love A Muslim* was published. Now, some nineteen years later, I have sought to address important issues that have come to our attention in recent years. I have also intended that the book may be useful as a serious introduction to the world of Islam.

The first two sections generally follow the pattern of the lectures, but have been substantially revised and expanded.

Part 1 deals with the religion of Islam as it presents itself. Any critical comment on Muslim beliefs and understanding is intentionally avoided. It is all too easy to cloud the issues and to perpetuate misunderstanding. It is assumed that readers are able to make their own value judgements and compare their own spiritual convictions with what they read.

Part 2 is a survey of the history of the British Muslim scene and its influence today. I hope that this proves helpful as Islam is making so much more impact on our lives today.

Part 3 is an assessment of the impact of Islam on women. This is an important consideration, especially in the light of the generally negative press they receive, that is born more of ignorance than knowledge.

Part 4 is devoted to an application of the gospel of the Lord Jesus Christ. I have attempted to show how it is possible to take the gospel of the Lord Jesus Christ to the Muslim. But remember, this is not the last word—only a contribution. The great need is not merely to acknowledge the opportunities. We must consider practical perspectives concerning the witness of the gospel. We have to overcome any negative feelings or ideas with respect to Islam, to deal with our own culturally-dictated sense of despair of being able to reach out to Muslims, and to face all the sensitive issues with a rich biblical understanding together with spiritual strength.

I firmly believe, and strongly uphold, those standards of biblical truth that are commonly termed the doctrines of grace. I believe these reflect the true teaching of the Bible—the revealed Word of God. I believe that there has been precious little serious application of this theological outlook to mission in general, but in particular to the challenge that the religion of Islam brings to us. I am firmly convinced that such an obvious deficiency needs to be both recognized and adequately dealt with. Perhaps this publication may help many faithful Christians to face the prospect of Islam with the boldness and confidence that a confident faith in the Word of God gives us, derived from a position of spiritual strength and deep conviction in the truths God himself has shared with us.

Edward Challen
Parkstone, Poole
October 2005

Appreciation

Serving the Lord in an Asian country gave many new insights and opportunities. While sharing the gospel, it was a privilege to learn from the people among whom we lived. I am very grateful to the Lord for giving this wonderful opportunity.

Among those who have been a support over the years, I thank Dr Phil Parshall for his leadership, friendship and encouragement, and other members of the team among whom I served. Thanks also to David Kingdon who encouraged the revision *To Love A Muslim*, contributing useful ideas, and Paul Simpson for his suggestions. Others include my wife Monica for her support and patience, Ron and Muriel Barnett and Solomon Nathaniel for checking the manuscript and enthusing over it, and everyone else who has helped put it together.

The book is a team effort. If it can be useful in the Lord's work, then that is all that matters. May the Lord continue touching hearts with his love and mercy, and add to the church those whom he will save.

The Muslim world
Introduction

We live in an outstandingly enlightened age. Knowledge is available on a scale never before experienced. We are extremely privileged to have the opportunities that are so readily available.

But with respect to the Muslim, what Islam teaches, and how Muslims live, we remain painfully ignorant. Many Christians in the western world seem to know very little of what Islam stands for, or what Muslims really believe. Nor do they really seem all that concerned. This is a sad indictment against the church—for did not the Lord Jesus Christ commission his church to take the gospel of grace to all people without distinction? We live in a cosmopolitan society in the UK. Immigrants from many nations have been coming into this country for many years. Are we as burdened to reach these unreached peoples as we claim to be? A great proportion of them are Muslims from Asia, Africa, the Middle East and Eastern Europe.

Recent history has made us more aware of the Muslim world. Many now see all Muslims as potential terrorists, reinforced in this view by events such as '9/11' in the USA, and subsequent wars against terrorism in Afghanistan and Iraq.

Many Muslims who have come from the Middle East and Asia and settled in Western countries are understandably objecting to the idea that all Muslims are extremists and terrorists. They claim to be peace-loving and tolerant, and that terrorism is not the real teaching of Islam. But on the other hand, it also seems that many who live in Muslim countries have been praising the terrorists' efforts, and see the results of their activity as their arch-enemy, the Christian West, getting its due. How do we balance these two claims?

We have a very complex picture emerging today in the Muslim scene. If we want to win Muslims for Christ then we must understand these people. We have to learn what the Qur'an, their holy book, has to say. We have to assess Muslim claims for their faith—and for their way of life—carefully.

The Muslim World
Most of the World's 1.2 billion Muslims are found in the Middle East, in Northern Africa, and in Asia. Young people from Islamic countries now form the largest group of international students in North America.

The first Mosque in the United States was built in Cedar Rapids, Iowa, shortly after the turn of the century. Also in Cedar Rapids is the first exclusively Muslim burial ground in the USA.

Canada's first mosque, Al Rashid, was constructed in Edmonton, Alberta in 1938.

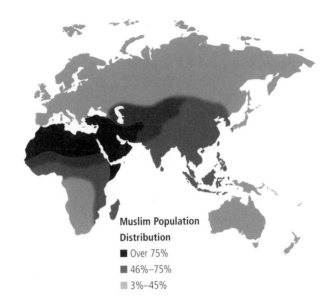

Muslim Population Distribution
■ Over 75%
■ 46%–75%
▨ 3%–45%

We have to listen to Muslims, to what they are really saying, and not what we think they ought to be saying! We also need to recognize that Muslims are going to be deeply suspicious about our motives and purpose when it becomes obvious that we show an interest in them and in what they believe. So we have to exercise great care, and approach Muslims with sensitivity and consideration.

Unfortunately, there is a very long-standing and deep-rooted intolerance and resentment against Muslims among Christians in this country. This is an attitude that has been perpetuated through successive generations. It could be claimed to be a hangover from the twelfth century Crusades.[1] A deep-seated suspicion of Muslims and a bias against them is still being maintained—even through contemporary books on church history.

Muslims strongly maintain that Mohammed was only the channel by which Allah brought them to know his will. The Qur'an, which for them encapsulates the will of Allah, was given to them through Mohammed, showing how mankind is to live before him. Mohammed is thus said to have only 'received' the revelation, being the channel by whom Allah chose to reveal it. But many well-intentioned people in the West, Christians included, describe Muslims as Mohammedans. The use of this term, and the associated use of the term 'Mohammedanism', gives great offence to Muslims. We neither win their respect or confidence by using it.

The reason why using such a term is so offensive is that Muslims do not consider they worship Mohammed. Worship is directed to Allah and him alone. Mohammed is simply respected as the one whom Allah chose, and used, to bring their attention to his will.

In our desire to 'preach the gospel to all the nations' we have a responsibility to take care how we refer to those who adhere to Islam. This is not a matter of indifference; it is vitally important for us to have a right attitude. On the other hand, we must take great care to have a balanced approach.[2] We cannot accept the claims that Muslims make concerning Mohammed without exercising some degree of discernment. Let us therefore seek to be objective in our approach. We must try to assess the real situation as it presents itself in Islam, and consider how we may address the problems it presents to us as Christians.

This book is not simply a case of attempting to paint a better picture of the situation—or to rewrite history. Rather, it is an honest and open-minded attempt to discover what Muslims really do believe, so that we as Christians may be better equipped to present the glorious claims of Christ to Muslims.

We may also consider the situation from another perspective. What does a Muslim see when he looks at us? Is he endeared to us as those who are willing to listen to his heartfelt needs with a measure of understanding? Or does he see us as a threat because of all that he misunderstands about us and our motives and our faith?

One missionary who works among these people records the following incident that took place in a restaurant in Washington, DC, USA.

'Why don't Christians follow the way of Jesus?' a Muslim asked. I was dining with a close friend, a Muslim, when he leaned close and asked that disturbing question. He continued slowly, pensively, 'When I read the gospel, I am overjoyed. The life and teachings of Jesus are wonderful, wonderful, really, truly wonderful. But please, show me Christians who are willing to follow in the sunna (way) of Jesus.' We sipped our cardamom spiced tea in reflective silence, and then he continued, 'I have met a few, very few people who try to follow Jesus. But they follow him only in their private lives. Consequently your American society has become very evil. It seems to me that you Christians really do not believe that the sunna of Jesus is practical. That makes me very sad.'3

Such a reaction would shock any Western Christian not familiar with the mind-set of a Muslim. This is a basic lesson we must learn. We must not compromise our understanding of the sovereign grace of God in order to win Muslims for Christ. Instead, we must seek to so raise the standard of our personal spiritual life and witness that Muslims and others will notice the difference in us. We surely want them to be attracted to the Saviour whom we love because he first loved us.4

This book will attempt to explain the general beliefs of Muslims, while encouraging a healthy respect for, and understanding of, biblical truth. These are both necessary for our task of reaching Muslims for Christ. To obtain a full understanding of the matters referred to, you will need an English version of the Qur'an.5

Notes

1 For an interesting and balanced view of the Crusades and the reason for them, see: **G. Riddell & Peter Cottrell,** *Islam in Conflict* (Leicester: IVP, 2002).

2 **Anne Cooper** (compiler), *Ishmael My Brother* (MARC Europe/STL/EA, 1985), pp.77–78, where a short history of Mohammed is given that gives the impression that Muslim claims are correct. It appears to claim that he received a genuine revelation 'from God' and had a genuine 'prophetic role'.

3 **David W. Shenk,** 'The Muslim Umma and the Growth of the Church', in Wilbert R. Shenk, ed., *Exploring Church Growth* (Grand Rapids: William B. Eerdmans Publishing Company, 1983), p.144.

4 1 John 4:10, 19.

5 All references from the Qur'an are taken from N.J. Dawood's translation (*The Koran,* Penguin Classics) unless otherwise stated. Note that **Mohammed M. Pickthall**'s translation, *The Meaning of the Glorious Koran*, is widely respected (see Additional Sources, p.265).

Chapter 1

The challenge of Islam

The history of the outworking of the Lord's commission to the Christian church sadly demonstrates the fact that there has been very little meaningful contact with the world of Islam. There have been wonderful but exceptional occasions when godly men have been burdened for Muslim peoples. Such outstanding men as Henry Martyn (1781–1812) and Samuel Zwemer (1867–1952) have made a considerable impression on us through their concern, passion and dedication to a difficult and unrewarding task.

It has to be said, with deep regret, that Muslim peoples have been a neglected mission field for far too long. This has been a tragedy for both the Christian church and Islam. Christians appear to have had very little to say to Muslims in any constructive sense. Great barriers of communication, and an immense prejudice against Islam, have been maintained for many years. As a result, the task of presenting the gospel to Muslims has been a somewhat weak, apologetic, and almost non-existent affair in many places.

There is no doubt that the challenge is immense. Islam constitutes a formidable opponent to the Christian faith. This problem should not be underestimated. We ought to admit that because historically the task has appeared to present so many difficulties, we have tended to formulate the word 'impossible' in our minds, if not actually on our lips. But why should this be so? It comes down to our lack of faith and vision, and this ought not to be the case.

As those who claim to believe in the great doctrines of the grace of God, are we not failing to apply them? We say that we believe in the God who is sovereign in the exercise of his authority, wisdom and power over all peoples. We must surely realize the implications of this truth and confidently assert that 'with God nothing will be impossible'.[1]

Islam is an issue that obviously faces us today. It will not go away. But what are we doing about it? Should we not admit that the prospect of coming to terms with this problem provokes a certain amount of fear in the hearts of many Christians? Yet, to not face the issue would surely diminish the importance of the missionary mandate given by the Lord Jesus Christ, and our responsibility to it. We would be undermining the explicit command he has given to us—that we are to 'Go into all the world and preach the gospel to every creature'.[2]

To ignore the challenge of Islam is to admit that we who are Bible-believing Christians doubt God's sovereign power as King of kings and Lord of lords. God's word plainly tells us that the Lord Jesus Christ faced the full wrath of God against all sin and all forms of rebellion against his majesty. He met the full force of the power of Satan and fully overpowered him. The Son of God himself overcame *all* the effects of sin; *all* the power of Satan. *Every* power that can be named was trodden under his feet. The Lord Jesus Christ *is* victorious. He is the sovereign Lord, the Redeemer and the only Saviour. It is on the basis of his triumphal conquest, his glorious work of redemption, that Christ himself now commissions us who believe. What he has achieved in principle we, by his saving grace, are to work out in practice. His conquest of the power of Satan is an accomplished eternal fact that is still being applied in space and time, through the powerful administrations of his Holy Spirit, according to his glorious will and purposes, and the outworking of his grace.

The very words of our commission are important: 'All authority has been given to Me in heaven and on earth.'[3] Here Christ's own personal declaration of his sovereign power is all the more gloriously expressed because of his completed work of salvation. As Paul asserted, the Lord is now 'declared to be the Son of God with power, according to the Spirit of holiness, by the resurrection from the dead'.[4]

It is important to notice that the apostle Paul goes on to speak emphatically about the effect that Christ's demonstration of power brings. It is through him that '... we have received grace and apostleship for obedience to the faith among all nations for his name'.[5] Paul continues to give us a further encouragement, a real stimulus to obedience, as he adds: '... among whom you also are the called of Jesus Christ'.[6]

This same power is available to us today. In the context of Muslim evangelism we make this particular application: that as we have been called by his grace, there is then no reason why he cannot call our Muslim friends also, as we all are sinners who may be called by his grace—there is no difference. The Lord sovereignly calls out his church from among all peoples. He builds his church. The gates of hell, he has promised, shall never prevail against his church.[7]

We need to affirm that we believe the gospel, for then there remains no obstacle to faith that cannot be surmounted. The gospel is the Word of God—and he has promised that his Word will not return to him void, that is, prove ineffective and without results. After his great affirmation of his belief in the power and sovereignty of Christ, Paul was also able to say, 'I am not ashamed of the gospel of Christ, for it is the power of God to salvation for everyone who believes.'[8] Paul then gives the reason for his being so firmly persuaded, drawing from the evidence of the gospel itself: 'For in it the righteousness of God is revealed from faith to faith; as it is written, "The just shall live by faith."'[9]

Here immediately we have an encouragement to take the gospel to the Muslim and say with humility, 'You claim to be righteous by what you do. We know the true righteousness of God which you sincerely seek. It is only to be found through faith in the Lord Jesus Christ. God has clearly said this himself in his revealed Word. Believe his Word for your salvation.'

Furthermore, the hope that is set before us gives us missionary vision. It gives us encouragement. We have been granted the privilege to share in that great vision which the apostle John was given in which he saw the Saviour, the slain Lamb of God, who reigns in heaven and continues to exercise his divine sovereign authority over every creature.[10] Who are the people John sees so vividly? The answer he receives is a clear affirmation of the Christian faith: 'a great multitude which no one could number, of all nations … standing before the throne and before the Lamb, clothed in white robes … and crying out …, "Salvation belongs to our God, who sits on the throne and to the Lamb."'[11]

No people who live on earth are to be excluded from the privileges of hearing and receiving the gospel message. Even those who once were Muslims will stand before the throne and they will also praise God. They will have come to the Father through faith in Christ. They too will be privileged to wear those white robes of Christ's own righteousness before his throne in heaven, together with us.

Notes

1 Luke 1:37.
2 Mark 16:15.
3 Matthew 28:18.
4 Romans 1:4.
5 Romans 1:5.
6 Romans 1:6.
7 Matthew 16:18.
8 Romans 1:16.
9 Romans 1:17.
10 Revelation 7:9–10.
11 Revelation 7:14.

The world of Islam

Islam entered the world in the Arabian Desert in the seventh century. Muslims consider Mecca to be the centre of the world. They see the impact of Islam on the world as being just like an earthquake in an ocean, for its shock waves have spread out from Mecca and its influence has spread all around the world.

Islam began in the two holy cities of Medina and Mecca. Mohammed was deeply concerned about moral decadence and many social problems among the Arabs of his day. Mohammed's puritanical reaction became consolidated into the religion of Islam.

History books tell us of the way a number of Arabs associated themselves with him: how they took Mecca by force and established it as the holy city; of their speedy conquests by the sword that took place after his death; of the internal bickering and argument that splintered the 'one brotherhood' into many factions. Interestingly, there is a tradition that Mohammed is alleged to have said, 'My community will divide into seventy-three sects of which only one is correct.' It is true that Islamic history has produced vastly more sectarian groupings than that traditional number. Muslims have been no less fruitful than other religious communities in multiplying internal divisions.

From the Saudi Peninsula, Islam spread west into North Africa and up into Spain. It spread northwards throughout the Middle East, through Palestine, up into Turkey and into Eastern and Central Europe. It spread eastwards through Persia and Afghanistan into many parts of India. It travelled via trade routes, reaching into China, Thailand, Malaysia, Indonesia, and the Philippines. In modern times its message has reached many African countries. More recently, as a result of immigration, there are now some 16 million Muslims in European countries. In the United Kingdom we now have over 1.5 million Muslims. Most of them have come from Pakistan, India and Bangladesh, together with an influential business population from Middle Eastern countries. In the United States, Islam is the third largest religious group with some 9.7 million adherents.

Worldwide there are about 1.5 billion Muslims—some 25% of the world's population. The countries with the greatest Muslim populations are Indonesia (201 million), Pakistan (140 million), Bangladesh (109 million) and China (76 million), which together constitute about 35% of the Muslim world population.[1]

Islamic numerical strength continues to grow, but it must be borne in mind that this is still overwhelmingly due to biological increase. It is said that in Britain 20,000 converts have come from the Anglo-Saxon population. These are mostly from middle-class backgrounds, and between 30 and 50 years of age, though younger Muslims point to conversions among students, highlighting the intellectual thrust of Islam. What is also significant is that two-thirds of these converts are women, especially in view of the way the West perceives Muslim women as down-trodden and despised. One convert to Islam, a graduate of St Anne's College, Oxford, claimed that Western feminism has robbed women of their rights, and she now feels liberated in Islam.[2]

London mosques have been reporting an increase in the number of converts to Islam, especially since the 9/11 attacks on America. Apparently, most of them were introduced to Islam by friends. Given that Islam is not generally considered to be a missionary faith, these were gentle personal introductions. For most of those reported to have become Muslims, conversion was born of curiosity, as an attempt to better understand the people around them. There is no doubt that some of the interest is sparked off by a disillusionment of life in the UK today. What is apparently attractive about Islam is its openness and lack of hierarchy. Some have suggested that there is generally an endemic suspicion of stuffy organized religion among the British, and yet there is great interest in 'spirituality'—whatever that might mean—and Islam seems to be meeting this need for some.

During the past sixty years Middle-Eastern Muslim countries have been pleased to realize that they have control over substantial amounts of the world's oil reserves. We have to understand that this awareness of economic power has gone hand in hand with a resurgence of a far more militant, fundamental form of Islam than has been seen for many a long day. The increasing presence of Muslims in the West has also brought added sophistication and sense of importance. Many Muslims are actively seeking to infiltrate western society by making their presence felt in the realms of education and politics, pressing, at the very minimum, for accommodation to their views, beliefs and values. On top of this, refugees from many Muslim countries, both exiles and economic migrants, have come seeking a better life.

That the Islamic world has been making a significant impact on recent history is obvious. There has been a resurgence of religious fanaticism in the twentieth century, as witnessed in Iran, Libya, the Palestine/Israeli conflict, and the Al-Qa'ida movement. Many countries in the Middle East and Asia are busy consolidating the place of Islam within their culture. We have also seen how it has affected economic and political stability in Central African countries.

Where did all this begin? To answer this question and also to understand something of the character of Islam, we need to look briefly at the life and circumstances of Mohammed, the prophet of Islam.

Mohammed[3] was born at Mecca in the year AD 570. His father's tribe was that of the Quraysh, who made strong claims to being direct descendants of Ishmael (the son of Abraham by Hagar, his wife Sarah's Egyptian maidservant). Mohammed's father died before Mohammed was born, and he was orphaned by his mother's death when he was only six. He was subsequently brought up in difficult circumstances by his uncle, Abu Talib. When he was old enough to work, the wealthy widow Khadijah employed him, and having noted his personal integrity she eventually put him in charge of her camel caravans. Later, when he was twenty-five years old, she rewarded him for his fidelity and business aptitude by marrying him. As he undertook this business, he was constantly coming into contact with both Jews and Christians—though the latter, very sadly, were unorthodox Syrian Nestorians and Monophysites.[4]

Through his marriage to Khadijah, Mohammed became a person of some considerable influence among his fellow countrymen. He earned a great measure of respect. As a result he was able to leave his business at times to those under his authority, enabling him to find time for serious meditation. It appears (contrary to the opinions of many critics) that he was no villain, nor did he act in any underhand way. He was well-liked and courteous. He was both eloquent and correct in his use of language. He was firm and prompt in making decisions. He was considered very faithful and generous to his workers, followers and friends.

When he reached the age of about forty, he became deeply troubled about religious issues. This was brought on through considering both the general attitudes of his people and their way of life, which were far from exemplary. So he began to withdraw frequently to a remote place, a cave on the slopes of Mount Hira, situated some three miles from Mecca, known particularly for its barrenness.

The Arabs at this time, as he noted, were very superstitious and idolatrous, worshipping heavenly bodies and stones, particularly venerating a Black Stone in the Ka'aba (a temple in Mecca). Therefore Mohammed's development of Islam should be understood in terms of a reaction to the idolatry and moral excesses of his day.

During his meditations on Mount Hira, Mohammed experienced trances, and an external power appeared to take hold of him. He discovered that he was able to express himself in eloquent and forceful language. On one particular occasion he claimed that he saw a vision of the angel Gabriel who commanded him to recite certain passages. At first he refused, but eventually complied.

Thus he learnt passages which he then recited to family and friends. The first that he claimed was transmitted to him was this: 'Recite in the name of your Lord who created, created man from drops of blood. Recite! Your Lord is the Most Bountiful One, who by the pen taught man what he did not know.'[5]

Mohammed continued to have visions, and the complete record of what are claimed to be his revelations now comprises the book that is known as the *Qur'an*, meaning 'recital'.

The resulting history of how Mohammed took Mecca from those he considered unbelievers and idolaters, and all the subsequent records, much of which we would consider very unsavoury and bloodthirsty, can be read from the various histories available.[6]

Much of the way that we see Muslims conduct themselves in many parts of the world today can be traced to the attitudes and actions of both Mohammed and his early followers. Some of it, however, must be understood not only in the light of Muslim teaching and attitudes, but also as a reflection of the temperament and culture of those who live in Middle Eastern countries, particularly ethnic Arabs.

The Muslim world is certainly complex. Many fixed attitudes and prejudices must be faced up to if we are going to undertake the task of presenting our gospel message seriously, and many problems need to be dealt with; but we will get nowhere if we do not make a serious attempt to understand the people who call themselves Muslims.

Notes

1 Statistics from the World Factbook 2002 internet site: www.cia.gov/cia/publications/factbook/fields/2122.html

2 *The Daily Telegraph:* www.telegraph.co.uk/news/main.jhtml?xml=/news/2001/12/30/nmus330.xml. Article: 'My dad buys me books about Islam' 30.12.2001, ¶21–23. See also Part 3: 'Women in Islam'.

3 Please be aware that because the Arabic character set is radically different from Latin characters it is difficult to transliterate Islamic words into English. Hence there are going to be different spellings of Islamic words and names from different sources. If you are searching for a subject on the internet, for example, it is worth putting in variations on a word.

4 Nestorians and Monophysites held unorthodox views concerning the person of the Lord Jesus Christ. Neither group could understand how Christ could be both fully human and fully divine—thus having two natures in one person. The Nestorians held that there were two distinct persons in the incarnate Christ, the divine and the human. They did not affirm the divinity of the man Christ Jesus. The Monophysites went to the opposite extreme, holding that Christ had only one nature, namely the divine. Both undermined the true humanity of Christ.

5 Sura 96:1–2.

6 See Additional Sources, p.265.

Who are the Muslims?

Muslims[1] are members of a community of people who hold to a system of religious teaching called 'Islam'. The word *Muslim* is an Arabic word, being the adjectival form of the noun *Islam*. Islam means 'submission': the surrendering of the complete person to Allah. It also carries the idea that one must accept Allah's will and be obedient to it.

Muslims consider that Islam is concerned with the direction provided by Allah for all mankind. Its principles guide and govern every aspect of individual and corporate living. The word *Islam* is strongly associated with the idea of 'peace' and it carries that connotation because this is the anticipated and assumed result of being totally surrendered to the law of Allah, and to Muslims it is the only true religion.[2]

Another definition seeks to give a greater appreciation of its meaning by referring to a root word *salama*, which can mean 'peace', 'surrender' and similar words.[3]

The term 'Islam' is derived from the Arabic root (SLM) which connotes 'peace' or 'submission'. Indeed, the proper meaning of 'Islam' is the attainment of peace, both inner and outer peace, by submission of oneself to the Will of God. And when we say submit, we are talking about conscious, loving and trusting submission to the Will of God, the acceptance of his grace, and the following of his path. In that sense, the Muslim regards the term Islam, not as an innovation that came in the 7th Century, Christian era, with the advent of Prophet Muhammad, but as the basic mission of all the Prophets throughout history (Noah, Abraham, Moses, Jesus, etc.). That universal mission was finally culminated and perfected in the last of these Prophets, Prophet Muhammad, peace be upon them all.[4]

so is Christianity = mutually exclusive

Islam is not seen as merely a religion, but a complete way of life. Muslims do not accept that Islam is one religion among many. The Qur'an states: 'The only true faith in Allah's sight is Islam.'[5] These comments show that Islam is universal, and did not start in the time of Mohammed, for the Old Testament prophets and our Lord Jesus were sent on the same mission, understood to be completed by Mohammed.

Thus Islam is a doctrine with universal application. Adam is considered to be the first Muslim. It is believed that the core message of the prophets and the messengers, from Adam through to Mohammed, is the same—i.e. obedience to Allah alone and submission to his law. The earlier messages had been sent to certain people only, and with time they had become distorted. Therefore Islam, as presented to the world by Mohammed, is understood to be the one universal and final religion, for it is the perfection of all that Allah originally meant religion to be.[6]

Because this concept is all-inclusive, Muslims never consider themselves as persons having individual responsibility. First and foremost they are members of a brotherhood, the *ummah*, a worldwide *community of believers*, who co-operate together in living for the glory of Allah. All that a Muslim does, he does corporately with other Muslims, and he will point to the testimony of the Qur'an:

Cling (hold fast) one and all to the faith of Allah and let nothing divide you. Remember the favours He has bestowed upon you: how He united your hearts when you were enemies, so that you are now brothers through His grace; and how He delivered you from the abyss of fire when you were on the brink of it. Thus Allah makes plain to you His revelations, so that you may be rightly guided.[7]

Muslims point out with pride the claim that their scriptures testify that they are the 'best community'. That same verse also gives a reason for this: 'You are the noblest nation that has ever been raised up for mankind. You enjoin justice and forbid evil. You believe in Allah.'[8]

The *ummah* establishes a sense of solidarity among Muslims. It brings a sense of belonging, that nothing must be allowed to spoil, bringing with it a sense of spiritual kinship that is much more than any sense of individual freedom.

Three virtues establish the faithful as Muslims: (i) correct conduct and right attitude, (ii) the forbidding of indecency, and (iii) belief in Allah. These criteria are not often referred to by Muslims directly, but the Qur'anic statement stands as a sociological reality which has the effect of bonding Muslims together, for the *ummah* is a mystical rather than physically defined community. Muslims consider that the links that join this community together are sealed for ever. The commands of the Qur'an summon up a keen sense of responsibility to the community, and instil a fear of breaking its bonds.

The concept of *ummah* is very important to Muslims who believe that their community has been raised up for the good of mankind; *ummah* is seen to be a model of righteousness. Therefore it is not only unforgivable, but incomprehensible to the Muslim mind that anyone should break away from Islam.

The strength of this idea of community is founded on the consideration that Allah[9] is the master designer and creator of the human race. He has formed those whom he created into social structures. Allah's purpose is clearly defined as creating a society in which all may come to recognize each other, and have a sense of belonging. As it is expressed in the Qur'an: 'Men, We [NB: the plural is used of Allah to denote great honour and respect] have created you from a male and a female and divided you into nations and tribes that you might get to know one another. The noblest of you in Allah's sight is he who fears Him most.'[10]

Muslims tenaciously hold on to the idea of community as a loosely knit brotherhood. Christians are used to such an idea, for the apostle Paul advocates the concept that all believers are members of one another in Christ.[11] Christians are encouraged to see themselves as members of one body or community, whose different members have differing gifts. The comparison is not absolute. As Christians we emphasize that we are building a spiritual house[12] and the spiritual body of Christ has a physical expression in the practical fellowship of local churches. This is different from the Islamic outlook that seeks for a physical identity, rather than a spiritual. They emphasize a social expression for their unity.

The Hadith (*ahadith*, Books of the Traditions of Islam, the sayings of Mohammed)[13] and the *sunnah* (examples from the life of Mohammed)[14] add another dimension to the idea of community—that of condemning racial prejudice while insisting on the primary importance of piety. The whole of mankind is to be embraced together without any distinction regarding colour or cultural differences. No difference can be recognized among the nations as they pray together before the one Allah. (This does not always work in practice, but that is the principle.)

What is the cement that holds this community together and how may we identify it? It is the bond of faith that must be seen as the integrating force behind the movement. This is the stimulus that brings together tribes and nations that are seemingly poles apart in every other way. Islam is one of the most theocentric religions of the world. Muslims are not worshippers of Mohammed, but only of Allah. They believe that Mohammed was merely the favoured vehicle of Allah's final revelation to mankind. Faith, to the Muslim, is the practical application of the principles of Islam to everyday life. It is expressed by their applied commitment to those principles (see chapter 4), through a meticulous observance of the legal requirements. There is an explicit trust, not in a person (as for the Christian), but in a system, with the unassured hope that a dedicated practice of all that the faith embodies may merit Allah's approval and acceptance for paradise. The Muslim considers such faith to be 'saving' faith, in that commitment and obedience expressed as good works is putting faith into practice and thus merits salvation. Their idea of salvation is understood, not as forgiveness of personal sinfulness, but that for an individual believer their good deeds outweigh their bad deeds.

An important question we must ask is, 'How does this faith express itself in practice?' One commentary on Islam answers it in this way:

Islamic Law governs (more or less) the worship, the belief, the customs, the trade, and even the politics. Everyone adopts a certain style of politeness and cleanliness, everyone has an Arabic name, everyone joins in the fast and festivals, and often everyone wears the same style of clothes: all these things show the solidarity of the community.[15]

This concept of solidarity is very important to grasp. It is the essence of Islam and pervades every aspect of life, so that the identity of an individual is always a secondary issue (if indeed it is ever considered!). This concept represents the greatest challenge that stands before us in our desire to win Muslims for Christ. Providentially, we discover through observation and experience that there is real inconsistency in the practice of Islam. But there is no room for complacency. If we are to face up to Islam then we must recognize the formidable presence of its community spirit.

Many people are drawn to Islam because they see in it a faith that gives believers a sense of security. The fact that there are strict, absolute rules, that there are specific practices to hold on to, that it is a system which appears to stand up to any test of logic and which unites people together, is appealing. Islam has intellectual, devotional and cultural significance. It appears to make sense of the world and give direction for life. The very strictness of Islam is one of its strengths. Its claim to being unquestionable truth attracts.

Notes

1 *Mussalman* is the Arabic term, and Muslims often use this word.
2 **Abu Ameenah Bilal Philips:** www.islamworld.net/true.html. Article: 'The True Religion'.
3 IslamicOccasions: www.ezsoftech.com/akram/meaningofislam.asp. Article: 'Meaning of Islam', 1¶.
4 *Fellowship of Ahl-ul-Bayt Islamic Organization*, Michigan, USA: www.fabonline.com. Article: 'Meaning of "Islam"'.
5 Sura 3:19.
6 **Abul A'la Mawdudi**, *Towards Understanding Islam* (Islamic Foundation, 1981), p.18.
7 Sura 3: 103–105.
8 Sura 3:110.
9 For a definition of Allah, see chapter 6: i. 'Belief in one God', p.50. We use the name Allah as the Muslim name for God, as it includes all that Islam teaches about him, which is different from a true Christian understanding of Almighty God, the Father of our Lord Jesus Christ.
10 Sura 49:13.
11 1 Corinthians 12:12–27.
12 1 Peter 2:5.
13 The *hadith* are an authoritative record of the utterances, actions or indirect approval (of an act) by Rasulullah (Mohammed) that affect the way a Muslim lives. They are second in importance to the Qur'an. There are several approved *ahadith* recorded by different followers of Mohammed (often referred to as Companions of the Prophet) who recorded what they heard him say and do.
14 The *sunnah* is the basis of the legal code of Islamic jurisprudence (*shari'ah*), depicting authoritative events in the life of Mohammed, and are compiled together with the *ahadith*.
15 *Christian Witness Among Muslims* (Africa Christian Press, 1971), p.78.

The expressions of community

What makes Islam so unique is the manner in which its doctrinal practices, known as the *Pillars of Islam*, influence the community. They are in fact expressions of *faith*, not simply practices. For in Islam faith and good works go hand in hand.[1]

These 'Five Pillars' consist of mandatory demands, or statutory obligations, that are imposed upon every Muslim. Thus there is a great emphasis placed upon them, and they are covered by detailed regulations. The five specific duties are detailed in the Qur'an. All the elaborate rules, or laws, that surround them are laid down in the large body of Traditions. These Traditions are the *ahadith* (or *hadith*)—recorded oral reports that have been passed on by contemporaries of the prophet Mohammed, describing various aspects of his life and thought. Muslims like to call these five pillars on which Islam stands their 'articles of faith'.

i. *Shahada*: the Confession, or Witness

la ilaha illa Llah, Muhammadun rasulu'Llah.

These seven Arabic words are reputedly the shortest creed in the world. This creed is certainly repeated more than any other.

There is no god but Allah, and Mohammed is the Apostle (Messenger/Prophet) of God.

Many Muslims express it in English as 'There is no god worthy of worship except Allah and Mohammad is his messenger'. The emphasis is on the idea that there is nothing or no one who may be worshipped apart from Allah, and that this message of  guidance has come through a man like us. 'To bear witness that there is none worthy of worship except Allah, and that Muhammad is his messenger to all human beings till the Day of Judgement. The prophethood of Muhammad obliges the Muslims to follow his exemplary life as a model.'²

The *shahada* is important in that its recital is the method of ascertaining whether a person is a Muslim. It is thus the method of admission to the community. Its recital in Arabic is the means of becoming a Muslim, by repeating these words in front of a judge, or two public witnesses. It is also continually used by Muslims in their prayers, and at countless other times in the day. It is even used as a battle cry; and by contrast, as an exclamation of joy at the birth of a baby. It is whispered into the ear of a deceased person at death, and heard as an incessant dirge at a funeral.

ii. *Salat:* Prayer

It is obvious to any observer that prayer has an important place in Muslim life. Many images representing Islam consist of a mosque with rows of worshippers lined up performing a prayer ritual.

The obligatory prayers are performed five times a day. However, before prayer can be performed, a Muslim must be ceremonially clean. So he first washes in the prescribed way to ensure 'spiritual purity' (*wudu*). Here is at least a recognition that he is coming before one who is altogether holy. He then has to pray a prayer of intention. This is to recognize the need to apply both mind and heart to the intended purpose, before such activity can be meaningful or meritorious. This is also the case before each statutory duty is performed.

Prayers are carried out barefoot on a clean floor or rug and consist of a set cycle of words and ritual gestures (each cycle being known as a *rak'ah*.³ The number of cycles completed depends on which prayer of the day it is. Muslims are called to prayer five times a day: at dawn, soon after mid-day, two hours before sunset, immediately after sunset, and two hours after sunset. The call to prayer, the *Adhan*, goes out from the mosque to remind the faithful that *Allahu Akbar:* 'Allah is most great.' It incorporates the witness, the *shahada*, and the dawn call also includes the injunction that *'prayer is better than sleep'*. Prayer is always performed towards Mecca, corporately, and theoretically with no distinction of class. Muslims proudly claim that the beggar stands shoulder to shoulder with the respectable classes.

Prayer stimulates oneness in the community. It gives an identity with that community. Prayer is the expression of the unity of faith, of the purpose of Islam, and a public declaration of the community itself.

iii. *Zakat*: Almsgiving

The word *zakat* means 'purification' and also includes the idea of 'growth'.4

In practice *zakat* takes the form of a compulsory payment, and is distinct from charity. It is an obligatory tax of some 2.5% on possessions in five categories of property, rather than on income: (1) food grains; (2) fruit; (3) camels, cattle, sheep and goats; (4) gold and silver; and (5) movable goods. The tax is payable each year after one year's possession. The proceeds are normally collected at the mosque, to be distributed to the poor, usually on Fridays. True free-will almsgiving is also encouraged over and above this statutory requirement.

The Qur'an specifies those who are to be the beneficiaries of this tax: 'Alms are to be used only for the advancement of Allah's cause, for the ransom of captives and debtors, and for distribution among the poor, the destitute, the wayfarers, those that are employed in collecting alms, and those that are converted to the faith. That is a duty enjoined by Allah. He is wise and all-knowing.'5

All property is considered to be on loan from Allah and not 'personal property'. Wealth and property ownership are privileges and on trust from Allah. All material possessions are to be used for Allah's purposes among the community. The concept of the self-possession of goods is considered a 'sin' against (or perhaps affront to) both Allah and the community.6 Here we see the community concern evidenced.

Zakat tangibly expresses the sense of responsibility that Muslims ought to have to one another, and especially to the less fortunate within the community.

iv. *Sawm*: Fasting

There is a regulation that states that fasting is decreed for all Muslims who are in good health above the age of thirteen for girls and the age of fourteen for boys. This obligation is to be honoured on several specified occasions, the most important being the celebrated month of *Ramadan*—the ninth month of the Muslim lunar calendar. This is the month during which the Qur'an is believed to have been revealed to the prophet Mohammed, and often the whole of the Qur'an is read by Muslims through the month. During this month it is claimed that the gates of paradise are opened, and those of hell are closed. It is believed that all Muslims who fast meticulously will be pardoned for their past venial (i.e., excusable) sins. The last ten days of the month are claimed to have special blessings, and the twenty-seventh night is the most holy night of the most holy month, called the Night of Power (*Lailat ul-Qadr*). On this night Muslims commemorate Mohammed's receiving of the first verses of the Qur'an, the night that is 'better than a thousand months'.

The Qur'anic injunction for fasting is 'Believers, fasting is decreed for you as it was decreed for those before you; perchance you will guard yourselves against evil. Fasting is prescribed for you as it was prescribed to those before you that you may learn self-restraint.'7

Fasting is thus seen as to have both a moral and practical purpose, in that it teaches 'self-restraint, self-control, self-discipline, self-obedience, self-education, and self-evaluation'.8

The Qur'anic instruction gives details of the qualifications, reasons and incentives for fasting:

Fast a certain number of days, but if any one of you is ill or on a journey let him fast a similar number of days later on; and for those that can afford it there is a ransom: the feeding of a poor man. He that does good of his own account shall be well rewarded; but to fast is better for you, if you but knew it. In the month of Ramadan the Qur'an was revealed, a book of guidance with proofs of guidance distinguishing right from wrong. Therefore whoever of you is present in that month let him fast ...

Allah desires your well-being, not your discomfort. He desires you to fast the whole month so that you may magnify Him and render thanks to Him for giving you His guidance.[9]

For the Muslim fasting is a very rigorous and demanding exercise. During the hours between sunrise and sunset nothing is to enter the body. The faithful are expected to spend as much time as possible in prayer, preferably at the mosque.

The fast is broken at night, as soon as 'a white thread becomes indistinguishable from a black one' and a 'break-fast' snack is taken. Later in the evening a large meal is consumed, if it can be afforded. This is often a most sumptuous affair, that more than makes up for what would normally be eaten during the day! Another meal is prepared at night, which is to be eaten about an hour before sunrise, in preparation for the next day's fasting.

At the close of the month of Ramadan a great celebration takes place— that of *Eid-ul-Fitr*. It is a wonderful day of great rejoicing and feasting and new clothes are often given to the children as presents. This festival is an expression of thanksgiving by the community for all Allah's blessings, especially for those obtained through the great fast.

Fasting is the collective recognition by the community of their utter dependence on Allah for every blessing, and an expression of a deep desire for personal forgiveness.

v. *Hajj*: The Pilgrimage

The annual pilgrimage to the holy city of Mecca (Makkah) is the largest multinational gathering of people on earth. There may be around 3 million people who gather, and they represent almost every ethnic group, political entity, economic stratum and skin colour known to the human race. It is considered to be tremendously exhilarating to attend, and a great spiritual blessing.

If financially feasible, every Muslim must make this Mecca pilgrimage at least once in a lifetime (more often if possible). This is the goal of all Muslims worldwide. Mecca is uniquely the Islamic holy centre. No non-Muslims are ever allowed within the city walls—immediate death is the penalty for breaking this sacred rule. This prohibition itself strengthens the concept of Muslim community.

According to Muslim tradition, Abraham was commanded to sacrifice his son Ishmael, but God provided a ram in his place. It is said that in gratitude to Allah, Abraham built a place of worship, called it *Ka'aba*, and requested that people make an annual pilgrimage to it. Since then local Arabs set up many idols in the Ka'aba, but Mohammed finally threw out the idols and restored monotheism and the pilgrimage.

The *Ka'aba* is an empty cube made of rough stones, with chalk filling the fissures, and with a black stone (*Hajr al Aswad*, usually thought to have been a meteorite) inserted into its eastern corner.[10]

The pilgrimage begins at Mecca in the eighth Muslim month *Dhul-Hijjah*. Every pilgrim has to prepare themselves mentally and spiritually for this act of ritual consecration. At every significant stage, prayers of intention are said. All the instructions are specifically detailed and include prayers at each significant moment. Each Muslim pilgrim shaves his head, washes completely (*gusl*), and subsequently wears two plain seamless white sheets of cloth (*ihram*), which leaves only his head and face uncovered. In the morning every pilgrim joins all others at the mosque in performing *umrah*—making seven walking circuits of the *Ka'aba* within the main mosque at Mecca, the Masjid-al-Haram. These circumambulations are done keeping the Ka'aba on their left, on each circuit kissing or touching the black stone in the wall. If this is not possible due to the volume of people, pilgrims should face the Black Stone and point at it.

This is followed by the ceremony of *Sa'i*, where pilgrims ascend the nearby hill of Safaa and descend towards the hill of Marwa, passing two pillars in the valley between which pilgrims move as swiftly as possible then climb to the top of Marwa. Then the procedure is repeated in reverse. Each part of this ceremony involves much praying. This ritual is to re-enact Hagar's desperate search for drinking water to give to Ishmael when she had been sent away by Sarah. Pilgrims then

find water at the well of Zamzam and take a drink, demonstrating the fulfilment of Hagar's search for water.

After noon, pilgrims make another full body wash (*gusl*) and then the pilgrims walk to Mina, where they pray and spend the night.

The next morning (day 2) the pilgrims make their way from Mina to Arafat, twelve miles from Mecca, where they spend the time from noon till night praying in the vicinity of Mount Rahmah (Mountain of Mercy), where Mohammed preached his last sermon. At sunset pilgrims travel back to Muzdalifah, which they have to reach before midnight, where they again stand to pray and meditate until sunrise. This is to honour Mohammed's standing in the community.

On day 3 they move back to Mina in the morning, to the claimed site of the sacrifice of Ishmael. There they do three things: (1) They each throw seven pebbles at Jamrah—three rock pillars that are claimed to be the largest symbol of the devil, situated

The Ka'aba

on the outskirts of Mina towards Mecca, saying 'Allah is the greatest' as they throw each pebble. Pilgrims hurl stones at each of the pillars. This is alleged to re-enact the scene when Ishmael hurled stones at Satan in his terror, to resist his temptations, when he was expecting to be sacrificed. (2) They slaughter the appropriate sacrificial animal, eating some of it, and giving some to the poor (in common with Muslims around the world)—this is the feast of *Eid-ul-Azha*. This commemorates the joyful sacrifice of the animal that Allah gave in place of Ishmael. (3) Pilgrims shave off their hair (a woman clips her hair the length of a finger tip). After these activities, pilgrims may discard their special *irham* clothing and wear ordinary clothes. Then they move back to Mecca to repeat a circumambulation of the Ka'aba. Then pilgrims return to Mina to spend the next two nights there (days 4 and 5). After noon on these days, stones are again thrown at the three Jamrah, beginning with the one farthest from Mecca, then the middle one, and lastly the Jamrah Al-Aqaba. If not in a hurry, pilgrims may stay a further night at Mina (day 6), on the afternoon of which more stone throwing takes place. To complete the ritual, pilgrims return to Mecca, and to the last circumambulation of the Ka'aba, completing seven circuits. Then they are free to go home having done the *hajj*.

Either before or after the *hajj*, pilgrims usually visit Mohammed's mosque at Medina where they pray according to a specific prayer ritual.

This pilgrimage is the focus of the realized hope of the community. Every *hajji*, as the pilgrim is known, believes that his total act of dedication in pilgrimage is the supreme means of obtaining the forgiveness of sins. Among the many traditions there is one which says that every step taken by the pilgrim in the direction of the Ka'aba blots out a sin. Also one who dies on this pilgrimage is enrolled among the martyrs and goes straight to heaven. This is why poorer Muslims often wait till they are much older before they undertake this pilgrimage. The Muslims' worldwide act of sacrifice at this time is considered to demonstrate: (i) the debt that the whole community owes to Allah, (ii) that Islam exhibits a remarkable solidarity of belief, and (iii) that the pilgrimage is itself a communal act of dedication to Allah. Though it is not officially considered to be a sacrifice for sin, or even a means of redemption, it is commonly thought to be so in practice.

The *hajj* is an affirmation of the Muslim's singleness of mind and purpose. It is designed to increase an awareness of Allah and give a sense of spiritual uplift. It is also believed to be an opportunity to seek forgiveness for those sins a Muslim accumulates through his life (one reason why the *hajj* is often performed by older men and women) Mohammed's claim was that a person who performs the *hajj* properly 'will return as a newborn baby', that is free of all sins.[11] The *hajj* is a representation of what is required to get to heaven: hard work, meditation, and the mercy of Allah. The logic then is that if a pilgrim dies on performing *hajj*, he or she will go directly to heaven, with their sins forgiven.

This is one Muslim's personal view of the pilgrimage.

The social significance of the Hajj is a glorious testimony of the social equality and universal brotherhood of Islam. Dressed in two white pieces of cloth men and women of different countries of the Muslim world; ... assemble together at Ka'aba testifying ... to the unity of Allah and also glorifying him and expressing their gratitude in him in the same breath at the top of their voices. They stand shoulder to shoulder as no distinction exists between the rich and poor, high and low. They are all humble creatures of Allah forming one fraternity of true believers. … Such a spectacle of social equality and brotherhood is nowhere to be seen in the world.[12]

This demonstration of the brotherhood of Islam is the public expression of the *ummah*. Where these expressions of community are seen, this is the evidence of the faith of the community that is seeking to establish Islam worldwide: the kingdom of Allah, who created all the world, is Islam. Thus the whole world must acknowledge Allah.

This leads to the concept of Islamic theocracy. This is defined as a country being run by Islamic leaders, so that all its citizens are under *shari'ah*, absolute Islamic law, and *fiqh*, a more relative Islamic legal philosophy. Not to put too fine a point on it, *shari'ah* (literally 'a path to life-giving water') refers to the Islamic legal tradition that must be adhered to, and *fiqh* (literally 'understanding') is Islamic jurisprudence, the process and rulings related to all aspects of Islamic life that ought to be observed. Terms such as *ijtihad* (exercising a judgement), *fatwa* (Islamic legal opinion), *qiyas* (legal analogy), and so forth are often associated with both *fiqh* and *shari'ah*.

Theoretically, for a country to be under such laws leads to peace and harmony within the community. Take Saudi Arabia, for example. That is a country under *shari'ah* law. Yet whenever news filters out from Saudi Arabia, we hear of injustices, and violent actions against citizens and immigrants, including harsh imprisonment, public whippings and beheadings. This is an extension of what it means to be *Islam*. The intention is to extend this rule of *shari'ah* to the entire world.

There is also some theological basis for viewing theocracy as an Islamic ideal type of government. Muhammad established the *ummah* (community of believers) as a holistic political community rooted in a faith that consciously sought to replace [everything else] as the primary social bond. Yet there is no single model for how a contemporary Islamic theocracy should be organized. There is no certainty that people will voluntarily accept [it] for long. There is even less agreement on whether theocracy is intrinsic to Islam or simply a historical phase. Some scholars argue that democracy is perfectly compatible with Islam, although this assertion is vigorously contested.[13]

Is there an answer to such a development of the Muslim *ummah*? We would wish that a more even-handed, kindly, considerate regime be established, based on truly humanitarian principles. But is there such a thing that can be established outside of the Judeo-Christian principles of law? There is no evidence. Yet the call of Muslims is for the whole world to be established under the reign of Islam, because the whole world is *Islam*.

Notes

1 About Islam: http://islam.about.com/blintroc.htm. Article: 'Five Pillars of Islam'.

2 Apna Islamic Network: www.apnaportal.com. Article: 'The Five Pillars of Islam'.

3 See Information sheet 4, p.227, for details of the prayer times, and the prayers and positions that constitute a *rak'ah*.

4 IslamiCity: www.islamicity.com. Article on *zakat*.

5 Sura 9:60.

6 In our experience of a Muslim country this was vividly portrayed. For example, one had to take care not to admire a certain ornament on visiting a Muslim family, or one was likely to have to come away with it, to one's personal embarrassment! This shows the reality of the principle, as well as their natural generosity.

7 Sura 2:183.

8 Islamic Server of MSA-USC: www.usc.edu/dept/MSA/reference/glossary.html. Article: *sawm*.

9 Sura 2:184–5.

10 See also chapter 8 'Life at the Mosque', p.78, for a more detailed description.

11 As reported at http://islamicity.com/mosque/hajj/hajjintro.htm. Article: 'Hajj Intro for People of Other faith'.

12 **Prof. M.N. Karim**, 'Hajj and Muslim Fraternity', *Bangladesh Observer,* 27 September, 1982.

13 *Congressional Quarterly: Theocracy: from Encyclopedia of Politics and Religion,* Robert Wuthnow, ed. 2 vols (Washington, DC: Congressional Quarterly, Inc., 1998), pp.733–735, published on their website: www.cqpress.com/context/articles/epr_theo.html, Article: 'Theocracy' ¶7.

Muslim Jihad

There is one other important observation to make concerning Muslim practice, for there is what has been loosely termed the 'sixth pillar of Islam'. It is something that we have heard a great deal about in recent years, and that is the concept of *jihad*.

The Khawarij would have been delighted to have *jihad* called the Sixth Pillar. They were a sect of Islam in the thirteenth century, descended from the Kharijites, the third most important group in early Islam, after the Sunnis and Shi'ites. They engaged in violence and political assassination in order to advance their cause. They derived from the Murji'ah, an early Muslim sect who used violence—even against Muslims. Interestingly, the modern Wahabbi are similar in outlook (see page 43).

In order for there to be a *jihad* there has to be a *fatwa*. This is an Islamic religious decree issued by the *ulema*, a recognized group of Muslim leaders. It can actually be the call of a single *mufti* (Muslim lawyer) but it must not reflect his own will or ideas, but be based on fixed precedent. Hence the call for the larger group, the *ulema*, to issue the *fatwa*, in order to bring consensus. Nominally a *fatwa* is something quite innocuous and is today of limited importance in most Muslim societies.[1]

However, in recent years we have heard of *fatwa* being proclaimed on Salman Rushdie and Osama bin Laden's *fatwa* of a *jihad* on Americans, whether Muslim or not. These were not quite as innocuous as suggested. It often seems that a *fatwa* may be issued whenever there is a perceived threat against Islam.

In the light of the fact that many Muslims like to refer to Islam as a system of peace, this concept of *jihad* is rather interesting. As soon as we hear the word today we immediately think of war and terrorism. But is it legitimate to think of Islam in terms of terrorism?

The word comes from the Arabic root word *jahada*, which means to struggle, or to strive, particularly for a better way of life. As far as Muslims are concerned the concept is of a struggle that is always on behalf of Islam and which seeks to advance Islam. Other meanings include 'endeavour, strain, exertion, effort, diligence, fighting to defend one's life, land, and religion'.[2]

Jihad is a religious duty for every adult male Muslim, to make war ☆ against *kafir* (infidels). There is a 'glory' in fighting under a *jihad* call, as those who die in such a war are assured of paradise.

There is a great deal of controversy over the concept: 'Jihad should not be confused with Holy War; the latter does not exist in Islam nor will Islam allow its followers to be involved in a Holy War. The latter refers to the Holy War of the Crusaders.'[3]

This statement is from the USA and is obviously very sensitive to any anti-Muslim feeling in the US, especially in the wake of 9/11. So their definition continues:

Not only in peace but also in war Islam prohibits terrorism, kidnapping, and hijacking, when carried out against civilians. Whoever commits such violations is considered a murderer in Islam, and is to be punished by the Islamic state. During wars, Islam prohibits Muslim soldiers from harming civilians, women, children, elderly, and the religious men like priests and [rabbis]. It also prohibits cutting down trees and destroying civilian constructions.[4]

Many Muslims like to express *jihad* as an 'internal struggle for piety'. As comforting as that may sound, there is another view being presented.

Jihad is 'holy war'. Or, more precisely, it means the legal, compulsory, communal effort to expand the territories ruled by Muslims at the expense of territories ruled by non-Muslims. The purpose of *jihad*, in other words, is not directly to spread the Islamic faith but to extend sovereign Muslim power (faith, of course, often follows the flag). *Jihad* is thus unabashedly offensive in nature, with the eventual goal of achieving Muslim dominion over the entire globe. *Jihad* did have two variant meanings ... one more radical, one less so. The first holds that Muslims who interpret their faith differently are infidels and therefore legitimate targets of *jihad*. (This is why Algerians, Egyptians and Afghans have found themselves, like Americans and Israelis, so often the victims of jihadist aggression.) The second meaning, associated with mystics, rejects the legal definition of *jihad* as armed conflict and tells Muslims to withdraw from the worldly concerns to achieve spiritual depth. *Jihad* in the sense of territorial expansion has always been a central aspect of Muslim life. That is how Muslims came to rule much of the Arabian Peninsula by the time of the Prophet Muhammad's death in 632. It is how, a century later, Muslims had conquered a region from Afghanistan to Spain. Subsequently, *jihad* spurred and justified Muslim conquests of such territories as India, Sudan, Anatolia, and the Balkans. Today, *jihad* is the world's foremost source of terrorism, inspiring a worldwide campaign of violence by self-proclaimed jihadist groups.[5]

Some of the foremost terrorist groups active today are:

The International Islamic Front for the Jihad Against Jews and Crusaders:	Osama bin Laden's organization;
Laskar Jihad:	responsible for the murder of more than 10,000 Christians in Indonesia;
Harakat ul-Jihad-i-Islami:	a leading cause of violence in Kashmir;
Palestinian Islamic Jihad:	the most vicious anti-Israel terrorist group of them all;
Egyptian Islamic Jihad:	killed Anwar El-Sadat in 1981, many others since then;
Yemeni Islamic Jihad:	killed three American missionaries in 2002.[5]

We could also quote from a more radical position. The World Islamic Front Statement of the Bin Laden group is extremely enlightening. This is the first paragraph:

Praise be to Allah, who revealed the Book, controls the clouds, defeats factionalism, and says in His Book: 'But when the forbidden months are past, then fight and slay the pagans wherever ye find them, seize them, beleaguer them, and lie in wait for them in every stratagem (of war)'; and peace be upon our Prophet, Muhammad Bin-'Abdallah, who said: 'I have been sent with the sword between my hands to ensure that no one but Allah is worshipped.'[6]

The statement continues in an inflammatory vein, and concludes with three Qur'anic quotations, which are all calling for war under the guidance of Allah.

So what do we make of all this? Is Islam inherently peaceful or militant? Where do such groups as Al-Qa'ida fit in?

The history of Islam has been largely one of triumph, except for the past 300 years. Mohammed's conquest of most of the Arabian Peninsula was achieved during his own lifetime. After the death of Mohammed, Islam became the dominant creed as it spread through the Middle East and beyond, reaching even as far as Spain. It was obvious who the victor was and who were the vanquished. This conquest steadily advanced for about 1,000 years. However, the lack of any further advance for about 200 years stunned Muslims, and they blamed themselves for the lack of progress—they must have been bad Muslims, and Allah was not pleased. With the coming of the modern age Muslims began to think of themselves as second-class citizens in the world. This was a tremendous challenge that faced them, and their answer began to develop into a call for Muslims to unite.

The modern movement of *jihad* has its origin in the general decline and final demise of the Ottoman Empire at the end of the First World War (1914–18). Turkey had made a fatal mistake in siding with Germany and had to capitulate to the British. Under General Allenby, the British began a campaign of slow conquest of the Ottoman Empire from out of British-ruled Egypt, liberating Jerusalem and Baghdad. The overall result was that the major Muslim countries (now known as Iraq, Syria, Lebanon, Israel and Jordan) became known as League of Nation mandates, which in practice meant that they were ruled by Britain and France. So Muslims had no power of self-rule. Many of the emerging leaders of the Muslim states were considered to be western stooges. Turkey's Muslim-born Kemal Ataturk abolished the Ottoman Empire in 1922, arranged a treaty with the West by which Turkey regained much of its lost territory, and ended the caliphate in 1924. The Hashemites gained Iraq and Jordan, but most importantly they lost their ancient domain of Hijaz, conquered in 1924 by King Abdul Aziz ibn Saud, leader of the Saudi dynasty. The Saudi family now ruled the holy shrines of Mecca and Medina, and were no longer under the control of the Hashemites, who claimed to be blood descendants of Mohammed. This caused much resentment and suspicion.

After the end of occupation by western powers, Muslim countries had several decades of independence when they had an opportunity to show the West that they were a political power that could be reckoned with. But that did not happen. The only major impact and influence they have made is on the world economy because of oil. Muslims found it very hard to make any impact on the western scene, much to their chagrin. Their vision had been that by being good Muslims, Allah would bless them and give them more blessings than the West had. But all they have seen is western powers dominating the world scene. Thus, due to a real sense of failure in making any impact, they have resorted to more overt means.

Muslims cynically adapted as survivors, not the conquerors they had once been. From 1918 in the Middle East, there was a deepening sense of Arab humiliation and betrayal. Muslims were particularly bitter with Britain for later establishing Israel as an independent Jewish state after World War II, displacing the mainly Palestinian Muslim occupants, and preventing Muslims from ruling their third most revered city, Jerusalem.

Yet Muslims are waiting for a new golden age of supremacy. It was from out of this scenario that Osama bin Laden began raising the hopes of many Muslims. After 9/11 he made this statement: 'What America is tasting now is something insignificant compared to what we have tasted for scores of years. Our nation [the Islamic world] had been tasting this humiliation and this degradation for more than 80 years.'7 Al-Qa'ida is therefore seeking to redress the humiliation felt by the Muslim world after the Great War (1918). It is not only their treatment from the West they are reacting to, but also the sense of betrayal by Muslim leaders. When the last Islamic superpower, the Ottoman Empire, was abolished and the ancient caliphate that goes back to Mohammed's successors, these were actions taken not by Western powers but a secularized Muslim, Kemal Ataturk. Hence Al-Qa'ida is believed by many Muslims to be not only putting the West in its place, but also dealing with the ultimate enemy, apostates within Islam.

Renewal movements within Islam had begun to rise back in the late eighteenth century. Jamal al Din Afghani (1838–97) was possibly the first pan-Islamist who wrote that all Islam was threatened by western power: in those days it was the British Empire. Therefore it was the duty of Muslims to discover the source of that power and use it to re-establish the supremacy of Islam. 'Pan-Islamists' taught there is to be no loyalty to nation, ethnicity, race or class. Loyalty to the one true faith of Islam was important, because Islam was the only thing that mattered.

Leaders of such renewal groups were resolved in their one aim to purify Islam—to deal with the perceived lack of 'faith' that was considered to be causing the failure of a continuing Muslim world take-over—in order to win Allah's blessing. Other distinctive militant groups were later to rise much later in the twentieth century. The following is a list of some major players.

- **The Wahabbi**—a strict conservative Sunni sect founded by Muhammad ibn-Abd-al-Wahab (1703–1792). They hold a particularly reactionary interpretation of Islam. Osama bin Laden belongs to Salafiyya, a subsidiary group of the Wahabbi.
- **The Muslim Brotherhood**—founded in 1928 by Hassan al Banna (1904–49) in Egypt, promoting the Qur'an and the Hadith as the proper basis for society; a distinctively Sunni group.
- **The Islamic Jihad**—founded in 1979–80 by Palestinian students in Egypt, who split from the Palestinian Muslim Brotherhood in the Gaza Strip, whose founders were highly influenced by the Islamic revolution in Iran, and the radicalization and militancy of Egyptian Islamic student organizations.
- **The Hamas**—formed late 1987 as an outgrowth of the Palestinian branch of the Muslim Brotherhood.
- **The Hizbollah (the 'Party of Allah')**—a Lebanese group of Shi-ite militants, formed in 1982 with Hussayn Musawi as leader, is an umbrella organization.

All these groups interpret *jihad* militantly, but there are other groups, such as the *Ahmadiyya*, started in 1879 in Punjab when Mirza Ghulam Ahmad claimed to be the *Mahdi* and the Messiah, who interpret *jihad* peacefully.

There are a number of Muslim internet sites that vehemently argue that *jihad* does *not* mean 'holy war' and that this is a false claim of 'western propaganda'.

However, Mohammed taught his followers to oppress or kill non-Muslims, and there are a number of supporting passages in the Qur'an.[8]

Generally, however, Jews and Christians were to be allowed to continue in their faith, provided that they paid a special tax (*jizya*), because they were seen to be the 'People of the Book'. Polytheistic cultures have been given the option of submission or death. Note what the Qur'an teaches:

Fight against such of those to whom the Scriptures were given as believe neither in Allah nor the Last Day, who do not forbid what Allah and His Apostle have forbidden, and do not embrace the true faith ... until they pay tribute ... out of hand [or willing submission] and are utterly subdued [with humiliation and feel themselves subdued to the government of Islam].⁹

So terrorism is not actually a distortion of the message passed down from Mohammed and his followers. It follows in the same vein.

The final object of *jihad* is to see the non-Islamic world—*Dar al Harb* (the domain of war)—turned into *Dar al Islam* (the domain of Islam). This is based on Qur'anic teaching—there are many verses which encourage belief in the universality of Islam. *Jihad*, then, is only concluded when the entire world is placed under submission to Allah. Jihad is seeking to impose Islam in every place and seeking to submit everyone to the laws of Allah.

Hassan al Banna (Muslim Brotherhood) taught that Islam thrives under the threat of its enemies. He claimed that every true Muslim must confront the infidel with an armed struggle—that anything less than this implies cowardice. It was straying from such a course of action, he firmly believed, that had left Islam divided and treated with contempt by the rest of the world. In keeping with all this, and since the United States of America is the present world super-power, it should not surprise us to read in a 1999 interview with Osama bin Laden that 'Hostility towards America is a religious duty and we hope to be rewarded by Allah for it'. In that same report, and in answer to a question about nuclear weapons, he said,

Acquiring weapons for the defence of Muslims is a religious duty. If I have indeed acquired these weapons, then I thank God for enabling me to do so. And if I seek to acquire these weapons, I am carrying out a duty. It would be a sin for Muslims not to try to possess the weapons that would prevent the infidels from inflicting harm on Muslims.¹⁰

The phenomenon of the suicide bomber is now evident worldwide. Many people ask, 'How is it possible that men and women can be so brainwashed into giving their lives in this manner?' The answer to that question is found within the whole ethos of Islam, in the *ummah*, the solidarity of the community. They see themselves as martyrs for Islam, doing their bit to further its cause, and to establish *Dar al Islam*.

In a *USA Today* interview, Boaz Ganor of the International Policy

Institute for Counter-Terrorism in Israel, explained, speaking of the inclusion of women as suicide bombers as well as men, 'If you analyze the motivations of the women who committed such attacks, it's the same as the men: They do believe, they are committed, patriotic, and this is combined with a religious duty.'[11] There are cash incentives for the families of suicide bombers, so they may be better off: 'Cash payments from Iraq and other Arab countries go to these families, many in desperate need of money, after the suicide-bombing mission.'[11] But what about any incentives for themselves? This is catered for in the promise of paradise:

Muslim men who volunteer to strap on explosives are promised unlimited sex with 72 virgins in the spirit world, he says. Even the women believe this. Not in the 72 virgins business, but that they are going to gain their place in heaven, ... Islamic leaders brainwash their constituency, telling them that this is a duty to Allah. You cannot persuade any Western-culture person to commit that act.[11]

'A duty to Allah'—that is the over-riding factor. And there are many verses in the Qur'an that support such a view. With regard to their personal reward for *jihad*, the Qur'an states, 'Those that have ... fought for Allah's cause with their wealth and their persons are held in higher regard by Allah. It is they who shall triumph. Their Lord has promised them joy and mercy, and gardens of eternal bliss where they will dwell for ever. Allah's reward is great indeed.'[12]

References to paradise in the Qur'an promise many pleasures, including virgins (*houri*) for the delight of a believer. The Qur'an does not define the number of *houri* for each believer, but there are traditions that claim 72— and all these add to the expectations of a Muslim martyr. (But note that these dark-eyed damsels are available for all Muslims, not just martyrs.) The promise of the *houri* is greatly emphasized, especially to would-be martyrs. The emphasis on sexual gratification is a powerful incentive.

According to the Hadith TIRMZI ...

1. A houri is a most beautiful young woman with a transparent body. The marrow of her bones is visible like the interior lines of pearls and rubies. She looks like a red wine in a white glass.

2. She is of white colour, and free from the routine physical disabilities of an ordinary woman ...

3. She is a woman characterised by modesty and flexing glances; she never looks at any man except her husband, and feels grateful for being the wife of her husband.

4. A houri is a loving woman ... [who] has the ability to put it into practice.

5. A houri is a recreated woman whose virginity has been restored. ...

6. A houri is an immortal woman. She speaks softly and does not raise her voice at her man; she is always reconciled with him. Having been brought up in luxury, she is a luxury herself.

To increase the sexual appeal of Islam, another hadith declares that man's virility shall be increased hundredfold. Thus, Islam equates salvation with carnal pleasures which houris, the paradisiac (sic) women provide, thus confirming woman's role in Islam as the object of sexual pleasures.[13]

All this becomes an amazingly powerful incentive to young men who are encouraged to give their lives for the sake of fighting against the perceived enemies of Islam.

Also there are a number of *hadith* that make specific promises of achievements for the suicide bomber, or the *jihad* fighter. One set of *hadith* promises:

(1) The souls of the martyrs are in the green birds dwelling in Paradise wherever they like. (2) That all their sins and faults are forgiven. (3) That he can intercede with Allah for seventy of his family members. (4) That he will come secure on the Day of Resurrection from the great terror. (5) That he will not feel the agonies and distress of death. (6) That he will not be horrified by the great Gathering (on the Day of Resurrection). (7) That he does not feel the pain of 'the killing' except like that of a pinch.[14]

This sums up the hopes of a martyr. Thus, in the days when Saddam

Hussein was a great hero who survived the first Gulf War in 1991, the then chairman of the Jordanian National Front, Ahmad Oweidi, said, 'Saddam talks about the things we feel; a Jihad against the US, UK and Israel. You westerners are keen to live, we Muslims are keen to die and go to paradise in the Jihad which will destroy the West.'[15]

To end this review of *jihad* and the reasons for it, note these observations on the whole concept of terrorism, particularly the Muslim variety.

People just don't decide to become terrorists. Terrorists are motivated by a doctrine that instils in them the hate and the will to kill. But you cannot hate so intensely unless you feel victimized. … That is why they are willing to die. Part of that victimization is justified, but the great part of that is induced in them by the teachings of the Qur'an. The Qur'an convinces the Muslims that they are the victims and exhorts them to fight against them and murder them, and it promises that despite their apparent weakness Allah will render them victorious. Armed with this intense hate … [they] become mindless machines ready to kill and ready to die.

We cannot combat this terrorism unless we stop this hate. We cannot stop this hate unless we stop the doctrine that promotes this hate. The Qur'an is a book full of hate of the non-believers. … There is no time for political correctness and appeasements. Not only our lives, but also the very existence of our civilization is in danger.[16]

We have seen that the concept of *jihad* is intrinsically connected with Islam and the teaching of the Qur'an. Muslim terrorists and suicide bombers genuinely believe what the Qur'an says.

Christianity is the specific enemy of Islam. Christians refuse to recognize Allah. These *kafir* cannot be tolerated[17] and so *jihad* is justified in eliminating Christians. There are countries in which this is systematically taking place (e.g. Sudan).[18] Such persecution is taught in the Qur'an.[19] Christians do not enjoy the same religious liberty in Muslim countries as Muslims experience in western countries. Persecution is justified by *jihad*.

***

This has been a lengthy statement on what used to be a relatively insignificant issue, but to ignore it is to misunderstand. We cannot afford to do that today, if we want to understand the Muslim mind, and the world in which we live.

Notes

1 Encyclopedia of the Orient: http://lexicorient.com/e.o/index.htm. Article: 'Fatwa'.
2 Islamic Server of MSA-USC: www.usc.edu/dept/MSA/reference/glossary.html. Article: 'Jihad'.
3 *Ibid.*
4 *Ibid.*
5 **Daniel Pipes,** www.danielpipes.org. Report, *New York Post,* December 31, 2002.
6 *Jihad Against Jews and Crusaders*: www.fas.org/irp/para/docs/980223-fatwa.htm. Statement: *fatwa.*
7 Quoted by **Christopher Catherwood,** *Christians, Muslims and Islamic Rage* (Grand Rapids: Zondervan, 2003), p.85.
8 Sura 9:3–5, Sura 8:65, Sura 2:216, Sura 8:38–39.
9 Quoted from the Tafsir Al-Jalalain—*the Al-Jalalain Interpretation of the Qur'an*: Sura 9:29.
10 *Time* magazine, January 1999. Interview with Osama bin Laden.
11 USA Today: www.usatoday.com/news/world/2002/04/22/cover.htm. Article, dated 22.4.2002: 'interview re suicide bombers'.
12 Sura 9:20–22.
13 **Anwar Shaikh**: www.derafsh-kaviyani.com/english/islamandwomanhood1.html. Article: 'Islam and Womanhood', ¶6.
14 The Islam Page: http://www.islamworld.net/jihad.html. Article: 'Jihad. Hadith: al-Bukhari and Muslim'.
15 Source: **Paul Simpson,** personal communication.
16 *Faith Freedom International*: www.faithfreedom.org/Articles/sina/mission.htm. *Mission Statement,* ¶5,6.
17 Sura 3:85; 4:89,101,102; 8:13–17.
18 **Ergun Mehmet Caner, and Fethi Emir Caner,** *Unveiling Islam* (Monarch Books, London, 2003), pp.176–177. See also www.persecution.org and www.projectpersecution.org.
19 Sura 4:171; 5:14,17,72–73,75.

The faith of the community

We now come to consider what binds the Muslim community. If we think of the 'Pillars of Islam' as the foundation blocks of the Muslim community, then their 'articles of faith' are the cement that holds them together. We have already noted in chapter 3 that faith in Islam is more than a belief in ideas.

One definition of faith as given by a Muslim apologist is as follows:

In the Qur'an, the term 'faith' means 'to consider something to be sure and reliable' without doubting. Faith can only be given by God, and means above all, that a human being acknowledges Allah's greatness and superiority, his own position as God's servant, who owes Him gratitude for His mercy towards man.[1]

As far as the Qur'an is concerned, mankind is divided into two groups, the Muslims, who are the believers, *al-mu'minun;* and the non-Muslims, who are unbelievers, *al-kafirun.* By definition the unbeliever is ungrateful towards Allah and does not acknowledge his goodness, in particular his gift of revelation, the Qur'an. The believer gives the thanks that he owes to Allah, in that he honours him as the source of all goodness and recognizes his revelation as law. Muslims believe that it is their faith that decides their fate on the Day of Judgement as to whether they will enter paradise or hell. This is a belief that is essential to the Muslim idea of salvation. But Muslim opinions differ on what constitutes faith (*iman*). There are several possibilities:

(1) The inner conviction of the truth of the revelation of Allah without any public confession being necessary.

(2) The declaration of the Islamic confession of faith, combined with the inner conviction being necessary.

(3) The fulfilment of the prescribed Muslim duties.

(4) The Muslim conviction of faith combined with the fulfilment of the Muslim duties and good works.

(5) The declaration of the Muslim confession of faith, inner conviction and good works.[1]

So besides the individual rules of behaviour, for which there are very stringent and lengthy instructions, the Qur'an does not formulate any particular tenets which a Muslim must believe in order to be considered a believer. We have already seen that reciting the *shahada* in Arabic before witnesses is what makes a person a Muslim, or else being born into a Muslim family. This in itself contains the items of faith that are absolute: (1) belief in Allah, and (2) belief in his prophet Mohammed. To these may be added (3) belief in angels, (4) belief in the holy books of revelation, and (5) the belief that every human being must appear before Allah at the last judgement. There are several subsidiary issues that come from these such as belief in paradise and hell, and in predestination.

i. Belief in one God

'*Allah*' (pronounced *Allaah*) is the Arabic word that translates our English word 'God'. But the question is, are the names really equivalent?

To the Muslim the name of *Allah* is indicative of his essential being. *Allah* is defined as the divine supernatural being and almighty creator who is sovereign over all. Etymologically, *Allah* is equivalent to, though not the same as, the Aramaic *alaha*, the Hebrew *El*, *Elohah (Eloah)* and the plural form *Elohim*. This immediately exposes a difference. For the word Allah is a somewhat unique word grammatically, for it cannot be made plural or given gender (i.e. masculine or feminine). This goes hand in hand with the Islamic concept of Allah. *El* is the Semitic name for the Almighty Sovereign God who is the Creator of all. Thus the Aramaic *El* and Arabic *Allah* have an equivalence.

The term *Allah*, Muslim sources indicate, is derived from two words *al* which means 'the', and *ilah*, which is said to relate to the Hebrew word for God, *Elohah*. So the claimed commonality between *Elohim* and *Allah* is *elohah* and *ilah*. *Allah* is probably a contraction of the Arabic *al-ilah*. There are also claims, possibly from a post-Mohammed period, in an attempt to justify the uniqueness of the term Allah, that it has no derivation whatsoever.

The English term 'God' and the Arabic word 'Allah' are technically synonymous. Our conflict is with the nature of God and the nature of Allah. It is with the Muslim understanding of *who* Allah is that we have to take care. Islam does not accept the same revelation of God as we do. It is the context that is given to a name that is important. The Allah of the Qur'an is not the same as the God and Father of our Lord Jesus Christ. Therefore we must be careful how and when we use the term *Allah*.

Allah is recognized by Muslims as the Almighty God, Creator and Sustainer of the universe. The most important aspect of belief about Allah is that he is one—*tauhid*—one in essence, not composed of parts; one in his attributes, not having a multiplicity of powers or will; one in his works, no other being besides Allah has any influence upon him. *Tauhid*, Muslims agree, is the very basis of Islam.

One chapter of the Qur'an powerfully expresses this idea of the unity of Allah: 'In the name of Allah, the Merciful, the Compassionate say: "Allah is One, the Eternal God. He begot none, nor was He begotten. None is equal to Him."'[2]

He has many *attributes*, and these are accorded to him as *names*. Each of them is to be found in the Qur'an—ninety-nine in all.[3] The hundredth name is hidden, only known to Allah himself. We may note that many of these attributes are also to be found in our Christian Scriptures. However, one significant name is missing: 'God is Love.' In Islam, Allah is called 'the loving One'—but the term is understood to be a characteristic of the divine will, rather than an aspect of his nature.

Many Muslims react against Christians making this claim.

Some non-Muslims allege that God in Islam is a stern and cruel God who demands to be obeyed fully. He is not loving and kind. Nothing can be farther from the truth than this allegation. It is enough to know that, with the exception of one, each of the 114 chapters of the Qur'an begins with the verse: 'In the name of God, the Merciful, the Compassionate.' In one of the sayings of Prophet Muhammad we are told that 'God is more loving and kinder than a mother to her dear child.'[4]

Yet it has to be said that this does not come across well in Muslim teaching or practice, and is thus an attempt to justify their teaching. Allah must not be considered in any negative way. The same brochure then goes on to speak of Allah as being just, and emphasis is put on his punishing evildoers, making the claim that 'God's attribute of Mercy has full manifestation in His attribute of Justice'.[4]

Out of all Allah's attributes, there are seven which are considered principal. They are fundamental to the expression of his being.

a. *Life:* He is without beginning and without end: eternal.

b. *Knowledge:* He knows all things, never forgetting, never negligent, never making an error.

c. *Power:* He is almighty, able to do all things. His power can never diminish: it is as everlasting as he is.

d. *Will:* He is able to do whatever he wills: making believers, or unbelievers, according to his will.

e. *Hearing:* He can hear any sound, high or low, without ears.

f. *Seeing:* He is able to see all things without eyes: even the steps of a black cat on a black stone on a black night.

g. *Speaking:* He speaks, without a tongue.

It is worth noting that the description of these aspects of Allah's nature is a rather hesitant anthropomorphism. The Muslim views Allah as so very unlike his creation that nothing in creation may be associated with him in any way. Therefore the Muslim theologian, attempting to relate who Allah is, and make him understandable to the human mind, has to resort to this somewhat hesitant use of human parallels. Muslims are very fearful of applying such concepts to Allah in a too hard-and-fast way.

There are three other important aspects of Allah that must be stressed, for they are ever in the Muslim mind:

a. 'Allah is Great'—*Allahu Akbar.* This expression is constantly to be found on Muslim lips. It indicates that whatever a man may possibly think, or whatever idea he may hold with respect to Allah himself, by definition Allah must be much greater. It is found as the opening words of the *adhan*, the Muslim call to worship that is given by the *muezzin* from the *minaret*, the tower at the mosque.

b. He is the Revealer of his Will. His revelation of himself and his will is the Qur'an, but only in the Arabic original (for Arabic is the language of heaven).

c. He is Transcendent. He is not knowable in reality and can never be known by man. Allah is so very different from whatever man can think about him.

His being is summed up by the first statement of the *shahada: la ilaha illa*

Allah—'there is no god worthy of worship except Allah'. One source suggests that four Arabic words are needed to help a Muslim to appreciate more fully what this means:

ilah = Deity, God; One to be worshipped; One who has power to satisfy your needs and answer your prayer; One who is in control of your affairs; One who can comfort you, provide protection and support you.

rabb = Lord, Master and owner; sustainer, provider and guardian; sovereign, ruler and administrator.

Ibadah = Worship and devotion; submission and obedience; subjection and servitude.

Din = ideology; government and constitution; complete system (way of life).

Thus these may be put together as follows: 'Allah is the *rabb* and the *ilah*. There is no r*abb* and *ilah* except Allah. To Him alone we make *ibadah*. Only His *din* we adopt and sincerely follow.'[5]

The distinctiveness of Allah is that he cannot reveal himself in three persons, he cannot have a son, and he is not a redeemer who takes away the sins of the world. For Christians, God reveals himself in three Persons, Father, Son and Holy Spirit, he determines to saves sinners, and makes it possible by grace through his Son becoming 'the Lamb of God who takes away the sins of the world'.[6] Allah, by the content that is put into the word, cannot be identified with the God of the Christian faith.[7]

ii. Belief in angels

The doctrine of angels is a very comprehensive one. Belief in their existence enters into the definition of faith itself: 'The apostle believes in what has been revealed to him by His Lord, and so do the faithful. They all believe in Allah and His angels, His Scriptures and His Apostles.'[8] Muslims teach that angels worship Allah continually and obey all his commands. They are unseen beings of a luminous and spiritual substance, they have no will of their own, and they act as intermediaries between Allah and the visible world. The Qur'an does not speak of the origin of angels, whereas it tells us that man is created from dust or clay, and the *jinn* (see below) from fire. However, on the authority of Mohammed we are told that the angels are created from *nur*—the divine light. Thus it is clear that the angels and the *jinn* are two different classes of beings.

It is said that the food of angels is celebrating Allah's glory, their drink is proclaiming Allah's holiness, their conversation is commemorating Allah and their pleasure is worshipping Allah. Angels hold a position of respect that is slightly inferior to human prophets. This is on the basis that they were, according to the Qur'an, commanded to prostrate themselves before Adam.[9] As regards their function, the Qur'an considers belief in angels as part of righteousness.[10] They help awaken the Muslim's moral consciousness.

As for those who say, 'Our god is Allah,' and take the right path to him, the angels will descend to them, saying: 'Let nothing alarm or grieve you. Rejoice in the paradise you have been promised. We are your guardians in this world and in the next. You shall find there all that your souls (*sic*) desire and all that you can ask for: rich provision from a benignant (*sic*) and merciful Allah.[11]

It is also said that every believer is attended by two recording angels, one sitting on his right shoulder recording his good deeds, while the other is on his left shoulder recording his evil deeds. '(Remember) that the two receivers (recording angels) receive (each human being), one sitting on the right and one on the left (to note his or her actions). Not a word does he (or she) utter but there is a watcher by him ready (to record it).'[12] The *hadith* attributes many functions to angels: the task of recording all deeds, whether good or bad; the 'seizing of the souls' of believers, and disbelievers; the gatekeepers and servants of the people of paradise; those who strive in *jihad* with believers; those who come down to witness the good deeds of Muslims.

There is a definite order of angels, with a hierarchy of *archangels* who have specific responsibilities: *Jibra'il* (Gabriel) is the angel of revelation, appointed to communicate Allah's message to mortal prophets; *Mika'il* (Michael) the patron, who looks after the universe, and the forces of nature (and a friend and protector of the Jews); *Israfil*, who places spirits within bodies, and will sound the trumpet on the last day; and *Azra'il*, the 'angel of death'.

Others include *Malik*, whose responsibility is to supervise *Cehennam* (Arabic of *Gehenna*, thus hell), and who has nineteen subordinates to assist him; Munkar and Nakir, who examine the dead in their graves on the night after their burial (or immediately after the funeral is over), to interrogate them about their belief in Allah, in the Prophet, etc., and to torture them if they do not give satisfactory answers. The throne of Allah is supposed to be supported by eight angels. There are others who intercede on behalf of man and celebrate the praises of Allah. In general, it is believed that angels act as guardians to man. Every child of Adam, except Jesus and Mary, is touched by the devil at its birth and this causes the new-born infant to cry.

We also need to mention the *jinn*. These have to be explained carefully. They must not be thought of as equivalent to angels. They are a wholly separate category of being, and supposedly created before human beings. The Qur'an states: 'We created man from dry clay, from black moulded loam. And before him *jinn* from smokeless fire.'[13]

They are creatures that have free will, who live on earth in a world parallel to mankind. Their name is derived from the word *janna* which means to hide or conceal. Thus, they are physically invisible. Occasionally they materialize and can be seen by mankind. It appears that every human being has a *jinn* counterpart. There is a large folklore surrounding the *jinn*. They are a significant feature in the *hadith*.

The *jinn* are essentially evil, and considered to be powerful, intelligent creatures, who possess freedom of choice. They are not necessarily antagonistic to men and women. They may be appeased. Muslims are very wary of them. There is an inbuilt, but little spoken of, fear of them; perhaps best described as animistic superstition. Some western Muslim thinkers play down the role of *jinn* in Qur'anic theology, even suggesting they might have been some earlier stage in the course of evolution.

Where does Satan, or the Devil, fit in? The Arabic names for Satan are *shaitan* or *iblis*. As you might expect, tradition also colours the Muslim doctrine of Satan. Some parts of the Qur'an itself seem to point towards Satan being an angelic being, but the Qur'an states that angels cannot disobey Allah. Satan, however, is a being who defied Allah, so Muslim theologians have held the opinion that Satan must have come from the *jinn*, for they have the ability to choose.

There is a discussion between Allah and Satan recorded in the Qur'an which describes the relationship between Satan and mankind, as well as his origin:

Your Lord said to the angels: 'I am creating man from clay. When I have fashioned him and breathed of my spirit into him, kneel down and prostrate yourselves before him.' The angels prostrated themselves except Satan, who was too proud, for he was an unbeliever. 'Satan,' said Allah, 'why do you not bow down to him whom my own hands have made? Are you too proud, or do you think he is beneath you?' Satan replied, 'I am nobler than he. You created me from fire, but him from clay.' 'Begone, you are accused!' said he. 'My curse shall remain on you until the Day of Reckoning.' Satan replied, 'Reprieve me, Lord, till the Day of Resurrection.' Allah said, 'Reprieved you shall be till the Appointed Day.' 'I swear by your glory,' said Satan, 'that I will seduce all men except your faithful servants.' Allah replied, 'Learn the truth, then, (and I speak nothing but the truth): I shall fill hell with your offspring and the men who follow you.'[14]

It is clear that Muslims believe that Satan was at the source and centre of evil even before the creation of Adam. He is the chief deceiver of mankind, seeking to lead mankind from the straight path of Allah's will.

iii. Belief in the books of Allah

Muslims believe that Allah has revealed himself and his will. The idea of revelation is a very basic tenet of Islam. The Qur'an is the ultimate revelation, but is the culmination of a succession of books:

This Book [the Qur'an] is not to be doubted. It is a guide to the righteous, who have faith in the unseen and are steadfast in prayer; ... who trust what has been revealed to you [Mohammed] and to others before you, and firmly believe in the life to come.[15]

Muslims are taught that the Qur'an is not the only revelation of Allah, but that it is the last in a succession.

There is no god but him, the Living, the Ever-existent one. He has revealed to you the Book with the truth, confirming the scriptures which preceded it; for he has already revealed the Torah and the Gospel for the guidance of men, and the distinction between right and wrong.[16]

Thus every Muslim is to believe in the divinely inspired books which Allah has sent down from time to time, to various peoples, through his many apostles and prophets. These books demonstrate Allah's greatest favour to mankind, for they are his means of guidance. The total number of books is believed, from the traditions, to be 104. Of these, only five are mentioned in the Qur'an:
  (i) The Scrolls of Abraham, now lost;
  (ii) The *Taurat*, the books 'given' to Moses (the Pentateuch);
  (iii) The *Zabur*, or the Psalms, 'given' to the prophet David;
  (iv) The *Injil*, or the gospel, 'given' to Jesus;
  (v) The *Qur'an*, 'given' to the last prophet, Mohammed.
Muslims teach that all other books, apart from the Qur'an, have been altered and corrupted in both language and content. This is particularly the case when these 'former' books differ from the Qur'an. It is the Qur'an that takes centre stage, and everything in it is the direct word from Allah for Muslims. It is the final revelation. The Qur'an is perfect.[17]

Muslims believe that the Qur'an in the Arabic language, as revealed to Mohammed, is an exact copy of the book which exists in heaven written on a special tablet. They teach that it was brought down to Mohammed by the angel Gabriel, who instructed Mohammed to recite it. They learn it by rote in Arabic, teaching it to their children from a very young age. As Muslims believe that Arabic is the language of heaven, any translation of the Qur'an is considered only an interpretation, because no *translation* can be perfect like the original.

Two points ought to be borne in mind. The first is that in spite of the fact that there is supposed to be only one Qur'an, there are around twenty versions of the Qur'an in Arabic. Muslims admit that there are seven variant yet authoritative 'readers' recorded by people who heard Mohammed (the Companions), and who wrote their own copy of his recitations. It became an increasing concern and it was considered that these differences were not acceptable. So in the fourth Islamic century, it was decided to return to the 'readings' (*qira'at*) handed down from those seven authoritative 'readers' (*qurra'*); in order, moreover, to ensure accuracy of transmission, two 'transmitters' (*rawi*, pl. *ruwah*) were accorded to each. Thus there are several accepted variants in existence.

... certain variant readings existed and, indeed, persisted and increased as the Companions who had memorised the text died, and because the inchoate (basic) Arabic script, lacking vowel signs and even necessary diacriticals to distinguish between certain consonants, was inadequate. ... There resulted from this seven basic texts (*al-qira'at as-sab'*, 'the seven readings'), each having two transmitted versions (*riwayatan*) with only minor variations in phrasing, but all containing meticulous vowel-points and other necessary diacritical marks. ... The authoritative 'readers' [were]: Nafi (from Medina), Ibn Kathir (from Mecca), Abu Amr al-'Ala (from Damascus), Ibn Amir (from Basra), Hamzah (from Kufah), al-Qisa'i (from Kufah), Abu Bakr Asim (from Kufah) [All these died within 200 years of Mohammed].[18]

Also, there are verses which contradict other verses in the Qur'an. Muslims have developed a doctrine of abrogation, whereby a later revelation supersedes and nullifies all earlier ones. This justifies any differences. For example, there are some 124 verses that teach some tolerance toward non-Muslims. But the striking fact is that all these verses are abrogated by Sura 9:5, as this is said to be the latest revelation to Mohammed.

Then there are the verses which upset many Muslims and which they try to cover up. These were brought to our attention infamously by Salman Rushdi in his novel *The Satanic Verses*. While not supporting the book, it does raise an issue concerning Sura 53:19–26.

Unimpeachable Muslim sources (Waqidi and al-Tabari) indicate that, prior to the flight to Medina, Muhammad was sitting with some important Meccan leaders, next to the Ka'aba, and he began to recite Sura 53, which describes the angel Gabriel's first and second visits to Muhammad.

The wording was: 'What do you think of Lat and Uzza and Manat the third beside? These are exalted Females, Whose intercession verily is to be sought after.'

These references were to some of the many gods the Meccans then worshipped, so the words seem to acknowledge the existence and even the importance of them, TOTALLY opposite of what Islam claims (of the One God, Allah). Islam says that Muhammad was later visited by Gabriel again, who reprimanded him and gave him the 'true' ending for that verse, which eliminated the praise for the gods and turned it into denigration. They consider those initial verses as being put into his mouth by Satan, i.e. Satanic Verses.[19]

These verses in the Qur'an are a serious problem for Muslims. They appear to demonstrate that Mohammed was carefully cultivating the Meccan leaders by saying things they wanted to hear—to be politically correct. But this is a claim that would greatly damage his credibility as a prophet, as his sincerity would appear to be in question. On the other hand, if Satan could so easily put words in the mouth of the Prophet, how much faith could anyone put in him? Also, such a situation implies that there might well be other passages where Satan affected the wording of the Qur'an. This is why Muslims want to vehemently defend their prophet—for they realize the fundamental implications of such a serious flaw. Muslims violently react to any such reference to their prophet, but the Qur'an also says:

Never have We sent a single prophet or apostle before you with whose wishes Satan did not tamper. But Allah abrogates the interjections of Satan and confirms his own revelations. Allah is all-knowing and wise. He makes Satan's interjections a temptation for those whose hearts are diseased, whose hearts are hardened …[20]

It is suggested that Gabriel comforted Mohammed when he realized how he had sinned:

They sought to entice you from Our revelations—they nearly did—hoping that you might invent some other scripture in Our name, and thus become their trusted friend. Indeed had we not strengthened your faith, you might have made some compromise with them and thus incurred a double punishment in this life and in the next. Then you should have found none to help you against Us.[21]

These references are an open admission that Satan could have such an influence on Mohammed.

iv. Belief in the prophets

The teaching of Islam is that Allah sent chosen prophets to the nations, at different times and in different places, to proclaim his message, and give guidance to his people.

The Apostle believes in what has been revealed to Him by his Lord, and so do the faithful. They all believe in Allah and his angels, his scriptures, and his apostles: We discriminate against none of his apostles. They say: 'We hear and obey. Grant us your forgiveness, Lord; to you we shall all return.'[22]

It emphasizes that all the prophets were thoroughly human.

Two types of prophet are recognized in Islam:

(a) The *nabi*. This group includes anyone directly inspired by Allah. It is only a very general term. The Lord Jesus Christ is recognized as a great *nabi*, though, sadly, Muslims do not believe him to have been more than this. But it is interesting to note that he is also included in the other category of prophet, namely,

(b) The *rasul*. These are distinguished prophets to whom a special message has been entrusted. To each of them Allah gave a book, that is described as a piece of scripture, the Word of Allah.

There were, according to tradition, 124,000 *nabi*, but only 313 of these are *rasul*. Some students of the Qur'an believe that there are twenty-eight prophets mentioned by name in the Qur'an, but others accept only twenty-five as referring to prophets.[23] Of these, a group of nine are singled out to be called *Ulu al 'Azam*, 'possessors of power'.[24] And of these, there are five who were granted special titles: Noah, the preacher of Allah; Abraham, the Friend of Allah; Moses, the Speaker with Allah; Jesus, the 'Spirit of God'/'Word of God'; Mohammed, the apostle of Allah.[25] All of these had identifiable books 'given' to them, except that the books of Noah and Abraham are no longer known.

Beside these, and outside these groups, there are three recognized prophetesses: Sarah, who received the news of Isaac's birth by revelation; Miriam, the sister of Moses, who received news of Moses' birth, and Mary, who received news of Jesus the Messiah from an angel.

As far as the Muslim is concerned, there has never been a time without Allah speaking to every generation.

v. Belief in the day of judgement

This is a vital article of faith in Islam: there is life after death, in a wonderful paradise for the Muslim. It is considered that 'Life on earth is meant to be a preparation for the *Akhirah* (life after death). Life is meaningless if people of good actions are not rewarded and people of bad conduct are not punished at the Day of Judgement.'[26] The purpose of Judgement Day is either to purify and give reward or to humiliate and bring shame. It is the day that Allah will show himself to be true to his revelation, demonstrating his characteristics of omnipotence, omniscience, wisdom, providence, justice and mercy.

The essential ingredients of this belief are:

a. There will be a Last Day, when life on earth will end and everything will be annihilated.

b. Allah will sit in judgement on that day. All human beings who have ever lived will be presented to him.

c. The full record of everyone's good or bad deeds will be presented to Allah.

d. Each person will be either rewarded if his good deeds outweigh his bad ones, or punished if his bad ones outweigh his good.

e. Those who are rewarded will go to paradise; those who are punished will go to hell.[27]

There are many graphic and highly colourful details ascribed to the Last Day. The righteous will be given his book of deeds in his right hand, but the damned will be forced to receive his in his left hand. His works having been weighed in the balances, everyone must walk the *syrat*, a path on the very brink of hell. Great care has to be taken, for this path is described as a tight-rope over the great chasm, a path sharper than a sword's edge, finer than a hair. The righteous with his book in his right hand will walk safely across into heaven, but damned sinners will fall into the fires of hell, and they will suffer there until they have been purified of their unrighteousness.[28] Then they too will be received into heaven.

Muslims believe that all men and women are born sinless, and that they will get to heaven by being at least 51% good. Sin is neither dealt with nor paid for in Islam, it can only be weighed on a balance. Islam has no promise of eternal life, and therefore eternity is faced with fear.

Eternity is never ending, and the destination of all is the Garden in heaven, or the Fire of hell. For Muslims, the situation is that all men and women have been given the truth of Allah through his prophets, and therefore there is no non-Muslim. Therefore those who refuse to believe (*kafir*, 'infidels', includes Christians), are going to hell, but there is no guarantee of heaven for the Muslim. It is wholly in the will of Allah, and hopefully a Muslim's good works will secure heaven.

Al-janna (lit., the garden) is the Muslim heaven, located at the macrocosmic centre of light. According to both the Qur'an and the *hadith*, it is a place of peace, great joy and ultimate satisfaction. It is a place of wonderful security and beautiful gardens, containing vineyards full of ripe grapes, a place of shades and fountains, an abundance of fruit, and beautiful maidens. All of this would have evoked many fond memories and extremely attractive images to the Arab living in the harsh desert, feeding vivid imaginations, and influencing many a Muslim to fight for Islam. There are often said to be seven divisions in heaven or paradise, and Allah's throne is above them all. It is believed that the greatest among Muslims will be on the highest heaven, and the less righteous placed on the lower levels.

There is no concept, as found in the Bible, of the saved believer sharing in the glorified life and worship of God.

Christians look forward to a new heaven and new earth in which righteousness dwells (2 Peter 3:13). However, from all that the Lord Jesus Christ taught, it is not a sensuous place. It is the place where worship is fulfilled and completed, as we focus our attention on him who sits on the Throne of God, even the Lamb of God (Revelation 7:9–17). Heaven is the glory of being in the presence of Almighty God. It is a vastly different hope from that of the Muslim.

Al-Jahanam, hell, the other extreme, is spoken of with great respect and fear. The Qur'an makes frequent mention of the fires of hell, and popular books wax eloquently on the awful torments of the doomed. There is much confused thinking, for although it is said that the righteous will pass over the hair's breadth bridge into heaven, orthodox teaching also states that all Muslims will spend time in hell, in a type of purgatory meant for their purification, but which therefore will not be everlasting.

There are seven divisions of hell described:

(i) *Jaheem*, the Muslim's purgatory. It is the shallowest level of hell, reserved for those who believed in Allah and his messenger, but who ignored his commands.

(ii) *Jahanam*, a deeper level where idol-worshippers are sent on the day of Judgement.

(iii) *Sa'ir*, is reserved for the worshippers of fire *(Sabeans?)*.

(iv) *Saqar*, where those who did not believe in Allah will be sent on the Day of Judgement.

(v) *Ladha*, the home of the Jews.

(vi) *Hawiya*, the abode of Christians.

(vii) *Al-hatama*, the deepest level of hellfire, where the religious hypocrites will spend eternity. The worst of Allah's creation are the *munafiqeen* (hypocrites), whether they be mankind or *jinn*, for they outwardly appear to accept, but inwardly reject, Allah and his Messenger.

The time spent in hell depends on the severity of one's evil deeds, though there is some distinct feeling that levels (vi) and (vii) will remain for ever. It is all a matter of some quite considerable debate, but it is stated that the infinite mercy of Allah is seen in the Qur'anic statement that those who have even a mustard seed's weight of belief in Allah will eventually be admitted to heaven.

The signs of the Judgement Day are also elaborate. There are about 70 minor signs of its coming, but about twelve major signs. These include

a. The appearance of a mighty conqueror (*Al-Mahdi*) who will unite Muslims to become a great nation.

b. *Al-Dajjal* (the Antichrist) will appear from between Iraq and Syria, roaming the world for forty days, laying it waste, before he is slain by the prophet Jesus.

c. Jesus himself will return, take a wife, and have children. He will call everyone to accept Islam. During his forty years on earth, there will be peace as never known before, such as described in Isaiah 11:6. Then he will die, and be buried alongside Mohammed.

d. The sun will rise from the west.

e. The Ka'aba will be destroyed. At the same time written copies of the Qur'an will be removed, and its words erased from people's memories.

f. This will be preceded by three blasts of a trumpet. The consequences of this will be: that at the first blast all creatures in heaven and on earth will be struck with terror; at the second blast all creatures in heaven and on earth will die; and at the third blast, forty years later, all will be raised again for judgement.

This Day of Judgement will last one thousand years (see Sura 22:47), or, maybe, even fifty thousand years (see Sura 70:4)—depending on which tradition one follows. When all are assembled for judgement the angels will keep them waiting for forty years (or another fifty thousand?). Then Allah himself will appear. At that time Mohammed will intercede for all Muslims, because Adam, Noah, Abraham, Moses and Jesus will all decline to do so, feeling they are unworthy of so great a task.

vi. Belief in predestination

Allah has timeless knowledge and it is in his power to execute his will. He is wise and merciful and whatever he does must have a meaningful purpose, even if mankind does not understand it. He determines everything.

Allah is absolute in his decree of both good and evil. He alone gives life and causes death. His decrees are inescapable, and everything that happens is determined by him and happens in accordance with his absolute foreknowledge.

A Muslim believes that Allah is not limited by any consideration whatsoever, moral or otherwise. It alone rests with Allah as to whether he forgives or damns. Allah is the sole 'decider' of a man's deeds and destiny. This doctrine places the responsibility of all that a man does, whether good or evil, entirely upon Allah. Man is therefore deemed not responsible for what he does. On the other hand, Allah cannot be accused of being unjust in judging those actions for which man cannot be held accountable.

This precept is totally cold and clinical, and has to be accepted blindly. It is pure fatalism. Allah is pleased to send people to hell. It is an event fixed in eternity, and human beings are powerless to alter such a decree. In practice then, Muslims understand that Allah sends to heaven whomever he pleases, and equally he sends to hell whomever he pleases.

This results in a sense of resigned insecurity. Everything a Muslim does is always with a sense of *insh'Allah* ('If God wills'). However much a Muslim fasts, prays, gives money to the poor and makes pilgrimage to Mecca, none of these things can keep him out of hell, if that is Allah's decreed will. For this reason, it is always that much more a reality to Muslims than heaven. Thus the promise of a passage to heaven by any means is an attractive proposition.

Despite this somewhat irrational and harsh dogma, it is interesting to observe that in the hearts of many Muslims there is a deep-seated desire to please Allah, and to know him in the sense of having a dependable relationship with him. Consequently, the practice of a great number of Muslims will be found to be inconsistent with this particular article of faith, though they will tenaciously hold to both a mental and verbal assent to it.

***

The 'Pillars of Islam' are merely the tangible expression of these doctrines. We have not been able to look too closely at all the teaching of Islam. The bibliography will indicate some useful books and internet sites that will help to give a broader and deeper understanding.

Notes

1 **Dr Christine Schirrmacher,** 'The Meaning of faith in Islam', 1997: www.visi.com/~contra_m/ab/cschirrmacher/faith.html.
2 Sura 112.
3 See Information sheet 3, Names of Allah, p.222.
4 MSA-USC: www.usc.edu/dept/MSA/humanrelations/humanrights/. Quoting *III&E Brochure Series, No. 2* (published by The Institute of Islamic Information and Education (III&E)).
5 MSA-USC: www.usc.edu/dept/MSA/fundamentals/tawheed/lailahaillaAllah.html. Article: 'Reflections on *la ilaha illa Allah*'.
6 John 1:29
7 See also Chapter 24, *Potential problems*, i. God ... or Allah?, pp.181–182.
8 Sura 2:285.
9 Sura 2:32.
10 Sura 2:177, Sura 2:285.
11 Sura 41:30.

Chapter 6

12 Sura: 50:17–18, quoting a readily available 'interpretation of the Qur'an' used on many internet sites.

13 Sura 15:26–27. Dawoo's word 'Satan' is changed to 'jinn', as other Qur'anic translations (Arberry, Pickthall, and Khalifa).

14 Sura 38:71–85.

15 Sura 2:2–4.

16 Sura 3:2–3.

17 Sura 10:64.

18 **Cyril Glassé**, *The Concise Encyclopedia of Islam* (San Francisco: Harper & Row, 1989), p.65, p.324.

19 BELIEVE Religious Information Source: http://mb-soft.com/believe. Article: 'Islam: Koran or Qur'an'.

20 Sura 22:52–53.

21 Sura 17:73–75.

22 Sura 2:285. See also Sura 10:47.

23 These include Adam, Noah, Abraham, David, Jacob, Joseph, Job, Moses, Jesus and Mohammed.

24 Noah, Abraham, David, Jacob, Joseph, Job, Moses, Jesus and Mohammed.

25 Some Muslims also include one other: Adam, the Chosen of Allah.

26 Islam@PakWatan.com, http://pakwatan.com/main/islam/principles.php3#_Sr674, Article: 'Principles of Islam: Akhira'.

27 Listed in **Anne Cooper**, *Ishmael, My Brother* (MARC/STL Books, 1985), p.42.

28 Notice the similarity with the Jewish concept of Hades (see Josephus) and the Roman Catholic concept of Purgatory.

Islam divided

Having looked at the basic principles of Islam, we must also consider the way Muslims and their beliefs vary worldwide. There are over 150 branches or groups in Islam, the main division being between Sunni and Shi'a, but these are also sub-divided. Some Muslims of both branches are grouped as Sufi Muslims.

Sunni Muslims

These follow the tradition of Mohammed as found in the *hadith*, and strongly maintain they alone follow the correct traditions. They are known as 'the people of the *sunnah*' ('custom', 'example').

In the early years following Mohammed's death, Islamic scholars worked to systematize the faith. In so doing, many thousands of *hadith* (traditions) had to be considered. Two scholars, Al-Bukhari (AD 810–870)[1] and Sahih Muslim (AD 817–875),[2] reduced the thousands to seven thousand, and by the tenth century these were given canonical status within Islam. Also two other partial collections were made by Sunan Abu Daawuud and Malik'I Muwatta, being about half the size of those of Bukhari and Muslim, which influence Islamic sects such as the Druze.

Over the same period, the *shari'ah* ('the path') were organized, these being the principles on which Islamic law is based. Rules of procedure were developed in four schools of law to decide on the details. All the laws were based on the Qur'an and the *sunnah*, and two legal principles became known as *qiyas* (analogy) and *ijma* (consensus).

Qiyas was an attempt to apply the law in situations not mentioned in the Qur'an, and might be considered as similar to the Jewish Talmud. Also *ijma* was used when no clear guidance was given in either the Qur'an or the *sunnah*, and the consensus of the community was sought. The four law schools accepted each other as orthodox, although they differed in outlook.

Today, Sunni Islam is often seen as giving the orthodox view of these matters, although many changes have been made. To describe other sects as deviant is therefore inaccurate. About 83% of Muslims are Sunni.

Shi'a Muslims

This group separated from Sunni Islam by recognizing a different caliph (*khalifa*) as leader over the Muslim state or government (*khilafa*) when Mohammed died. A minority group in Medina wanted a cousin of the prophet, Ali ibn Abi Talib, feeling he was better qualified to be their leader. They came to be known as *Shiat 'Ali* (the party of Ali) and then as the *Shi'a*.

The Shi'a believe that Mohammed actually chose Ali. On this basis Ali and his associates were obliged to protest against the practice of choosing the Prophet's successor by election. This protest separated them from the majority Sunnis. So the Shi'a believe that Ali was the first true Caliph, who was followed by a hereditary succession of eleven others. They also believed that he was divinely inspired and immune from error, which made him infallible in his knowledge and in his authority to teach Islam after Mohammed.

Some twenty-four years elapsed between Mohammed's death and Ali finally becoming caliph. His leadership was both charismatic and controversial, but he was murdered in the fifth year of his caliphate. Following his assassination the caliphate was reorganized under the rule of Mu'awiya who established the *Ummawiyy* dynasty (lasting to AD 750). His rule brought new innovations to Islam, and the old supporters of Ali formed the nucleus of opposition. Ali's eldest son al-Hassan came to an agreement with Mu'awiya. When he died, Ali's second son al-Husain became the leader of the opposition. After Mu'awiya died in AD 680, Husain left Medina to travel to Kufa, but was trapped in the desert at Karbala, on the bank of the river Euphrates, by soldiers of the new caliph, Mu'awaiya's son Yazid. Without water and hopelessly outnumbered, al-Husain and his followers fought a desperate but hopeless battle. Yazid's troops both killed and desecrated al-Husain's body. At this point a distinct Shi'a Islam came into being. In the succeeding decade they were persecuted by the Sunnis. The Shi'a became the focus of opposition, and many disaffected Sunnis joined them, mostly *Mawali* (non-Arabs), who were as such being treated as second-class citizens.

An important theme in Shi'a Islam is the ideal of suffering and martyrdom. This has been focussed on the martyrdom of Ali, and the massacre of Husain and his followers. The battle of Karbala is remembered at *Ashura*, celebrated on the tenth day of Muharram, with a wailing *imam* whipping the congregation into a frenzy of tears and chest beating.

In Shi'a teaching, the *Imam*s (Ali and his descendants) were the only authoritative source of religious instruction and guidance. As all Muslims do, they believed that the teachings of the Qur'an and the sacred law of Islam (the *shari'ah*) came from sources beyond man and thus contained truths that could not be grasped by human reason. But in applying this they concluded that it was necessary to have an authority in religious guidance, namely the *Imam*. Their *shahada* (confession) also differs slightly: 'There is no God but Allah, Mohammed is the Messenger of Allah, Ali is the Friend of Allah, the successor of the Messenger of Allah, and his first caliph.'[3]

Because of these beliefs, these Shi'a became known as the Twelvers, based on the twelve hereditary caliphs. This line of special *imam*s came to an end in AD 878. A collective body of Shi'ite religious scholars, known as *ulema*, assumed his office, as they awaited the return of the *Mahdi*, 'rightly-guided one'. The present day *Ayatollah*s (Signs of Allah) see themselves as joint caretakers of the office of the *Imam*, who, it is anticipated, will return at the end of time.

There are some significant differences between Sunni and Shi'a Islam. They both believe in the five Pillars of Islam. However, they only share three main doctrines: belief in the undivided unity of Allah, the revelations of Mohammed, and in the resurrection on the Day of Judgement. They hold to a different set of *hadith*. Sunni Islam gives far more importance to Mecca and the *Hajj*; while the Shi'a insist that there are some other important pilgrimages as well. Sunni Muslims revere Ali, but they do not hold that he is the true continuation of the tradition from Mohammed. Shi'a Muslims insist that he received divine light from the Prophet, and that his successors, the Imams, are fully spiritual guides and inerrant interpreters of law and tradition. An important characteristic of Shi'a Islam that differs from Sunni Islam is that doctrine can be continually expanded and reinterpreted.

On a practical level, Shi'a have a different call to prayer, they perform their washings and prayer (*salat*) differently, by placing the forehead on a piece of hardened clay from Karbala, not directly on the prayer mat. They also tend to combine prayers, sometimes worshipping three times instead of five times a day. Shi'a Islam also allows a fixed–term marriage (*muttah*), which is now banned by the Sunnis, but which was apparently permitted in the time of Mohammed. It is now being promoted in Iran by an unlikely alliance of conservative *mullah*s and feminists.

Another important characteristic is the emphasis on the visitation of shrines that are dedicated to the various Imams. In Iraq, these include the tomb of Ali, in An Najaf, and that of his son, Imam Husain, in Karbala. Before the Iran-Iraq War (1980–88), tens of thousands of Iranian Shi'a used to visit them each year. In Iran, pilgrimage sites include the tomb of the eighth Imam in Mashhad and that of his sister in Qom. Some of the reason for the popularity of these shrines was the huge expense and practical difficulty of poorer Shi'a Muslims making the *hajj* in the early days of Islam.

But all was not happy in the ranks of the Shi'a, and they were not all agreed on the idea of *Imam* succession. So a group broke away and became known as the Seveners or Ismaeli, because it was their view that the rightful seventh and last Imam was not Musa al Kazim, but his elder brother Isma'il who died as a child.

To summarize, we can see that Sunni Islam believes that the Qur'an is the final authority—that there is no further revelation. However, Shi'a Islam believes that the rightful *Imam* has both divine inspiration and the authority of Allah to add to the message of the Qur'an. Thus Shi'a Islam is the more radical of these two main branches of Islam, and it is not surprising therefore that many conclude that Sunni Islam is the more orthodox Islam. Also down the centuries within Shi'a Islam there have been those who claimed to be the next *Imam* and attempted to rally Muslims to their particular cause. This has often been expressed as a *jihad*, and thus Shi'a Muslims have often been seen to be the more militant stream.

In today's world, Iran is overwhelmingly Shi'a. Shi'a Muslims also form the majority population in the Yemen and Azerbaijan, and constitute up to around 50% of the population of Iraq. There are also significant communities of Shi'a in Bahrain, the east coast of Saudi Arabia and in the Lebanon (where the militant group Hizbollah is based). Worldwide, there are estimated to be anything from 10% up to 16% Shi'a within the overall Muslim population.

Divisions and sub-divisions

From the early years of Islam many other groups fragmented the Shi'a.

The Khajirites (meaning 'secessionists') withdrew from the 'party of 'Ali' because they claimed that their leaders did not follow the Qur'an strictly, and leave major decisions to Allah'.4 They believed that Islam should be a community of saints and that those who commit grave sins should forfeit their identity as Muslims. There were those who differed on this, emphasizing the importance of faith over works, arguing that the decision on 'grave' sinners should be deferred to Allah at the Day of Judgement. This latter group came to be known as the Murji'ites ('postponers of those who have hope'). But those who emphasized human responsibility over predestination were known as Qadarites (determiners). The Kharijites exist today as a small sect in North Africa.

The Ismaelis, mentioned above, developed their own distinctive ideas. Flourishing in the tenth century, they were influential in establishing the Fatimid dynasty in Egypt, Palestine and Syria. They have been active missionaries for Islam, and their influence spread to southern Arabia and East Africa. They divide into two branches, namely the *Musta'li* based in Bombay, India, and the *Nazari,* led by the Aga Khan. Other groups that derived from Ismaelis include the Nusayris, mostly found in Syria, and the Druze.

The Druze call themselves *muwahhidun*, 'monotheists', but are rather an obscure sect of Islam, and many Muslims actually regard them as non-Muslim. They meet on Thursdays for prayer instead of Fridays. They hold firmly to monogamous marriage. Their theology is called *hakim*, the main theme being that Allah incarnated himself in the Shi'a (Fatimid) Caliph al-Hakim, who disappeared in AD 1021. Most Muslims believe he died, but the Druze maintain that he is alive and waiting to return to the world to bring in a new golden age for true believers. The Druze believe that Allah's qualities cannot be understood by man. Al Hakim is worshipped in Druze religion, called 'Our Lord' and his cruelties and eccentricities are interpreted symbolically.

The *Hashshashin* ('assassins') broke away from the Ismaelis in Syria and Persia during the period of the early Christian crusades of the eleventh century. They received their name from their use of hashish. They became famous for seizing the Crusader forts and assassinating Christians. Today they are known as Khojas or Mawlas and live mainly in the Bombay area, though some still live in Syria and Iran.

The Ahmadiyya movement is generally called Qadianism by Muslims. Established in 1889 by Mirza Ghulam Qadiani in what is now Pakistan, they have become a strong voice for Islam in some places, being very missionary-minded, preferring debate over the concept of *jihad*. However, many Muslims consider them to be heretical, much of their teaching not being truly Islamic. Indeed, their teaching is highly syncretistic. This is a messianic movement, Qadiani claimed he is the *Mahdi*, and the Messiah, and the avatar of Krishna, and even an improved incarnation of Mohammed.

But the divisions did not occur only among the ranks of the Ismaelis. Sunni Muslims also divided into various groups. One of the earliest of the Sunni groups was formed by Abu Hanifah, who died in AD 767. This became known as the Hanafi, and is considered to be one of more liberal schools of thought, when compared with more fundamentalist groups. This is the school that dominated Muslims in the Turkic peoples of Central Asia, Turkey and in the Arab countries of the Fertile Crescent, lower Egypt and also in India.

The Malakite school, formed by Malik ibn Anas (died in AD 795), developed around the idea that it was more important to depend on the traditions of the Companions of Mohammed, rather than on the Prophet himself. When they were faced with conflicting traditions, Malik and his followers took a rational view and made an arbitrary choice. Followers of this school are still very strong in North Africa, particularly in Algeria.

The Shafi'ites were founded by a follower of Malik, one Al Shafi'i, who died in AD 820. He made a considerable impact on the developing Islamic Law, giving influential input into defining the *shari'ah* (the fundamental Law of Islam) and the *hadith*. They can be found in lower Egypt, Syria, India and Indonesia.

Sufi Islam

In Arabic, adherents to Sufi Islam are known as *tasawwuf*. Sufi Islam is a mystical form that began to make an impact within the first 100 years of

Islam, but their origins are as mystical as their practice, with no clear history.

The great Sufi *tariqa* (paths, orders, groups) were founded in the twelfth century by scholars who became disillusioned in their search for truth through the intellectual application of legalistic practices advocated by the various schools of Islamic doctrine. They reacted against a purely transcendent Allah, preferring to believe that knowing Allah must have a more personal and subjective aspect. Their central doctrine is *wahdat al-wujud*, the unity of being—a oneness of man with Allah. Therefore they sought to develop a religion of the heart, and not merely of the mind, where men may become 'drunk' with the love of Allah. A keyword therefore is passion in worship. They continue to believe that the Qur'an is the means of spiritual guidance, but to this they add the need of instruction and help from a wise and experienced 'master' or guide.

Thus Sufi Islam is wisdom orientated, centring on a spiritual guide, or learned leader known as a *sheikh*, or a *pir* (Persian word). The call is for a life of love and pure devotion to Allah. Sufis developed a spiritual path to Allah, consisting of various stages of piety (*maqamat*) and gnostic-psychological states (*awal*), through which each Sufi must pass. This concept of stages in piety led to a perception of sainthood in Islam. Hence there are pilgrimages to the shrines of such *pirs* who have attained sainthood, prayers to the saints, and belief in miracles obtained through such things.

Strict orthodox Islam frowns on any use of music in religious rituals. The only acceptable 'musical' form is the chanting of the call to prayer by the *muezzin* at the mosque, and the recitation of Qur'an where the spoken Arabic has an inherent 'beauty'. But Sufis have developed a wide variety of ritual observances that involve singing, drums and other musical instruments. There are also trance-making dance forms, the best known being the Turkish Mevlevi order, often called the 'whirling dervishes'. There are also forms of meditation, reciting of sacred phrases, and even breathing exercises.

The mystical teachings of the *pir* guide students, who are known as *murid*, along the *tariqa* that leads to the ecstatic experience of a personal moment of intimacy with Allah. The relationship between *pir* and *murid* is a very close one. Many famous *pir*s attract large followings, their brotherhoods becoming centres for spiritual institutions, and provide social services. The practice of receiving gifts from pilgrims often means that such a *pir* becomes wealthy and powerful.

Sufi practices are found among both Sunni and Shi'a communities, but tend to be more widespread among Sunnis. This may be because the Shi'a already attach great value to the intercession of saints and most Shi'a already embrace some form of mysticism.

Many Muslims see Sufism as a threat to the *ulema* (religious authorities), and undermining the concept of a universal, unified Islamic community (*ummah*) in following the *shari'ah*, the 'straight path' of Islamic law. But Sufis argue that their expression of Islam is the real basis of orthodox Islam.

It is extremely difficult to determine the percentage of Sufism in Islam, but many Muslims, if they are serious about wanting to know Allah, demonstrate some form of Sufi interest. One estimate is a total of 5 million Sufis around the world which seems a conservative figure.[5] If you identify Folk Islam with Sufism, then the figure is going to be much higher for it is estimated that 70% of Muslims practice Folk Islam to some degree or other.[6]

Folk Islam

What is Folk Islam? It is the belief system of those who claim to be Muslims, but go beyond even the 'felt religion' of Shi'a Islam. Muslims in many countries of Asia and Africa have absorbed into their Islamic religion practices that are not Islamic. Sufi Muslims describe the special gift that Allah gave to the founders and heads of Sufi orders as *baraka*, a special gifting or blessing. Such a leader who has *baraka* has the power to bless others, such as in granting healing, giving financial blessing, and enabling childbirth—but there is a potentially harmful side; *baraka* can be used to curse others, and thus bring evil or injury upon them.

Fear is one of the reasons that much Sufi practice came into being. Sufis follow their leader (their *pir* or *sheik*) in order to receive blessing so that they might not have any negative experiences that could be attributed to Allah's displeasure. All Muslims, it is true to say, have a conscious hope of heaven and a fear of hell. In Sufism, there is a greater personal consciousness of this, for they have the hope of knowing the presence of Allah in this life, and subsequently, there is an even greater consciousness of knowing evil personally through Allah's disapproval. Take that a step further, and you enter what we are describing as Folk Islam, or if you like, 'popular Islam'. So for many ordinary Muslims there is a close relationship between well-being and Allah's blessing on the one hand, and misfortune and Allah's disapproval on the other.

Most Muslims think that Allah really can be known. Formal Islam keeps Allah at arm's length, but reason argues that we can be in touch with Allah, leading to a real tension.

Not to understand this aspect of Islam is to miss something extremely important.[7] It is reckoned that across the Muslim world some 70% are influenced by and practise some form of Folk Islam, including those multicultural neighbourhoods in our own western countries. It may be described as the grass-roots, or popular, form of Islam that is practised worldwide.

New Age practices have made an impact on western society: people buy spells, love potions and gem stones, assuming they have mystical powers. These are also sold widely in Muslim countries by *pirs* to assist their followers in everyday life issues. Folk Islam addresses the fears and longings of Muslim hearts. Many of these people live in deeply superstitious communities.

So what can we identify as popular Islam? On the *hajj* pilgrimage the Ka'aba is kissed by pilgrims. Why? Was it not part of the superstitious worship Mohammed criticized? It is argued that a kiss is a sign of respect. One writer observed that Mohammed was against idolatry rather than pagan practices.[8]

Another contributor replied in defence of kissing the Ka'aba:

However, people want to touch or kiss it with respect because this stone bears a memory of Prophets Adam and Ibrahim. Therefore, this black stone is not sacred nor has it any importance in Islam other than being a memory. Any form of veneration or any worship associated with this black stone should be treated as blasphemous.[9]

The reality is that there is little practical difference between remembering and worshipping in the minds of ordinary Muslims. Mohammed allowed 'veneration' of the meteorite stone as an act of appeasing the inhabitants of Mecca when he re-entered with his army 'without a fight' in AD 630, and declared an amnesty. This practice, to an unbiased observer, could well look to be a remnant of pre-Muslim idolatrous, animistic practice.

In spite of Mohammed's aversion to idolatry, most of his earlier followers were open to the teaching of 'other gods', as this had been inherent in their upbringing. Today, a vast number of Muslims find the official doctrine of Allah too cerebral, and hence too distant, to meet their personal needs. So they have adapted Islam, knowingly or unwittingly, to be 'more practical', for their personal needs demand attention. Thus they have turned to what may described as a more earth-orientated mysticism— a spirituality that has a 'helpful' mix of elements that are foreign to pure Islam, but which promise 'power' that will affect them directly. So there is a practical interest in spirits, in dead saints, and even ancestors. Protection is sought against spells, omens, the 'evil eye', and other problems caused by detrimental spirits.

So in Folk Islam there is a high dependency on the esoteric qualities of experience, such as dreams, visions and divinations. Occult powers are sought through the use of amulets, charms, magic, astrology, sorcery and witchcraft. Verses of the Qur'an are worn on the body in amulets, or written on paper and eaten to ward off evil spirits or to accomplish different purposes including healing. The power of the 'evil eye' is so great as to be enormously crippling. Therefore some use of animistic means is required to redress the balance. The impact that Folk Islam has on ordinary Muslims is revealing.[10]

Summary

In this chapter we have simply been attempting to give an overview of a very perplexing and complex issue. I have tried to show how the different strands of Islam have developed, and how we get to the very varied Muslim scene of today. Whenever Muslims are encountered, we need to listen carefully to the things they say and understand concerning Islam—and not assume that we know what they believe.

Notes

1 Full name: Abu Abdullah Mohammed bin Ismail bin Ibrahim bin al-Mughira al-Ja'fai. His *hadith* is the work of 16 years, comprising 3,295 *ahadith*, divided into 97 'books' with 3,450 chapters. He applied to his collection the most stringent rules, putting them into four categories: sound (*sahih*), good (*hasan*), weak (*da'if*), and fabricated or forged (*maudu'*).

2 Full name: Abul Husain Muslim bin al-Hajjaj al-Nisapuri. He was a student of al-Bukhari. His collection is much larger, based upon less stringent criteria than used by Bukhari, accepting about 12,000 *ahadith*, from out of some 3,000,000.

3 Their *shahada* (creed) is much more extensive according to Hussein Abdulwaheed Amin. A fuller statement on the Shi'a *shahada* and their beliefs is given on the *Islam For Today* website at www.islamfortoday.com/shia.htm#shiabeliefs. Many other interesting details are given.

4 The Unreached Peoples Prayer Profiles:
http://www.ksafe.com/profiles/a_code/islam.html#Divisions, 'An Introduction to Islam: Divisions and subdivisions', ¶1.

5 Encyclopedia of the Orient: http://lexicorient.com/e.o/index.htm. Article: 'Sufism'.

6 Compare **Phil Parshall**, *Bridges to Islam* (Grand Rapids: Baker Book House, 1983), p.37 and the reviews of books on Folk Islam by Jenny at http://home.vicnet.net.au/~efac/folkislam.htm.

7 I commend **Phil Parshall**, *Bridges to Islam* (Grand Rapids: Baker Book House, 1983) for a deeper study of this phenomenon and to understand its importance in Muslim evangelism.

8 **M.S.N Menon**, www.tribuneindia.com/2002/20020721/spectrum/main3.htm. Article: 'Was the Prophet misunderstood?' *The Sunday Tribune*, 21 July 2001.

9 See **Badaruddoza and Arshad Chouhan**, (Amritsar):
www.tribuneindia.com/2002/20020825/spectrum/feedback.htm. Article: 'Understanding the Prophet', *The Sunday Tribune*, 25 August 2002, Feedback, ¶5.

10 For a deeper treatment and enlightening illustrations of Folk Islam see **Bill Musk**, *The Unseen Face of Islam* (MARC, 1989).

Life at the Mosque

Islam has an all-encompassing influence within any Muslim country or tribal group. The Islamic requirements for life and worship become an intrinsic part of Muslim society. Especially, the Qur'anic commands to pray five times daily have a visible impact. Wherever Muslims are, at home or travelling, they will stop, and after a ritual washing, get out their prayer mat, face the *qibla*, and do their *salat* or *namaz*.

Mohammed taught that worship should be focussed at a mosque (*masjid*, 'the place of prostration'). He built the first one at Quba, south-east of Medina. Two others are mentioned in the Qur'an, the Masjid al Haram—the home of the *Ka'aba* at Mecca)—and the Masjid al Aqsa—the site of the Jewish Temple in Jerusalem from where Mohammed ascended up to heaven (*miraj*). Here he received the command to pray five times a day and the revelation which encapsulated the beliefs of Islam:

Al Aqsa Mosque, Jerusalem

The Apostle believes in what has been revealed to him by his Lord, and so do the faithful. They believe in Allah and his angels, his scriptures and his apostles; we discriminate against none of his apostles. They say: 'We hear and obey. Grant us your forgiveness, Lord; to you we shall all return.'[1]

The site in Jerusalem thus became a sacred spot for Muslims, who peacefully conquered Jerusalem after a short siege in AD 638, and subsequently began to build the famous Dome of the Rock mosque on what was considered to be this sacred spot in AD 685.

Just as Christians identify themselves as the universal body of Christ (the Church) which has its practical expression in the local church, in a similar way, Muslims view their community as being based on a local mosque, which becomes a local expression of the *ummah*.

The Dome of the Rock, Jerusalem

A *masjid* is therefore the place where the pulse of the Islamic community can be felt. The mosque has always been a religious and social centre. The most obvious feature of the mosque is that it is the place for *namaz* (or *salat*)—the worship of the community: the ritual prayers. It is also the place of learning, whether secular or religious, and the place where important historical occasions are celebrated. It also provides a platform for political pronouncements, which often take place at the Friday midday prayers.

So the mosque, besides its obvious religious role, is the hub of society. It may be compared with the Greek Agora or the Roman forum. Similarly, St Peter's Church at Rome is still the place where political and social, as well as religious, pronouncements are made by the Pope.

Praying at the mosque holds special value. As one *hadith* expressed it, 'The reward of the prayer offered by a person in congregation is twenty times greater that that of the prayer offered in one's house or in the market.'[2] The community has to be reminded of their deities. If they did not pray five times a day, believers would soon forget about Allah and his greatness.

All mosques take their significance from the Ka'aba (*Masjid al Haram*). This place of worship is claimed to have been built by the prophet Ibrahim (Abraham)—this is made as a categorical statement, not a speculation. In the centre of the present mosque is the simple cube structure which has gone through several renovations and expansion, though supposedly maintaining its original style, the last major reconstruction being in 1996.

And today there is an exclusion zone (*haram*—prohibited area) around the Ka'aba, in some directions extending up to twelve miles, into which only Muslims are allowed to enter; any foreigner enters it on pain of death.

The Ka'aba measures about 13.5 metres (45 ft) by 16.5 metres (55 ft) around the base, and about 11.7 metres (39 ft) high.³ It is built so that its corners are set to the four points of the compass. The stone walls are 1 metre (3 ft) thick and built with grey stones hewn locally from the hills around Mecca.

On the inside of the Ka'aba the stones are unpolished, while outside they are polished. The floor is covered by marble, making a base which is about 25 cm (10 in) high. The ceiling and roof are made out of wood. These were reconstructed with teak and capped with stainless steel. A door is set in the north-eastern wall 2 metres (6.5 ft) above the surrounding ground. Two (three?) wooden pillars hold up the roof, accessed by a ladder. The upper part of the inside walls is covered with some kind of curtain with the *kalimah* (the statement of faith) written on it.

On the outside, at the eastern corner, is the Black Stone, set 1.5 metres (5ft) above the ground. This Black Stone is now in pieces, three large parts and smaller fragments, which are tied together with a silver band. There are several theories on the origin of the Black Stone: (1) a meteor; (2) lava; or (3) basalt. It is reddish black in colour, with some red and yellow particles. Its original diameter is estimated to have been 30 cm (1 ft). There is another stone, too, built into the Ka'aba, in the western corner: the Stone of Good Fortune. This is far less sacred than the Black Stone. The wall between the door and the Black Stone is very sacred, and is considered to have a lot of *baraka* (blessing).

The Black Stone in the Ka'aba

The black cover over the Ka'aba, called the *kiswa*, is made of pure natural silk dyed in black, and produced in Egypt annually. The cloth is some 14 metres high, fixed to the ground with copper rings. Over the upper third of the cloth is the 95 metres (300ft) wide and 45 metres (140 ft) long

80 Love your Muslim neighbour

hazam or belt, which is made of 16 pieces and surrounds the *kiswa* from all sides. This *hazam* is embroidered with protruding designs that are enamelled with silver threads covered with gold, with some Qur'anic verses in Arabic calligraphy. Under the belt, at each corner of the Ka'aba, the Sura 112 *Ikhlas* (Purity of Faith) is written inside a circle surrounded by a square shape of Islamic embellishment. At the same height, also under the belt, there are six verses from the Qur'an—each of which is written in a separate frame. On the areas separating these frames there is a shape of a lamp on which other Qur'anic phrases are written. In an interim period which lasts a little more than two weeks, the *kiswa* is taken off and the Ka'aba is covered by a white covering. At the end of *hajj* the new *kiswa* is presented.

This mosque takes centre stage in all Muslim activity. It is the most holy shrine to Islam, but Muslims stringently maintain that they do not worship the Ka'aba. To untrained eyes it would appear that the veneration given to the Ka'aba is worship.

The Door of the Ka'aba

In every place where there are Muslims around the world, there are mosques. Each is built with a *qibla* that faces the Ka'aba in Mecca. The model of all early mosques was the courtyard of Mohammed's house in Medina, constructed in AD 622. At first it was organized with a *qibla* that faced Jerusalem, but when the Jews refused to accept Mohammed as a prophet, he changed the *qibla* to face Mecca. This Medina mosque also had social, political and judicial functions.

Mosques developed into something more complex and even more uniform in their shape. The following descriptions are of the different parts of a mosque. Inside along the 'back' wall (towards which prayer is made) is the *mihrab* which is a niche in the mosque wall which indicates the direction of *qibla*. The *minbar* is the pulpit, sited next to the *mihrab*, from which the weekly Friday sermon is presented. Before this wall and the *mihrab* are rows of beautifully designed carpets often with Qur'anic quotations, where the worshippers stand, kneel and crouch while performing their prayers. But note that no figurative art is permitted in a mosque. And if no carpet is provided, each Muslim takes his own prayer mat. These are often designed with Islamic calligraphy, and may even have a picture of the Ka'aba.

Friday is Islam's holy day. A Muslim is required to visit the mosque on Friday to offer prayers, if he possibly can. In fact the main mosque in any city is called the *Jama* (Friday) mosque, where Muslims gather for communal prayer (*jum'a*) at mid-day, the congregation of a mosque being the *jama'at*.

The local *imam* leads the *namaz* (prayer ritual), after which he stands on the lower steps of the pulpit (*minbar*), for the top step is symbolically reserved for Mohammed. From there he delivers his sermon (*khutba*), which traditionally involves moral denunciation of wrongdoers— including officials and leaders—and this is designed to have a powerful impact on listeners. Today, recordings of these sermons are often circulated.

Towards the front of a mosque, or perhaps at the side, is a place where shoes are kept, for these are removed before entering the prayer area. Ablution areas are provided near the entrance for both ritual washing and for drinking.

Another feature of traditional mosques is an associated school where the young are given Islamic teaching, and learn to recite the Qur'an. Such a school is called a *madrasa*. This is presided over by an *alim* (scholar) whose job it is to ensure that the traditions and ritual are preserved within each generation.

Another important feature of the mosque is the *minaret*, a tower structure from which the call to prayer is given and which is usually situated at the side of the entrance. So the *muezzin* mounts the steps and proclaims the *adhan*—the call to prayer—at the appointed time of each of the five prayer rituals during the day. It is his responsibility to call the community to prayer. The reciting of *adhan* is also considered as an art form, reflected in its melodious chanting.

In a large mosque, the *muezzin*, after he has given the call to prayer from the minaret, goes in front of the *mihrab*, to a platform called the *dakka*, from which he also gives the call to prayer, and from where he imitates the movements of the *imam* as he leads the prayers. As a result, the faithful can both see and follow the ritual actions. Next to the *dakka* is a *kursi* (lectern) on which the Qur'an can be placed, and there is sometimes a seat for the reader.

As every mosque is within a local community, it is the community that is responsible for the building and running costs. Most of this money comes as donations from the people. A box is sometimes passed around after the Friday sermon. Mosques are usually established by means of *waqf*, an endowment that brings in revenue. Such endowments were normally agricultural land, often administered by the donor or members of his family, and in some cases may be situated far from the mosque which they finance.

Many mosques in early Islam were originally churches. This often happened through the forced conversion of Christian communities. However, in the West, many redundant churches are becoming used as mosques.

The outside appearance of a mosque is quite striking with the slender minaret rising up, often richly decorated with a crown on top, and the dome that dominates the roof. The dome, sometimes made of shining copper or even gold, is usually situated above the *mihrab* which indicates the direction of Mecca, and on the top of which is the moon symbol of Islam.

There are sometimes reliquaries, where bodies, or even parts of bodies, or even the personal belongings of past religious personalities, may be kept. Incense is used, especially in association with festivals. On these special *Eid* days the community meets for prayer and instruction, to celebrate the particular event, such as Mohammed's birth and death (commemorated the same day) or *Eid-ul-Fitr*, *Eid-ul-Azha*, and the atmosphere is saturated with incense.

Each mosque is connected with a *jama'at* (society). Even though every mosque is theoretically open to any type of Muslim, in practice mosques are built to serve a particular recognized group of people.

Mosques have often officially been administered under local rulers who had them built, but because of their economic independence through w*aqfs*, direct control has been difficult. The main donor and his family were in many cases considered the legal owners of the mosque, but that was often as far as their influence went. In other cases it was the *qadi*, the judge of *shari'ah* law, who acted as the main administrator, *nazir*, of the mosque. The power of a *nazir* was considerable and this position has often been the cause of intense internal conflicts between groups and individuals. The one considered to be the actual leader of a mosque, however, is the ruler, who holds the title of *imam*. Then there is also the *khatib* (orator, speaker), a position which arose as the result of the *imam* being unable to perform the special midday *salat* (*namaz*) on Fridays, and give the *khutba* (sermon), thus acting as the *imam*'s deputy. The Friday prayer and *khutba* is considered to be compulsory for all Muslim men.

There is often a mosque committee that oversees the affairs of the local mosque and which usually deals with everything pertaining to its running. They usually appoint the local *imam* who conducts prayers, the *muezzin* who calls to prayers, as well as a local arbitrator (in Asia called a *moulvi*) who is conversant with Muslim law and who will deliberate on local disputes among the community.

Mosques are centres of Muslim life, whether in the city or village. Very few mosques are found in open areas of countryside, and very few mosques do not develop shops and commercial activities in the streets around. In some places this commercial activity is in properties owned by the mosque and the income from the tenants' rents go towards funding the mosque. People's homes are often found in a second 'circle' outside the mosque and the shops. As well as the *madrasa*, law courts, hospitals and lodgings for travellers are often connected to mosques.

The practice of entering a mosque is governed by regulations. First, worshippers must take off their shoes or sandals. Entrance is made with the right foot first, while uttering blessings to Mohammed and his family. Then they must ritually wash, if they intend to pray. Once inside the main area of the mosque, two *rak'ahs* are to be performed. A person in a mosque shall talk softly, so that he does not disturb people praying. Also for the Friday prayer, best clothes are the order.

Women are not prevented from entering the mosque, but there are specific regulations as to how they should behave in a mosque. Mosques segregate women from men, either in time or in space. But through much of Muslim history, women entering mosques have not been welcomed by men.

Mosques have in many cases been closed to women, either by local rules or by tradition. Women have therefore had to pray in their homes. However in some modern mosques, especially those built in western countries, there is a special area that is designated for women, behind an ornate partition or veil.

While *salat* or *namaz* can be performed at home, or wherever a person may be, it is considered that prayer in a mosque—that is, praying together with other people—gains more merit.

Simply put, Islam and the mosque is the very life and soul of being a Muslim.

Notes

1 Sura 2:285.

2 **George Braswell,** *Islam* (Nashville: Broadman and Holman, 1996), pp.59 60.

3 These measurements may be somewhat inaccurate. A search on the internet for the size brings up a wide variety of claims, but these figures are the rough consensus. I doubt the measurements are actually variable! Example 1: 35 ft wide x 40 ft long x 50 ft high (10.5m x 12m x 15m). Example 2: 33 ft wide x 50ft long x 45 ft high (10m x 15m x 13.5m). There is even a repeated claim that the base is 627 sq feet, which is somewhat difficult to reconcile with any of the figures given!

Conclusion

In this first section we have looked at Muslim beliefs and practices. If it has given the reader an appetite to know more, then it has fulfilled its intention. We live at a time when it is vital that Christians look more closely at the teaching of Islam, because we are all coming into contact with Muslims in our communities to a far greater extent, and thus we have more opportunities to share our lives with them. We ought to have a willingness to learn more about Muslims—what they believe and the way they live. We should have a desire to understand them, our purpose being that we may then be able intelligently to lead them into an understanding of our own faith and of God's way of salvation. Let us not feel that we are being presumptuous in this task, for our Scriptures categorically state—and we are convinced of their truthfulness—that Jesus is the true revelation of God, and the only Saviour.

We need to be aware that not many Muslims know the real doctrines of Islam. For many, Islam is very much a practice of ritual. As long as they are seen to be doing the right things, they are thereby acceptable to the Muslim community, and all will be well. Islam is very clearly a system that proclaims salvation through works. This also proves to be the reason why there is much ignorance on the finer points of Muslim doctrine.

As those who are seeking to present Christ to Muslims, we need to know what they theoretically believe. However, we must be careful not to fall into the trap of teaching a Muslim his own religion, when we are talking to him with the express purpose of presenting Christ. Sharing the gospel may prove to be an easier task than we think, especially if we are considerate to him, listen to him, while praying that the Lord will prepare his heart to hear God's Word.

Part 2

Islam in Britain
Introduction

The aim of this section is to examine the situation with respect to Islam and its impact that it has in our own country of Great Britain.

We will be examining something of the impact that Islam has made upon these shores over the past centuries, and at the much greater rise in the number of Muslims settling in Britain in the nineteenth and twentieth centuries.

Many facts and figures will be needed to illustrate these matters, and it will be necessary to treat many of them with care. Some may be taken from a national census, others may be affected by the perceptions of the provider, but they will all give only an approximation to the truth.

We shall be looking at what it means to be a Muslim in Britain today. We therefore need to understand the situation because Muslims are part of our nation and their culture affects us all.

And finally, but not least important, we shall be considering a few guidelines on how to reach Muslims in Britain with the gospel.

Beginnings

Three are claims that Muslims make about the early influence of Islam on the British Isles. Some of these, while interesting, are difficult to substantiate. Therefore the following information needs to be considered in the light of real history. However, it is necessary to refer to these claims, because it affects the Muslim's view of Britain.

The influence of Islam is said to reach back to the times of Anglo-Saxon Britain. The claim is made that coins minted in the time of the powerful King Offa of Mercia (died AD 796) bore the *shahada*, but it is likely that the coin was produced in order to facilitate trade with Islamic Spain.

Muslim map-makers were aware of the existence of the British Isles from an early period. Around AD 817 one map records a number of place names in Britain. Another claim made about Islamic influence in the region concerns the Ballycottin Cross on the southern coast of Ireland that appears to bear the Arabic inscription *bismillah*.

Around AD 1125, Adelard of Bath (AD 1075–1160), the tutor of King Henry II, travelled in Syria and Muslim Spain, and translated a number of Arabic texts—and is thus known as a scholar in Arabic with an interest in Muslim science.[1]

During the time of the Crusades there was some cross-fertilization of ideas taking place, but by the fourteenth century, Muslim scholarship was renowned among the educated in Britain.

William Caxton, having learned printing skills at Cologne, returned to England in 1476, setting up the first printing press in England at Westminster. The first book he printed, dated 1477, was the 'Dictes and Sayings of the Philosophers', being a translation of a popular Arabic manuscript, *Mukhtar al-Hikam Wa mahasin al-Kalim* by Abul Wafa Mubashir ibn Fatik.

While this shows that there were early contacts with the Muslim world, it does not imply any more than a gradually growing acquaintance with Islam and its adherents. During the sixteenth century, trade with Muslim countries was growing, especially with Istanbul at the very centre of the Ottoman Empire. Other trade routes used by Britons also included Aleppo, Syria (a crucial silk trade route), Beirut, Jerusalem (the city of pilgrimage),

Cairo, and Fez (Morocco). This was a time when Muslim naval power dominated the western Mediterranean. Thus when the Spanish Armada loomed in the mid 1580s, Queen Elizabeth made a request to the Ottoman Sultan Murad for naval assistance against the Spaniards.

The first verifiable convert to Islam was one described as the 'son of a yeoman of our Queen's Guard. ... His name was John Nelson.'[2] Other early allusions to a Muslim presence in Britain appear to come some time after 1586. Sir Francis Drake 'rescued' (captured?) a group of some 500 people, a disparate group of some South Americans of both sexes, Spanish and Portuguese soldiers, and a small group of African slaves, but the majority were Moors and Turks, who had been taken to South America. He apparently planned to settle them as a colony on Cuba with the intent of interfering with further Spanish settlements there. When storms prevented him from reaching Cuba, he sailed northward along the American Coast. He deposited his human cargo at Roanoke Island, off North Carolina, to make room on his ships for the English garrison there, who implored him to take them back to England. There is evidence that a substantial number of these deposited foreigners eventually found their way to England, but it is not known how much impact they had while in England.

Throughout the medieval and renaissance periods English scholars of mathematics, astronomy and medicine relied heavily on books that were translations from Arabic originals. In recognition of this, a Chair of Arabic was established in 1636 at the University of Oxford, and Edward Pococke was the first incumbent.[3] Charles I collected Arabic and Persian manuscripts. Indeed, the Bodleian Library in Oxford has a manuscript letter to King Charles from Sultan al-Walid of Morocco, which in part reads 'To our exalted presence has come your noble servant, John Harrison, well and in good health and with far-reaching, sincere hopes. He has taken up residence with us, encompassed by kindness and treated with all manner of generosity...'.[4]

The Civil War brought a period of terrible turmoil in England. It may be that some Englishmen, because they were disturbed by the unrest and violence, were encouraged to break with traditions. There was at this time deep antagonism between varying Protestant views, and some may have considered looking elsewhere for truth. However, we do not learn a great deal about such an interest. There was an account written in 1641 that described 'a sect called Mahomatens (sic)' who were discovered to be living in London. After the royalists were defeated, the 'Council of Mechanics' of Cromwell's New Commonwealth voted for the toleration of various religious groups, including the Muslims. Then in 1649, the first English translation of the Qur'an by Alexander Ross was printed, and reportedly received a wide circulation, though widely criticized as inaccurate.[5]

After the English Civil War, Cromwell and his Parliamentary Party were attacked for their disrespect of parish priests and for their rejection of high Anglican beliefs. Their critics argued in a very interesting way:

And indeed if Christians will but diligently read and observe the Laws and Histories of the Mahometans, they may blush to see how zealous they are in the works of devotion, piety and charity, how devout, cleanly and reverend in their Mosques, how obedient to their Priests, that even the Great Turk himself will attempt nothing without consulting his Mufti.[6]

Thus the Puritans who made an independent stand against the formalized high Church of England were contrasted with the Turks who were seen to submit themselves to their religious leaders. But there was with Cromwell a remarkable scholar of Latin, Greek and Hebrew, Henry Stubbe, a friend of Edward Pococke (see above). Henry Stubbe wrote a book entitled *Rise and Progress of Mahometanism*,[7] thought to have been written around the time of his imprisonment in 1673, although it was never published. He gave an account of the character of 'Mahomet', identified the bias and ignorance of the times concerning Mohammed and Islam, and included a chapter entitled *Concerning the Alcoran & Miracles of Mahomet, the Prophecies Concerning Him and a Brief Account of His Religion and Policy.*

There is a claim that Cromwell was familiar with the Qur'an because of a letter he had written to the ruler of Algiers in June 1656, concerning commercial agreements. In his letter Cromwell wrote 'who have declar'd your selves hitherto in all things to be men loving righteousness, hating wrong, and observing faithfulnesse in covenant'. However, the idea that this means his familiarity with the Qur'an is somewhat fanciful, as these moral standards are common to Christianity. But the modern Muslim author Nabil

Mata, in seeking to show the influence of Islam in Britain, has attempted to claim that 'from sectary to antiquarian to Lord Protector, the Qur'an was a text widely consulted and quoted: it had legitimacy for addressing not only Muslims overseas but Christians in England and the rest of the British Isles'.[8]

It is true to say that there was a strong influence of Muslim thinking in the areas of mathematics, astronomy, chemistry and medicine, at least up to the seventeenth century, a period in which Muslim scholarship was much more sophisticated than in the West: 'In medieval times ... Islamic civilization in terms of material comfort, hygiene, medicine, and technology in general, was far in advance of anything European.'[9]

So Islam had a considerable intellectual influence on Britain. The fields of science and medicine in particular show the changes it brought through the words that are still used to this present day, such as alchemy: *al-kemia*, alcohol: *al-kuhul*, algebra: *al-Jabbr*, and alkali: *al-qali*. Arabic has influenced ordinary English vocabulary,[10] but so have French and other languages.

The movement of Muslims into Britain began at the end of the seventeenth century, particularly from the Ottoman Empire. A Turkish bath opened in London in 1679, testifying to the presence of Turks. Sake Deen Mohammed (1750–1851), came and settled in England. He set up an 'Indian Vapour Bath and Shampooing Establishment', *Mohamed's Bath*, in Brighton, even, it appears, acquiring the status of 'Shampooing Surgeon to His Majesty George IV'.

During the nineteenth century the number of Turkish sailors and traders visiting British ports increased, and some of these began to settle in various places. For example, according to the census of 1881, forty-four Turks and eight Egyptians were living in Merseyside.

The East India Company, as far back as the seventeenth century, had employed Asians who became known as *lascars*.[11] Recruited from various Asian countries, they were employed as seamen to serve on European ships, and paid through an Asian agent, known as a *Ghat Sarhan*.[12] *Lascars* were promised a fixed wage en route from India to London, where they were promised bounty money and maintenance while waiting for a return passage to their point of origin. In reality, many were simply abandoned in London or other ports. By 1842 there were 3,000 *lascars* visiting Britain every year, and a substantial number were finding themselves destitute and alone in Britain. Thus in 1885, the Church Missionary Society founded the Stranger's Home for Asiatics, Africans and South Sea Islanders in London, to provide for them.

In 1869 the Suez Canal was opened, giving unprecedented opportunities for increased trade between Britain and its colonies. As a result, Yemeni seaman employed on British ships began to settle in small communities, especially in London, Liverpool, Cardiff, South Shields and Tyneside. It is estimated that between 1890 and 1903, some 30,000 Yemeni seaman spent part of their lives in Britain. There was of course a language barrier between them and their employers, so in tribal fashion, they grouped together around a particular recognized leader, who helped them receive their daily needs and work requirements. Their leaders, chosen because they had better communication skills, were better able to understand their employer's and the government's requirements. At first, they were in transit for just a few months, but this period lengthened, and some of the Yemenis began to settle for longer periods, and even married local women. At first they set up small prayer rooms, but by 1860 a mosque had been built in Cardiff.

Muslims also began to enter into Britain for other reasons. Indian civil servants who worked for the British Raj came to visit Britain, either to seek work experience, or to take the Civil Service examination in order to obtain promotion and improve their job prospects. Some of them, seeing what life had to offer in Britain, stayed and settled.[13]

Not only was there an increase in the small numbers of Muslim immigrants coming into Britain, but also an increasing number of British nationals were becoming fascinated and interested in Islam. Others who visited Muslim countries were attracted to the mystical dimension of Islam. Still more came into contact with Muslim professionals and students here in Britain as they mingled with the British aristocracy (for many of them who could afford to come shared a similar background). By 1886, the *Anjuman-I-Islam* was founded in London, which later became known in 1903 as the Pan-Islamic Society. At the turn of the century it is estimated that there were some 10,000 Muslims living and working in Britain.

The objects of the Pan-Islamic Society were:

(a) To promote the religious, social, moral and intellectual advancement of the Mussulman world.

(b) To afford a centre of social union to Muslims from all parts of the world.

(c) To promote brotherly feelings between Muslims, and to facilitate intercourse between them.

(d) To remove misconceptions prevailing among non-Muslims regarding Islam and Mussulman.

(e) To render legitimate assistance to the best of its ability to any Muslim requiring it in any part of the world.

(f) To provide facilities for conducting religious ceremonies in non-Muslim countries.

(g) To hold debates and lectures, and to read papers likely to further the interests of Islam.

(h) To collect subscriptions from all parts of the world in order to build a mosque in London, and to endow it, and to extend the burial ground for the Muslims in London. Its members are ordinary, extraordinary and honorary.[14]

William Henry Quilliam, a British solicitor from Liverpool, became a Muslim while visiting Morocco on business in 1887. He returned to Liverpool and started the Liverpool Mosque at Mount Vernon Street that very year. Two years later the mosque moved to Brougham Terrace, opening its doors on Christmas Day 1889, and was in use until 1908. Quilliam also went on to found the Muslim Institute, which established a Muslim College, enrolling both Muslim and non-Muslim students. He also became editor of the *Islamic World* and the weekly publication *The Crescent* (1890), and founded Madina House as an orphanage in Liverpool.

Notes

1 For a reference to this interest see www.fordham.edu/halsall/source/adelardbath1.html.

2 **Nabil Matar**, *Islam in Britain 1558–1685* (Cambridge University Press, 1998) quoting *The Voyage made to Tripoli* (1583).

3 LoveToKnow Free Online Encyclopedia: http://64.1911encyclopedia.org/P/PO/POCOCKE_EDWARD.htm, for an account of Edward Pococke's life and achievements.

4 Sala@m: www.salaam.co.uk/themeofthemonth/september03_index.php?l=22. Article: 'The Historical Roots of British Islam: Sixteenth & Seventeenth Century', ¶2.

5 **Nabil Matar,** *Islam in Britain 1558–1685.* **S.M. Zwemer,** *Translations of the Koran,* Muslim World, V (1915), p.250.

6 Sala@m: www.salaam.co.uk/themeofthemonth/september03_index.php?l=22. Article: 'The Historical Roots of British Islam: Sixteenth & Seventeenth Century', ¶4.

7 Stubbe's book remained in manuscript form until 1911 when it was edited and published for the first time by **Hafiz Mahmud Khan Shairani** (London: Luzac, 1911, and a second edition was printed in Lahore in 1954).

8 Muslims make extravagant claims as to the historical influence of Islam has had on Britain in the past. Another example concerns Sir Isaac Newton who held Arian views on the Trinity—but there are Muslim authors who put this down to 'being influenced by Muslim scholarship'.

9 **Christopher Catherwood,** *Christians, Muslims, and Islamic Rage* (Grand Rapids: Zondervan, 2003), p.51.

10 Such words include: admiral, alcove, algebra, algorithm, alkali, almanac, amalgam, aniline, apricot, arsenal, arsenic, artichoke, assassin, aubergine, azure, borax, cable, calibre, camphor, candy, cannabis, carafe, carat, caraway, checkmate, cipher, coffee, cotton, crimson, crocus, cumin, damask, elixir, gauze, gazelle, ghoul, giraffe, guitar, gypsum, hashish, hazard, jar, jasmine, lacquer, lemon, lilac, lime, lute, magazine, marzipan, massage, mattress, muslin, myrrh, nadir, orange, safari, saffron, sash, sequin, serif, sesame, shackle, sherbet, shrub, sofa, spinach, sugar, sultana, syrup, talc, tamarind, tambourine, tariff, tarragon, zenith, zero—to name but a few. See **W. Montgomery Watt,** *The Influence of Medieval Islam on Europe* (Edinburgh University Press, 1982). Also of interest: The Vocabula Review: www.vocabula.com/VROCT00salloum.htm. Article: Salloum, Habeeb, 'Arabic influences in the English Language'.

11 This is a term probably derived from the Persian word *lashkar* meaning an army, or a band of followers. The first European use of this word goes back to the early 1500s through the Portuguese employment of Asian seamen.

12 *Ghat Sarhan:* an Asian term. Literally: Indian *ghat*=landing place; Persian/Indian *sarhang* =commander).

13 One such civil servant, Abdullah, came to live in Britain, married and died here. He is notable for his translation of the Qur'an into English.

14 Mahatma Ghandi website: www.mkgandhi.org/cwm/vol6/ch098.htm. Article: *Pan-Islamic Society Minutes,* Contents Vol.06: No.98: ¶4.

Chapter 10

The rise of modern
Muslim Britain

By the start of the twentieth century a number of significant English intellectuals had turned to Islam. *The Guardian* newspaper of the 21st November 1913 reported: 'We have no doubt that many a prayer for Lord Headley will go up from humble Christian hearts that he may return to the way of truth; unquestionably that is the proper attitude of mind towards a profoundly regrettable incident.'

The Rt Hon. Sir Rowland George Allanson-Winn, the fifth Baron Headley (1855–1935) was a leading British peer, statesman and author. He converted to Islam on the 16th November 1913, adopting the Muslim name of Shaikh Rahmatullah al-Farooq, under the tutelage of Khwaja Kamal-ud-Din. Having been educated in Cambridge, and becoming a peer in 1877, he served in the army, rising to the rank of Lieutenant Colonel. By profession he was an engineer, and had wide literary tastes, being one time editor of the *Salisbury Journal* and the author of several books, the most significant being *A Western Awakening to Islam*. In the 1920s, he toured Muslim communities in many countries, including India. In the company of the Khwaja he performed the *hajj* in 1923.

These actions were unthinkable in the heady days of the British Empire, where Britain was ruling over those countries where other religions were prominent, and the Christian faith was assumed to hold a superior intellectual position.

Khwaja Kamal-ud-Din, born to Muslim parents in 1870 in India, had been a successful barrister in Lucknow. He had been influenced by Christian missionaries, but had come across some Ahmadiyya literature, and his doubts about Islam disappeared. He came to Britain in 1912 to plead a court case before the Privy Council, the highest court of appeal for India at the time, after which he stayed on to establish a Muslim mission in England, seeking to promote the Muslim cause. He associated himself with the Woking Mosque.

This Mosque at Woking had been the inspiration of Gottlieb Leitner (1840–1899), a Hungarian scholar, who had wanted to establish an Institute for Oriental learning and literature. When the Royal Dramatic College, a home for retired actors in Woking, closed in 1877, he took it over and established his Institute, building a mosque next to it in 1889. This was Britain's first purpose-built mosque, and its funding was met largely by Shah Jehan, the then ruler of the Bhopal State in India, and leaders of the state of Hyderabad Deccan. After Leitner's death ten years later, the work declined, as also did the mosque.

But Khwaja Kamal-ud-Din discovered that the Woking Mosque was about to be sold to a developer and, in a landmark court case, had it declared a place of worship. The court set up a trust to manage the mosque and its property. Khwaja Kamal-ud-Din repaired the mosque and started the Woking Muslim Mission, a body set up to help new Muslims. He also began publishing the *Muslim India and Islamic Review* (later, simply *Islamic Review*). Lord Headley became an active supporter of the Woking Mission, taking a prominent role along with other high-profile Christian converts. Worshippers came to the Shah Jehan Mosque, as it was known, from all over the country to the 'centre' of Islam in Britain.

Lord Headley, after his conversion to Islam testified that it was 'the intolerance of those professing the Christian religion, which more than anything is responsible for my secession.'[1] He came to an independent conclusion that becoming a Muslim was the 'tolerant' thing to do! 'It is possible that some of my friends may imagine that I have been influenced by Mohammedans; but it is not the case, for my convictions are solely the outcome of many years of thought. Even my friend Khwaja Kamal-ud-Din has never tried to influence me in the slightest degree.'[2] He concludes his testimony in this way: 'Having briefly given some of the reasons for adopting the teachings of Islam, and having explained that I consider myself by that very act a far better Christian than I was before, I can only hope that others will follow the example.'[3]

In 1914 Lord Headley established the British Muslim Society, whose aim was to give a credible image of Muslims and Islam as part of British society. It is claimed that following Lord Headley's conversion, there was something of an Islamic renaissance, centred on the mosque at Woking. In

1916 he made a request to Austen Chamberlain, Secretary of State for India, for an allocation of funds to be given so that a Mosque might be constructed in London in 'memory of Muslim soldiers who died fighting for the Empire'.

During the same period, Marmaduke Pickthall produced an English version of the Qur'an which is still greatly respected today. He was the son of an Anglican clergyman, a distinguished poet and novelist, and he had already become politically active on behalf of Muslims in the First World War. He openly declared his own conversion to Islam in 1917, after delivering a talk entitled 'Islam and Progress'. He also had been in constant touch with the Woking Mosque. He published a journal (as appeared to be the fashion) called 'The Muslim Outlook'. So in these ways, Britain's contact with Islam continued to deepen at both the intellectual and grassroots level.

After the Great War, political activity on behalf of Muslims increased. Lord Headley formed the London Mosque Trust Fund in 1928, which made a significant transfer of funds to the London Central Mosque Fund, leading to the Islamic Cultural Centre in Regents Park.

Nor was all the activity confined to London. In 1930 a branch of the Western Islamic Association was formed in South Shields by Khalid Sheldrake, and also a Sufi meeting place (zawiya) was established there. By 1938 this northern Muslim community numbered 700.

Various organizations began to be formed to look after Muslim interests in Britain. The Muslim Society of Great Britain, under the presidency of Ismail de Yorke, organized Islamic events at the Portman Rooms in Baker Street, London, in 1933. The next year saw the formation of the Jamiat Muslimeen in east London, under the presidency of Dr Qazi. Branches were formed in Birmingham, Manchester, Glasgow and Newcastle. Also in 1934, following the death of Lord Headley, Sir Hassain Suhrawardy became chairman of the London Nizamiah Mosque Fund. Lady Evelyn Zaineb Cobbold was the first English woman to go on pilgrimage to Mecca in 1934.

What was causing such an interest? Why were educated and high-society people turning to Islam? It seems that many were attracted to the apparent simplicity of much Muslim teaching, in contrast, for example, to the 'conundrum' of the Trinity. Also Islam did not appear to have the infighting and arrogance among the denominations that Christendom demonstrates.

Abdullah Yusuf Ali, born in Bombay, was an Indian Civil Servant who trained at Cambridge University. Having travelled throughout the British Empire as an itinerant educationalist, he settled in Britain in 1937. This was the time when those who were now identifying themselves as British Muslims initiated their first political campaign. They were expressing their opposition to the Peel Commission's proposals for the partitioning of Palestine. So Yusuf Ali, who had first-hand experience of the mandates drawn up by the League of Nations, lectured extensively on the subject at various venues, including London, Cambridge and Brighton, representing the British Muslim community. He also became the only non-ambassadorial trustee of the London Central Mosque Fund. His famous translation of the Qur'an into English was first published in Lahore in 1934.

In 1940, during the Second World War, Prime Minister Winston Churchill authorized the sum of £100,000 to be unconditionally set aside for the acquiring of a site for the proposed London mosque. After the war, the Mosque Committee registered the London Central Mosque Trust Limited as a Trust Corporation, with seven representatives from six Muslim countries acting as Trustees. The work of building the Mosque was not to begin until 1974.

Meanwhile the East London Mosque, established in 1910 in Commercial Road, East London, moved to a purpose-built Mosque in Whitechapel Road in 1941. This mosque became well established, and by 1985 it had been replaced with a larger mosque nearby.

Muslim activity around the country was also beginning to increase in pace. Glasgow received its first mosque in 1943, and in November 1944, King George VI gave Muslims a moral boost by visiting and officially opening the Islamic Cultural Centre in Regent's Park, London.

Many things changed in post-war Britain, especially on the religious scene. There was an even greater disillusionment with the established church and all that it stood for. After the terrible loss of life in the war, many positively rejected the Christian gospel (though most did not know the truths they were rejecting). Scientific thinking was leading to an increasingly humanist society. The scientific claims of evolution, however unsubstantiated they were in reality, became the replacement faith of many. However, for some, there was a deep hunger for a 'faith' to replace the Christianity they were rejecting.

In the early 1950s there was real hope for revival when the Billy Graham Crusades of 1954 and 1955 took place at Harringay and Wembley. On another front, people were rediscovering the doctrines of grace and men like Dr Martyn Lloyd-Jones put their weight behind the renewed interest. The Banner of Truth Trust was established and began printing books that had long been lost and forgotten, but which taught solid biblical truth. So there was a real spiritual breath of fresh air, and many Christians enjoyed the boost they experienced, but it was all to be very short-lived. By the 1960s there was a distinct decline setting in among the churches of Britain.

The shift in religious thinking, and the subsequent change experienced in social, educational and welfare institutions, lent itself to a more protagonist approach by Muslims. And yet in that complacent post-war period of the 1950s very few people were aware of any real impact of Islam on Britain. The churches generally considered that Islam was a foreign mission field, never thinking that it could ever make any significant contribution to the religious scene in Britain, and the majority of people were not concerned about it.

As the years passed, Muslims showed greater openness. By 1962, groups of university students from six major cities met in Birmingham to form the Federation of Students Islamic Societies in the UK and Eire (FOSIS). This was something of a shock to Christians in the university scene, for here was a Muslim alternative to the evangelistic approach of the InterVarsity Christian Fellowship. Later in 1962, the UK Islamic Mission was formed. The Muslim Educational Trust was established to address the needs of Muslim schoolchildren. Its landmark publication was the First Primer of Islam in April 1969. Islam had arrived.

This was also the period of rebellion among young people: pop music and the 'hippie' culture. The charismatic movement was more firmly established bringing spice and excitement into the churches. These things prevailed, and as a result the power of the true gospel of grace appeared to be diminishing. Churches felt the decline, experiencing a hardening of people against even hearing the gospel which continues today. This was the time when Muslim power was increasing.

Notes

1 The Lahore Ahmadiyya Movement: www.muslim.org/woking/headley.htm. Article: 'The Obituary of Lord Headley from the Islamic Review', September 1935, pages 322–325: ¶4 (gives personal quotations of Lord Headley).

2 *Ibid.*, ¶5.

3 TheTrueReligion.org: www.thetruereligion.org/headley.htm. Article: 'Men who have embraced Islam: Lord Headley Farooq', ¶8.

Muslim immigration

T he connection between north-east India and Britain started in 1839 when the first imports of tea arrived. The British East India Company had established the trade, initially from Assam (India) and soon after from the Sylhet region (now in Bangladesh). The effects of the 1947 partition were felt here as well, and a Sylheti population settled in Britain. Further upheavals increased the flow of immigrants, many settling in Whitechapel, part of the East End of London. British immigration policies at the time were relatively easy.

The hope of many of them, mostly unaccompanied males, was to make money in Britain and then return, but economic decline in the 1960s and 1970s made this hope hard to realize. As immigration policies were tightened up, the Commonwealth Immigration Act 1961 was passed, but there was an eighteen-month 'window' before implementation. Many immigrants took this opportunity to bring their families to Britain and settle permanently.

The arrival of families changed the situation. Muslim families wanted to share religious education with their children by teaching the Qur'an, and the beliefs and practices of Islam. This meant allocating a house in the area for their children's education—and that same house began to be used for the five daily prayers. Also, to maintain the requirements of Muslim dietary laws, they set up *halal* meat shops. Thus Muslim neighbourhoods began to develop.

In East Africa the newly independent countries with their policies of 'Africanization' made life difficult for the many Asian businessmen who had settled there. This situation culminated during 1972 in the forcible expulsion of Asians in Uganda on the orders of President Idi Amin, who claimed that Asians were controlling the economy for their own benefit. As many as 60,000 holders of British passports were affected, and they sought refuge in Britain, further increasing the numbers of Muslims in this country.

In addition, many Muslim countries wanted to send their students to Britain for higher education. The student population was swelled by those coming from Malaysia, Iran, Pakistan, Iraq, Saudi Arabia and the Gulf States. These students, wanting to keep company with other like-minded students, and keen to express their Muslim faith, formed Islamic Societies in various British universities. In 1962, these Islamic Societies consolidated, forming the Federation of Islamic Societies in the UK and Eire. The purpose of this organization was to give guidance to new Muslim students arriving in Britain, and to provide facilities for Friday prayers in universities. As Muslim students grew in strength they began to hold Islamic Weeks, consisting of lectures, exhibitions and video shows, with the general aim of giving support to Muslim students, and promoting Islam.

The number of organizations for Muslim students has grown steadily:

The UK Islamic Mission: 1962;

Muslim Students' Society: 1962;

The Union of Muslim Organizations: 1970;

Islamic Council of Europe: 1973;

Young Muslims: 1984;

The UK Action Committee of Islamic Affairs: 1988;

The Islamic Party: 1989;

The Islamic Society of Britain: 1990;

The Islamic Parliament:1992;

World Islamic Mission; the Jamiat 'Ulama-i-Islam; Muslim Council of Britain: 1997;

and many others.

Recent notable events

The following is a brief summary of key Muslim events that have affected British society in recent years:

1969: In order to address the educational needs of Muslim children in Britain, the Muslim Educational Trust came into being. They published the 'First Primer of Islam', a book that aimed to provide elementary but basic knowledge of the important principles of Islam, written especially for children who are being taught in the English language.

1970: Martin Lings, a British convert to Islam—also known as Abu Bakr Sirajuddin—was appointed to the post of Keeper of Oriental manuscripts at the British Museum. Also that year the Union of Muslim Organizations was formed. In Glasgow, Bashir Maan was elected as the first Muslim councillor.

1971: This year marked the start of building a mosque in Victoria Park, Manchester, by the Jamiat-ul-Musilmeen. Also in May the authoritative Muslim magazine *Impact International* was launched in London. The *ulema* association Jamiat Ulema Britain was formed. The Muslim population of Britain was estimated to be somewhere between 369,000 and 390,000.

1977: The London Central Mosque finally opened in Regent's Park, London, at a cost of £6.5 million. It became the focus for Islam in the UK, being an inspiration to many. The design capacity was to enable 4,500 people to pray, not only in the main hall, but also in the basement foyers and the extended open wings. In practice it is estimated that it accommodates some 6,000 worshippers during a summer period when 1,000 or more may pray in the open forecourt of the mosque. At the *Eid* festivals,[1] up to 50,000 Muslims offer their *Eid* prayers in about six batches. A new Educational and Administrative block was added, being completed in 1994.

1984: The organization *Young Muslims UK* was founded, with the express aim of reaching and involving young people in Islam. 'We are a British Muslim youth organization sharing in the vision of the Islamic Movement. We follow the aims and objectives of our parent organization the Islamic Society of Britain, whose vision is: to inspire and enable people to live by Islam.'[2]

1985: An application for State funding for the Islamia primary school in Brent, London, was turned down. This was seen as a setback. There was uproar in the Muslim community over Salman Rushdie's book *The Satanic Verses*. It caused a deep divide in Muslim Britain, with many Muslim community leaders backing the Iranian Ayatollah Khomeini's *fatwa* to hunt down and kill the writer, who went into hiding. Many mosques burnt his books, and a £1.5 million bounty on his head was announced (lifted 1998).

1990: Islam made further inroads into British society, challenging British norms. Kalim Siddiqui issued the Muslim Manifesto, and called for a parliament similar to the Jewish Board of Deputies.

1991: Disquiet and opposition was shown by many Muslims over Britain's involvement in the Gulf War.

1992: The Muslim Parliament was founded to bring Muslims together and act as a voice in the political arena, seeking to implement Muslim requirements in Parliament, schools and the workplace. More pressure was put on the Department of Education by parents at the Al Furqan Primary School, Birmingham, voting to apply for grant-maintained status. This school had been established by Yusuf Islam, otherwise known as the rock star Cat Stevens, who had converted to Islam in 1977.

1996: The Runnymede Trust set up a commission to investigate the problem of British Muslims and Islamophobia. It reported the next year that Muslim communities suffer more racist violence than any of the other minority communities. It also demonstrated that Muslim communities mistreat women, while other religious cultures have outgrown patriarchy and sexism. This report did not put the Muslims in a good light.

By the mid-1900s there were more than 800 mosques of various persuasions and around 950 Muslim organizations giving support to Muslims in Britain.

1997: Mohammed Sarwar became the first Muslim MP, representing the Glasgow constituency of Govan for Labour. The Muslim Council of Britain (MCB) was founded as an umbrella group to represent the interests of the various Muslim groups. It was set up to highlight the problems facing the Muslim community in seeking to be recognized (for Muslims wanted to assert their own claims upon society). The MCB has been a voice for a moderate understanding of Islamic Law.

Muslims in Britain were estimated to be around 1.5 million at that time. The Muslim communities were mainly in Greater London, the West Midlands, West Yorkshire and central Scotland. There were growing tensions, because many Muslim immigrants still looked back to their home countries for their roots, but they were becoming more British in identity. The majority of British Muslims were intent on living their lives without interference, and wanted to be thought of as being faithful adherents to Islam as well as loyal citizens. The MCB wanted to highlight their claim to be an asset to the nation, also to stress the contribution already made to society:

It is hoped that the MCB will concentrate on the urgent issues, problems and challenges facing Muslims in Britain and that it will be seen to be working for the interests of the wider society of which we are a part. 'Seeking the common good' was the theme of the Inaugural Convention.3

Despite opposition from some fringe groups, around 350 out of 500 Muslim organizations had joined the MCB by 2002.4

1998: The MCB held its first General Assembly meeting at Brent town hall. That year also saw the appointment of the first two Muslim peers, Lord Nazir of Rotherham and Lady Uddin. The two Muslim schools, already mentioned seeking government funding, were awarded grant-maintained status.

2001: In the northern England 'mill and mosque' towns of Oldham, Bradford and Burnley, damaging race riots erupted. These were followed by the 9/11 attacks on America. The MCB issued a press release, expressing their shock and horror, and saying of the attackers, 'we condemn them utterly'. 'The Holy Qur'an equates the murder of one innocent person with the murder of the whole of humanity. ... We utterly condemn these indiscriminate terrorist attacks. ... The perpetrators of these atrocities ... stand outside the pale of civilised values.'5

The Council was bold, but the reports were that the majority of Muslims quietly approved, even if openly giving lip service to condemnation. In the wake of this atrocity there were more than 300 assaults on Muslims in Britain, most of the victims being women.

Notes

1 See chapter 7, *Life at the Mosque*.

2 Young Muslims UK Organization: www.ymuk.net/: Article: 'About YM: Our method of work in YM'.

3 UKACIA: www.ukacia.com/page7a.html. Article: 'Press release on OIC Summit', ¶15–17.

4 ISLAM Transforming Great Britain: www.masada2000.org/IslamicGroups.html. A list of the affiliated Islamic groups.

5 RE_XS for Schools: Islam News: Muslim Council of Britain: http://re-xs.ucsm.ac.uk/news/mcb.html/. Article: 'Press release 11.11.2001: Muslim Council of Britain condemns terrorist attacks': ¶1,3.

Chapter 13

Muslim communities in Britain

The many different Muslim communities in Britain may not have much in common culturally, linguistically, or even socially, but share a common Islamic ethos. So we must first recognize the differences. For example, the Bangladeshi Sylhetis and Pakistani Punjabis do not easily get along with each other. The Sylheti national dress for women is a *sari*, whereas the Punjabi women wear *shalwar qamis*. Eating differences are reflected in the way they might ask you whether you have had a meal. The Sylheti will ask, 'Have you eaten *bhat* (rice)?', and the Punjabi will ask, 'Have you eaten *roti* (bread)?' These simple examples reflect many differences that can be found between these two groups.

However, both groups will co-operate to establish local mosques and schools. Such co-operation will be upon distinct and more important 'denominational' lines (Sunni, Shi'a, etc.), rather than on any common ground of geography or language. They will fight their own ground with the local authorities, rather than unite together, in order to obtain grants to benefit their communities, and for their specific language and cultural needs. This is because the local authorities are set up to give help on ethnic, language and racial, not religious grounds.

It is beyond the scope of this book to enter into an assessment of the interaction with the British community of these groups, or any other, in terms of 'race'. As Christians, we understand that God created all humankind in his image, and that the term 'race' covers all mankind without distinction. Sadly the wrong idea of 'race' has taken hold in today's materialistic and humanistic society, and this is the reason why many Muslim immigrants have suffered abuse from ethnic Britons. We must also realize that the somewhat insular attitude of many Muslim communities has been influenced by their experiences. In 1976, the Race Relations Act was passed, seeking to improve relationships between the different cultures now in Britain. The complex issues of racial discrimination were summed up by the phrase 'race, colour, nationality (including citizenship), ethnic or national origin'. This seemed to be an extensive definition, but religious distinctions were not considered to be so important. As a result many Muslims felt that the Act did not help.

Muslim communities in dialogue with Christians

Some Muslims, seeking to meet with Britons in the area of religion, have been involved in interfaith initiatives. Many Christians in Britain who have not fully understood the dangers of ecumenism have involved themselves in approaches to Islamic peoples by such means. Their intention is to encourage Muslims into religious dialogue and understanding, which, in turn, they believe might lead to common worship. Muslim immigrants arriving on British soil have been a source of curiosity for churches, leading to an interest in the way Muslims worship, and what they believe. Organized dialogue was intended to bring Muslims and Christians together, giving greater understanding of one another. This initiative particularly came from local churches in the cities where there are many Muslim immigrants. These churches identified a similar challenge that faced the local authorities over community relations, and this encouraged them to seek discussions with Muslims with the intention of seeking to live in harmony together. However, this same period has been one of overall decline for the churches. British society has been consciously divorcing itself from any Christian identity. The direct result of rejecting Christianity has been a decline in moral standards, resulting in the loss of personal respect and dignity. So Muslims look out upon 'Christian' Britain, and openly reject what they see, identifying what they perceive as 'Christianity', giving rise to Muslim communities not wanting to be involved in British society.

Nevertheless, there has been a deepening concern for understanding between churches and Muslim communities. The first identifiable public discussions between Muslims and Christians took place in May 1973. These were given the theme 'Islam in the Parish', and held in co-operation with the local authority. This led to the formation of a panel of Muslims and Christians. The proceedings were edited by the Community Relations Chaplaincies of Bradford and Wakefield, and the report was published by the Bradford Metropolitan District Community Relations Council. This was followed up by two more discussions on the themes of 'The Family in Islam and Christianity' in 1974, and 'Worship and Prayer in Islam and Christianity' in 1975.

Thus churches, or at least their leaders, were waking up to the impact of Muslim communities, and decided to do a survey of Muslims in Britain. The British Council of Churches appointed an advisory group led by the Bishop of Guildford who was also a member of the panel of Muslims and Christians at the earlier dialogues. He had experience among Muslims in the Middle East and Africa, and therefore was thought to be a good choice.

However, in 1976, before the panel could publish anything, the attention of British people was caught by the 'World Festival of Islam', which was opened by HM The Queen. This event raised the profile of Muslims immensely and caused the panel to consider the possible impact that the festival might make.

Their findings were published later in 1976, entitled 'A New Threshold: Guidelines for the Churches in their relations with Muslim Communities'. It identified major problems among relationships and also issued a Code of Practice. There has been an ongoing dialogue between the two communities since then, with both formal and informal discussions taking place over many issues.[1]

Other discussions have involved the Jewish community. A grass-roots initiative in 1972 formed 'The World Congress of Faiths'. Jews, Christians and Muslims met together on a regular basis, with the stated aim of providing a discussion forum in Europe for the members of the three communities. The *raison d'être* was that they all shared a belief in one God, with a common basis in the historic figure of Abraham. The forum has been meeting bi-annually in Bendorf, Germany, attended by many young people from Germany and Britain. There is an autumn meeting exclusively for women. The week's gathering has the purpose of observing each other's way of living and praying, seeking to understand what the other holds precious.

In Britain there is also The Leeds Concord Inter-Faith Fellowship. This is an even wider group of interested parties that include Hindus, Buddhists and Sikhs as well as Muslims and Christians. This is somewhat startling, considering the major differences between them all—but it apparently gives opportunity for many to examine other faiths to seek common understanding.

Such interfaith activity prompted the British Council of Churches to establish formal links with interfaith groups. As a result yet another organization was set up, Interfaith Network. Its purpose is to provide a platform for all its affiliated organizations to discuss current relevant issues among themselves and to be represented collectively with government bodies, secular institutions and the media.

So churches, other religious groups, the government and local councils have all come to have a growing realization that Muslims are here to stay, and that they have already made an impact on British society. How that impact has been received has depended to a large extent on the background of those involved, but there are now overt demands that the requirements of Muslims should be met on an official basis. Today, most people are aware that Muslims have special dietary requirements (for example, halal meat), that they have special requirements in education (including the segregation of boys and girls, and for girls to wear 'appropriate' dress), and special arrangements for prayer times at the workplace. Many of these things would not have been considered fifty years ago, but Islam is now a force to be reckoned with.

Notes

1. **Ataullah Siddiqui**, *Fifty Years of Christian-Muslim Relations: Exploring and Engaging In A New Relationship*: village.flashnet.it/~fn026243/com.htm (English version second half of web page).

Chapter 14

Mosques in Britain

It is difficult to quantify the total number of mosques in the British Isles, although one source lists over 1,500.[1] The following list has been drawn up to show towns and cities where there are at least 3 mosques,[2] but it is likely to be out of date already. The list does, however, show how many places have an Islamic presence.

Accrington	5	Glasgow	16	Oldham	14
Batley	9	Gloucester	3	Oxford	3
Bedford	4	Halifax	3	Peterborough	4
Birmingham	100	High Wycombe	6	Portsmouth	3
Blackburn	21	Huddersfield	11	Preston	11
Bolton	10	Hull	3	Reading	3
Bradford	44	Keighley	7	Rochdale	13
Brighton	5	Lancaster	4	Rossendale	3
Bristol	6	Leeds	18	Rotherham	6
Burnley	5	Leicester	19	Sheffield	21
Burton-on-Trent	3	London (Greater)	183	Slough	4
Bury	4	Loughborough	3	Stoke-on-Trent	6
Cardiff	6	Luton	9	Swansea	3
Coventry	5	Manchester	39	Tameside	3
Crawley	3	Middlesbrough	3	Wakefield	5
Derby	7	Nelson	4	Walsall	11
Dewsbury	17	Newcastle-upon-Tyne	7	Warley	4
Doncaster	3	Northampton	4	Wolverhampton	4
Edinburgh	5	Nottingham	10		

Number of towns in Great Britain that have 3 or more mosques: 56
Number of towns in Great Britain that have 2 mosques: 25
Number of towns in Great Britain that have 1 mosque: 65
Total Number of towns in Great Britain that have mosques: 145
Total Number of mosques: **848**

These figures probably do not take into account the many shops and homes that set a room aside for 'public' prayer.

Time and space do not allow for a detailed history of the development of mosques in Britain. Some are small, perhaps just a modified house, while others are ornate and large buildings capable of holding thousands of worshippers at one time. Much money has been used in their construction, and they have become features in many places. Some individual mosques have already been mentioned in earlier chapters.

Notes

1 Sala@m: www.salaam.co.uk/mosques/. For finding mosques in the UK.
2 Islamic.co.uk—a site dedicated to British Muslims: www.islamic.co.uk/mosques/search.asp. Accessed 2nd May 2005.

Present situation

We have so far been considering the situation of having Muslims in Britain from a British point of view. But we need to ask, what kind of perception do Muslims have of Britain? This question needs to be looked at from various viewpoints.

How Muslims in Britain see themselves

The greater majority of Muslims living in Britain are immigrants, with preconceived ideas of this country, particularly that it is Christian. In other words, they expect to see every Briton as a practising Christian, with churches being full. Other concerns include language, culture, education and money. Often they feel overwhelmed by their new surroundings.

It is a shock to realize they have joined a modern, secular, materialistic culture where Christianity is marginalized, where humanistic values have taken over, and which is dominated by evolutionary thought. British culture has lost its religious sensitivity, pagan influences have taken over, and if they see any Christianity at all it is damaged by unbiblical ideas.

They discover that everything about the Christian faith is publicly undermined. As they meet people in their work, they find that Christianity is mocked, that important truths are sneered at, that the name of the Lord Jesus Christ is blasphemed. They discover an utter disdain for the Christian faith.

Now, rightly or wrongly, that is how the majority of Muslims see 'Christian' Britain. As far as we are concerned, the reality is different. We know there are thousands of faithful, Bible-believing Christians in Britain, who seek to be obedient to the Word of God, who have a genuine desire to worship God on the Lord's Day, and who are very active in the life and ministry of their church, including the need to share the gospel with others. But we have to face up to what Muslims perceive, and the reasons for it, because such negative first impressions often become confirmed in the Muslim mind.

Also, we must bear in mind that a Muslim's own understanding of Islam is permeated with Islamic culture, and many find it almost impossible to make any differentiation. Their own Muslim customs and traditions have had a defining influence on the way they comprehend Islam.

Christians in Britain, seeing Asian or Middle Eastern immigrants, cannot easily make any valid distinctions. They simply see them all as being 'different'. Very few Christians understand the differences that being a Sikh, Muslim or Hindu actually means. The immigrants themselves are aware of this. They believe, from what they see in Britain, that the indigenous community has no real interest in them. And, seeing the moral and religious problems within British society, Muslims prefer to keep themselves to themselves, thus preserving what is precious to them.

The rapid growth of Muslims in Britain has created something of a generation gap. In the earlier days, Muslims imported *imams* to run their local mosques and teach their children. Because these were Muslim leaders who had been brought in for a specific purpose, they themselves had a very narrow understanding of their role. Having been brought up in a strong Muslim society, they have seen their role as protectors of the society out of which they have come. These *imams* made many assumptions about the children whom they were teaching in the mosque and the *madrasa*. One was that they considered them as they might have been in their 'home' countries, but these were children of two cultures with two lives. In the day school they were encouraged to question and reason about the things they were taught, but these same children were invariably discouraged from questioning and reasoning in their evening classes at the mosques, especially about religion. Traditionally, Islamic teaching is done by rote. The conservative attitude of the *imams* caused a rift among the generations. Muslim children were learning English better than their parents, and now in the third generation, English is their first language. The interesting thing is that in a large number of *madrasas*, the *imams* are still teaching them in Asian languages. So it is not surprising that there is an increasing frustration among the younger people.

In spite of this, there has been a surprising increase in the use of *imams* from villages of the Indian sub-continent. At the same time, the adult congregations of these local mosques rely even more heavily on day-to-day *fiqh* (Islamic jurisprudence) issues, wanting to know how to work out Islamic principles in their lives. But these two opposing concerns are developing a deeper problem, rather than producing a cure. The 'foreign' *imams* are dwelling on theological issues, rather than developing Islamic legal issues concerning what it means to be a British Muslim. So the *imams* are comfortable leading daily prayers, conducting marriages and funerals, and performing other similar requirements. However, very few *imams* possess the necessary skills to help Muslims integrate. They do not address the issues of great importance for a Muslim living in Britain, or understand the demands of living as a Muslim in a pluralistic society. This results in an increasing divergence between the practical and religious needs of Muslims.

Muslim communities, as they recognize this need, have tried opening seminaries to train their *imams*. But the tragedy is that the traditional syllabus of these seminaries does not reflect contemporary needs. Thus the only difference between an imported *imam* and a locally trained *imam* is in the fact that the latter can convey his message in English, but the real needs of the Muslim community are still not being addressed.

This exceedingly unsatisfactory situation has led to a dilemma. There is either a strong reaction by Muslim youth against the traditions of Islam, or, as we have seen in more recent days, there is an even deeper commitment to the religion of their parents with equally disturbing consequences. So there is a real questioning of Islam by some who demand a more British identity, but for others there may be a new sense of attachment to Islam. Either way, there is an increasing identity crisis. Some therefore become British over their Muslim upbringing, but others place their Muslim identity over and above their being British. The former become nominal Muslims, the latter can easily become fanatical and turn to terrorism as an expression of their Islam.

Many families are torn apart by reasoning children who do not want to accept the unquestioning attitude of their parents in religion. They want to enjoy the freedom of the relationships they find in Britain. Therefore they buck against the strained (and restrained) relationships between the sexes, and the maintained *status quo* of arranged marriages that their parents and grandparents accepted, or had been forced to accept.

Then again, other families are equally bewildered by the extremism that they discover in their children. These families 'cannot believe' that *their* sons were involved in such overt terrorism, but radical *imams* were actively inciting young men to such acts. There are British Muslim young people who became actively involved in Islamic activities during their college and university experiences, who have discovered a renewed sense of attachment, as well as pride, in their Muslim faith. These sometimes appear to become 'born-again' Muslims, with such a zeal that shows up their families' commitment to Islam. This leads them on further to seek a change in their commitment to Islam, actively challenging their way of practising it. Such missionary zeal convinces them to see themselves as right and others as wrong, considering their fellow Muslims as either lapsed or inadequate. On the other hand, they consider non-Muslims as potential enemies of Islam, seeing them as conspiring against the wider Muslim community, and even Muslim leadership collaborating with them.

Bringing all these differing strands together, we gain an overall picture of Islam in Britain. Even though many Muslims are seeking to live as harmoniously as possible within British culture, even maintaining that Islam is a system of peace and harmony, there is real tension, centred on the way Muslims practise Islam. Islam is community based. The sense of *ummah* is fundamental, and is diametrically opposed to any co-existence with a 'Christian', or even secular, community. Islam has to make its mark. Islam is a territorial religion. Because everything is perceived to be *Islam*, Muslims must make every effort to claim territory for *Islam:* to establish the ideal of *Dar al-Islam* (a state under Islamic law), and the *ummah* must stand together.

Therefore the reality is that Muslims remain within a community group, consolidating together. The community becomes all-important, because it is their identity. Therefore the group is their protection as well as their character.

Among Muslims there is a strong motivation to impose this sense of community on the state, because, without the support of the state, they simply cannot express their Islam adequately. Hence the lobby to establish places of worship, *halal* shops, and education methods which Muslims require. The move of Muslims to get involved in politics, both on the local and national level, is deliberate. Not only do they want a voice in the British community, but this is the only way that they can obtain what Islam dictates. They need to demonstrate *ummah*. And *ummah* is only valid if it is state based. Islam must be imposed on the state. Muslims cannot separate *ummah* and state, and therefore they experience an identity crisis when isolated. 'A regime in which an individual Muslim lives ought to be one following the Islamic faith.'[1]

For Christians, living in a non-Christian state is no problem.[2] Christians do not need a Christian state in order to be effective and faithful Christians. The kingdom of God is not of this world, and Christians are citizens of God's spiritual kingdom, only passing through this world.

We perceive Muslims as gathering together in closely confined groups, for support and protection, to experience and enjoy a common culture and identity. They have a persecution complex and are very suspicious about the motives of British people who may only want to offer help and support. It is also true to say that they have a 'ghetto' mentality, feeling threatened by the Christian majority.

From a Muslim perspective, Dr Ghayasuddin Siddiqui, as leader of the Muslim Parliament, described how the hatred of Islam and Muslims had deep roots in European civilisation and psyche, in a keynote speech in October 1997. He spoke about the difference between non-Muslims living under *Dar al-Islam* and Muslims living in Britain (a non-Muslim country—a place of *Dar al-Harb*). He described how non-Muslims, basically meaning Christians and Jews, enjoyed compassion and tolerance under Muslim rule, but that Muslims who come to live in the West experience intolerance and feel persecuted.[3]

One of the reasons Muslims in Britain feel threatened is the Muslim practice of *dhimmi*, which is a formalized regime under Muslim rule that allows Christians and Jews to enjoy a protected status. However, in practice this means that they are denied important civil rights, pay an extra imposition tax, are denied any status in society, are prevented from holding leadership, and are not permitted to evangelize. Knowing that this is how Christians are treated in an *ummah* state, Muslims anticipate similar treatment here, and feel themselves to be second-class citizens. After all, this is how they would expect to treat others in *Dar al-Islam*.

On the whole, Britons accept Muslims as having equal status. We try to include them into British society, but problems arise when our efforts are spurned. This results in British non-Muslim people believing that the Muslims are actively promoting racism.

How we must consider Muslims in Britain

There is great diversity among Muslims in Britain. The different ethnic origins, identities and backgrounds will all colour the way they both view themselves and the way they live. Muslims are not all the same—they never have been and never will be a homogenous unit. We must realize this.

It is all too easy to try stereotyping Muslims into one kind or another. The high profile of terrorism in recent years has coloured the way British people perceive Muslims. The fact remains that the majority of Muslims are not 'fanatics'. They are not all 'fundamentalists'. Many Muslims are deeply upset at the way other Muslims have been acting.

A recent poll of Muslims in Britain indicated that 87% considered themselves supportive of the action that Britain was taking against terrorists.[4] This shows that we cannot make sweeping statements about where their loyalties are.

British Muslims reflect the world situation. All the different schools of Islamic thinking are represented. Sunnis are by far the greatest number, but also there are Shi'a groups and differing Sufi orders. There are also sects such as the Ahmadiyya and Nation of Islam (a Black Muslim movement).

In considering how and where Muslims live in Britain several factors need be taken into account. We can provide facts and figures to illustrate the situation, but we must realize that Muslims will be living near us all.

Muslims in Britain today are comparatively younger than the majority white British population. The 1991 census showed 43% of Pakistanis and 57% of Bangladeshis were under 16 (compared with 19% of the white population). At the other end of the scale only 2% of Pakistani and 1% of Bangladeshi were over 65 (compared with 17% of white British people). More recent studies show that 52% of Pakistanis and 44% of Bangladeshis were born in Britain.

Family life is also significant. Over 83% of Pakistani and Bangladeshi families live in traditional families, compared against 65% of white people and 66% of all ethnic minorities. Larger families are normal, with South

Asian women having children earlier and stopping later. Separation and divorce are much less frequent among South Asian and Turkish communities.

There are, however, higher rates of unemployment as well as illness and disability, which mean greater dependence on social security benefits. It seems that many Muslims live in housing that is socially challenging. Studies done in 1996 show that 65% of Bangladeshi families and 45% of Pakistani families live in overcrowded housing conditions and lack amenities. Many Muslim families would appear to be more deprived, as 28% of older Pakistani and Bangladeshi families live in homes without central heating. They were three times as likely not to have a phone as non-Muslims, before the mobile phone became commonplace.

As regards house-ownership, it appears that only 45% of Bangladeshis were owner-occupiers and 43% live in council or housing association properties. However, Pakistanis fare better with 77% being owner-occupiers, though an overall 42% live in cheap terraced houses. The number living in local council or housing association properties was less.

Muslim minorities appear to suffer discrimination at the institutional level. Many experience problems of unfair treatment by landlords, local authorities and housing associations and even estate agents. They experience much prejudice and ill-informed opinion instead of sympathy. Consequently, there is a felt alienation and frustration within Muslim communities.

Regarding employment, the majority of Asian Muslims work in semi-skilled and unskilled jobs. This is one reason why so many live in poor housing. Too many have low educational qualifications. On the other hand, a significant minority of Pakistanis are in professional occupations, and do better than their white counterparts. This enables them to move into the more affluent suburban areas. Others are successful in business, particularly property, food and fashion. Among the Arab settlers in Britain there is a large proportion who are highly skilled, who are employed as professionals in engineering, medicine, higher education, as well as running businesses of various kinds. Over 5,000 Muslim millionaires live in Britain with liquid assets of more than £3.6 billion.[5] Interestingly, the proportion of Muslims who are self-employed (especially South Asians) was much higher than among white and Afro-Caribbean ethnic groups, mostly in small businesses that serve the requirements of their own communities.

One important factor of interest is their religious identity, because the way they conduct themselves as Muslims varies enormously. Muslim expression of religion ranges from the devout adherence to the nominal. The situation is fluid, and we must treat each individual separately and assess how they live out their Muslim identity in a non-Muslim state. They may be very different Muslims than they would otherwise have been in their own country of origin. We need to recognize that coming to Britain has fundamentally changed them, and many are struggling with their new identity. This leads to their being defensive of themselves and their families. They have settled in the country and faced unexpected problems, have suffered rejection, experienced disadvantages and felt excluded. These factors have caused them to develop their own perceptions about their identity as Muslims. Older Muslims have tended to withdraw from what they consider the difficulties of British culture, but young Muslims are more likely to try to tune in to what it means to be British. These younger Muslims tend to criticize the religious and cultural beliefs and practices of older generations, and take on some of the 'norms' of British society, even those that are at severe odds with Muslim teaching, such as interaction between sexes and even premarital sex.

Young Muslims are working out new ways of being Muslim in Britain. Indeed, British elements of their identity form a most important part of the equation. But Britain today is itself changing in this post-modern era, and the input of Muslims in Britain is part of that change. Many young Muslims see themselves as culturally and socially British, and would defend their position strongly, but there is uneasiness among many Muslims that Britain is not the place they thought it was.

Young Muslims are indeed making a stand. They are not prepared simply to accept their parents' position of unquestioningly accepting everything, so there is a spirit of questioning among them, and some of it comes from the education they have received in British schools. What is the meaning of Muslim rituals? Why the segregation of the sexes? They even go as far as raising the taboo subject of homosexuality, some showing gay, lesbian, and bisexual tendencies. This is an open challenge to the traditional stand of Islam.

Among Muslim women in Britain, there is a greater desire for openness and self-expression. The standard picture of female submissiveness and oppression in Islam is not the experience of most Muslim women in Britain. They have learned to construct their own system of how they relate to other women, to men, and to their families. These women have been shaped by the cultures and social structures of the regions from which they came, and their own interpretations of traditional Islam.

In Britain, most Muslim women have escaped at least some of the traditional restrictions. Outside the home, many older Muslim women have struggled to manage on limited English, depending on their husbands and other male relatives or children. However, they hold a strong position in the maintenance and transmission of cultural and religious values. Many of them seek to shield their families from undesirable western influences. They give their communities a sense of cohesion and they shape its domestic life, which is the same role they played in the country of origin. They are learning to find their own niche in Britain.

Arranged marriages still take place, as this is seen as a means of protecting the family and also their Islamic identity. This practice is controversial, and it has attracted much negative media attention. Arranged marriages, however, are on the decline, as more and more Muslim young people are objecting to the system. It appears to be the less educated families that maintain the practice, while the better educated and those among professional families are freer to choose their own partners. Of course, there is still parental pressure to make a match that is consistent with being Muslim.

There is a tendency for young Muslims to criticize what they see as double standards in relation to the way men and women are treated within their communities. They see a wide gap between the freedom that men enjoy and the insistence that young women stay at home. Islamic teaching is used to give legitimate control to men in asserting themselves over women. So younger women especially are challenging the system of an overwhelmingly male leadership, and they are demanding that their voice be heard. A form of 'women's lib' is developing within the Muslim communities.

But we must not think that Muslim women are trying to break the system. Many young women wish to assert their religious identity, as a way of addressing their concerns. Those who are well educated are questioning the position of women in British society. What they see out there is not what they like. They see the excessively loose way of living between men and women and make value judgements accordingly. Many refer back to the Qur'an and the *sunnah* and apply the methods of *ijtihad* (independent enquiry) to shape a new strategy. This has led economically active young women to develop a willingness to wear the *hijab*. In this respect Islamic teaching has been relatively successful—and helps young women extend their personal choices. The popularity of the *hijab* among young Muslim women as a symbol of their femininity was described thus:

Some use it simply as part of their worship; others as a strategy to loosen the bonds of patriarchy, to resist cultural practices such as arranged marriage, and to re-assure parents and communities that they will not be 'corrupted' by [British] culture. ... For other Muslim women it helps to reshape the cultural space in which they operate by indicating to young Muslim men how they wish to be treated—with respect.[6]

Others are not so convinced about the *hijab*. Some see it as a way to maintain control over them. While *hijab* does allow women to enter public places, it also legitimizes and strengthens the difference between the private and public place. It demonstrates that a woman's place is in the home, and that they should only go out to work from necessity. Hence the only way to assess why *hijab* is being used is to listen to the views of those using it. This is the principle we should be apply to everything: be a good listener.

Some Muslims in Britain are making educational, economic and social progress in the Britain of today. That progress may be slow and hesitant, but it is progress, and seen in all walks of life. This is in part due to the rest of society recognizing Muslim concerns, while acknowledging the contribution they are making to British society. In spite of this, there are still many negative attitudes against Muslims.

Many Muslims now realize that standing apart does not help their cause, and become more involved. Such involvement is actually motivated by certain principles of Islamic teaching. The values of equality and justice are highly valued in Islam, and some Muslims are recognizing that these important values might be better promoted through using strategies within democracy. Instead of a 'city under siege' mentality, they have moved into the mainstream. Younger Muslims have realized that failing to participate in politics is detrimental to Muslim interests. There has been a steady increase in voting at elections, party membership and even standing as candidates. But Muslims do not just vote for Muslim candidates: many realize that they must be more widely involved. It is not surprising that many joined the Labour party as the party of the 'working class', and that Muslims perceive Labour to be less racist in attitude. More affluent Muslims, however, support the Conservative Party, because of policies that place a greater emphasis on self-employment, home-ownership and family life.

The statistics of the 2001 General Election are interesting. A record fifty-three Muslim candidates stood. There were now two Muslim MPs (both Labour), one MEP (Conservative), and four Muslim peers, all Labour. Baroness Uddin was the only Muslim woman in the British Parliament. In the country overall there were 217 (Labour: 161, Liberal Democrat: 27, Conservative: 23, others: 6)7 out of 25,000. Muslim councillors have been typical of politicians in Britain as a whole, being predominantly middle-aged and male, and belonging to the more well-off groups of society, and many would describe themselves as 'secular Muslim'.

In 1992 the Muslim Parliament was set up under the leadership of Dr Kalim Siddiqui, but after his death in 1996, internal disputes caused the organization to collapse before the end of 1998. The whole affair was regretted by some Muslim observers.[8]

This institution had only marginal support across the mass of British Muslims. The organization had no democratic principles, and was entirely at odds with the British parliamentary system. Though it sought to influence that traditional institution, it was diametrically opposed to it in principle because of its autocratic stance. There was never any room for discussion for there are Muslim groups who sincerely believe that any democratic system is not worth messing with. Some even more extreme Muslim groups have said that the democratic system is 'based on the creed of separating religion from life, it is un-Islamic, and political participation in general, in a democratic but non-Islamic state, is forbidden to Muslims.'[9]

This underlines the fact that Muslims think differently in terms of state. On the local scene, the *imam* of the mosque is the guide for all affairs of life. He is chosen by the congregation, but he can exercise a very strong power over them while holding that position.

The Muslim Parliament failed because it proved unable to mobilize enough support from other Muslim groups to realize its strategy. The Muslim scene cannot be considered as cohesive, for it is ethnically and culturally too diverse to develop one effective self-contained institution.

One problem for Muslims is education. Western educational ideas are seen as materialistic. Multiculturalism in schools is claimed to dilute Islamic teaching, and thus Muslims are looking for state support for Muslim education through the voluntary aided grant system. Only in this way can Islam be taught as they want.

Another problem is that of legal rights. Muslims are campaigning for a greater acceptance of Islamic religious law within British society. In other words, they want to change the historic British system so that it suits their needs better. This constitutes a real challenge, for many Muslims in Britain understand Islamic law to be an integral part of living in accordance with God's revealed will. *Shari'ah* law governs human behaviour, both with respect to God and to society. Individual duties and responsibilities should be within the context of *shari'ah* law. This thinking impinges on a secular society such as we have in Britain. No real guidance is given to Muslims about how they should live in Britain, as those who have settled permanently in a secular society. In British law there are no safeguards for faith except those provisions that protect the freedom to practise it. So Muslims perceive a real difficulty.

Many Muslims feel that important aspects of Islamic law are not covered by English law, for example, the giving and taking of interest, which is prohibited in Islamic law; and polygamy, which is permitted in Islamic law but is unlawful according to English law, unless it takes place outside the UK. Some elements of English law appear to be in conflict with Islamic principles: laws relating to usury, gambling, the sale and consumption of alcohol, and the absence of capital punishment. In addition the law in

Britain, unlike *shari'ah* law, does not consider certain forms of behaviour to be criminal, such as fornication, adultery and homosexuality.[10]

However, a study in 1989 revealed that if there was a case of conflict between English and Muslim laws, 66% of those Muslims questioned would follow English law. The Muslim Parliament even accepted that Muslims should comply with the laws of a non-Muslim state 'as long as such obedience does not conflict with their commitment to Islam and the *ummah*'.[11]

Family law affects the procedures for divorce, polygamy, and important provisions concerning inheritance. Permissions under Islamic law may be prohibitions under state law—or they may not even be recognized by British law. While the situation is complex, the majority of Muslims in Britain accept that they do not need separate legislation to meet the demands of Muslim family law.

The present law in Britain concerning Muslim marriage means that the official legal marriage often takes place in registry offices, and the religious celebration takes place elsewhere. About 25% of mosques are registered for marriages, but an official of the local Registry Office has to be present. There are very few mosques who have sought to have a recognized 'Registered Person' who is able legally to witness a marriage. Perhaps the *imam* sees a conflict with the requirements of British law over and against the requirements of the *shari'ah*. Muslims have set up their own organization to facilitate arranged marriages; and others provide 'crisis intervention' and marriage guidance, as well as advice to the elderly regarding the interpretation and obtaining of social security payments.

Muslim divorce is not recognized by British law, but marriages contracted in Muslim countries are normally accepted. Similar ceremonies taking place in this country are not. This leads to a situation where marriages accepted by Islamic law are not recognized in Britain if there has been no civil ceremony according to British law. Concern has been expressed that those wives involved lose their Islamic rights if they then divorce, because bodies who deal in Islamic family law have no legal standing. So Muslim women want to see their marriage by religious Islamic ceremonies acknowledged and respected by British law. Then, if they want to divorce they will come through the experience with their dignity intact, and be able to enforce their Islamic rights.

Blasphemy is another serious issue, highlighted by the Salman Rushdie affair. Muslims were outraged at the 'blasphemous' content of his book, and some demanded that Britain should recognize the *fatwa*, and sentence Rushdie to death. Britons saw this as an attack on our laws concerning freedom of speech. There are therefore continuing calls from Muslims for a change in British law on blasphemy, as it appears only to protect Christianity. Such matters cause Muslims to claim discrimination, and this leads to further feelings of injustice.

The next problem for Muslims is their treatment by the media. British people realize that the bias and over-simplification so common in the media applies to everybody, with some newspapers intent on stereotyping and destroying the integrity of their victims. Muslims feel that this applies only to them, and are particularly upset when by implication all Muslims are branded as 'terrorist' or 'extremist'. They feel hurt, and further alienated. This is yet another reason why Christians need to understand the point of view of individual Muslims.

The events of 9/11 in the USA, and other incidents in Britain and Europe, have not only made these feelings stronger, but have also led to the enactment of anti-terrorism laws which allow people to be detained without trial. Again, many Muslims feel that such laws are aimed specifically at their religion.

Quite naturally, Muslims have tended to find places to live in the same vicinities, each ethnic and cultural group gravitating together through the things they share in common. But such physical segregation causes isolation too. As a result, ghettos tend to form in inner cities, producing so-called 'parallel communities'. Muslims also find that they have to work hard at sustaining their religious beliefs and practices, since modern British society has virtually rendered the idea of religion obsolete. The Christian faith is marginalized, and true biblical Christians have a hard time being recognized. So if this is true of Christians in a 'Christian' country, is it surprising that Muslims have a hard time, even moderate ones? Here is a Muslim perspective:

The more that Muslim communities have become rooted in Britain, the more their members have striven to put structures in place to enable them to live their lives according to their own understanding of Islamic practice. Space in public life has been 'stretched' to include Islam, and facilities now exist in Britain enabling Islam to be practised in diverse ways.[12]

This means there has been some acceptance and accommodation for Islamic belief and practice. This has come about through the activities of various agitation groups in the past twenty years or so. In fact there is actually a more willing accommodation within society for the beliefs of Muslims, Hindus and Buddhists, than there has been for expressions of Christian practice. For example, Christians are not permitted to speak on the media and in the press so openly about the meaning of the gospel and about how Christ has changed their lives, but Muslims are given much more freedom in this respect.

It is the desire for Islamic law to be accommodated within British law that has met with much more resistance. In practice Muslims have attempted to bypass the British legal institutions, and set up their own parallel structures to deal specifically with legal matters and concerns in connection with Muslim requirements. These have been established on both a formal and informal level, and command respect and legitimacy within certain Muslim communities because they are different, and are seen to be addressing legal issues that are specifically Muslim.

So Muslims have responded to the challenges of living in Britain in a variety of ways. Some have sought greater secularization, while others, especially younger Muslims, have sought to discover 'true Islam' through their own interpretation of the Qur'an and the *hadith*. Far too many of them feel undervalued and even humiliated by mainstream society, and they have explored strategies to resist the onslaught of what is antagonistic to their way of life. The conclusions that these Muslims have come to, especially the younger element, are that appropriate solutions can only be found in 'religious extremism'. The principle of *jihad* holds an amazing appeal for many younger Muslims because they feel disaffected by British society. They understand *jihad* (whether it may be the more pacifist type, or the more especially violent expression) to be the legitimate way that

Muslims are to defend themselves when under threat. Because worldwide communication is very easy, British Muslims can respond quickly to conflicts involving Muslims anywhere in the world. In this way they gather support among the disillusioned and alienated within society, and this helps to account for the *jihad* mentality.

Many different viewpoints on the world and society in general can be found among Muslims, depending on age, ethnic background, social position, economic standing, personal circumstances, education and gender. There is freedom of thought and expression in Britain that previously they may not have enjoyed. This allows them to assess, or perhaps reassess, their beliefs, traditions and practices. This produces a real mixture of perspective, from polarization, to growing interaction and dialogue with British society.

As always, when coming into contact with Muslims, we must make no assumptions or apply prejudices, but simply listen. Sometimes we may be surprised by what we hear and learn. But only in this way can we begin to understand who we are dealing with, and how we can interact with them. We have to respect their social norms (even if we disagree with them), and we have to learn ways in which we can adapt to Muslims, or move towards them. This is fundamentally necessary if we are going to be successful when we share the gospel with them.

So how do we seek to understand them? We must recognize that some British Muslims see themselves as Muslims first and then British, but others hold the opposite view. The rest are between these two extremes. Different Muslim groups learn to adapt in various ways. There is no hard and fast rule. Muslims in Britain are still finding their identity, acceptance and means of self-expression. We must never treat them as if they are unimportant, or as if they have no contribution of any worth to society.

Another issue that Muslims have to face in this country is that there is an already established religion. Muslims are very much aware that they are a minority faith in Britain, but they take great encouragement that in the last census in 2001[13] they come out as the second largest religion in Britain. The figure that was given is 1,591,126—as opposed to those claiming to be Christian coming to 42,079,417. The total number of other religions (Jewish, Hindu, Buddhist, Sikh, etc.) comes to 1,492,352. The number claiming to have no religion is 13,626,299. The total population of Britain is given as 58,789,194.

In Britain there is an officially recognized Christian denomination, the Church of England. This is perceived as being 'the dominant faith' in England. The link between the Church of England and the state goes back to Henry VIII. The present situation is that the Head of State (the Queen) is the Supreme Governor of the Church of England, and appoints its leaders—archbishops, bishops and deans, on the advice of the Prime Minister. The two archbishops and twenty-four bishops also have a legal and political role, for they sit in the House of Lords, and make a major contribution to the work of Parliament. One of the concessions is that a minister of religion can celebrate marriages which are then legally recognized. Also, the 1988 Education Reform Act required that religious education should be compulsory and school assemblies should be 'mainly and broadly' Christian acts of worship. Muslims perceive the Church of England as enjoying a privileged, powerful and dominant position.

The Church of England, as the established church, is not a voluntary society. Its laws are part of the English legal system, as are its courts. On the other hand, all other religious bodies are voluntary associations, and so make their own rules. Muslims must understand that it is not only they who come under this category, but also all *non-conformist* churches. Muslims, however, also see that the State is committed to contributing towards the activities of the Church of England, and that it is responsible for 40% of the upkeep of the country's churches which have been designated as listed buildings.

Muslims envy this privileged position—that one 'faith' is being privileged over another, which they see as degrading to these others. So they subscribe to the view that in plural Britain it is no longer appropriate for the monarchy to be so closely linked with one religion. 'The symbolism of the Queen as head of the Church means that other religions, even if more vigorous, have the appearance of being second class.'[14]

Muslims therefore see all major religious events in Britain as being biased towards the Church. Everything points to Britain being a Christian country—even such things as singing the national anthem and the performance of religious rituals at public events such as royal funerals,

coronations, royal weddings, remembrance day services—even the opening
of Parliament—and conclude that all other faiths are not fully British.
Muslims thus feel they have little status, and even less that they are really
British. They argue, how can they be faithful citizens?

... by reinforcing the image that they are not really British, and therefore cannot be
trusted to understand or cherish Britain, its history and its people, or have a lesser
birthright to it, and so may be legitimately denied some of the available jobs, prizes,
distinctions and may legitimately be objects of suspicion in times of political and
international tension.[15]

Muslims are challenging the status quo, and demanding equal religious
rights. Thus, in this sense, they are seeking to undermine that very
establishment as it is historically perceived. Yes, it is true that Britain is a
pluralistic society. Yes, it is true, from a non-conformist perspective, that
the Church of England is in an untenable position being tied into the
political scene. But is it really true that Muslims are being treated as
second-rate citizens because the Church of England is the established
religion? What do the majority of the population think who never enter any
church? They do not see themselves as second-rate citizens. They see the
Church as out of date, and simply dismiss it as being unimportant.

However, Prince Charles has made it known that he wants to change
things.

Prince Charles is known to be keen to modernise the monarchy and has spoken about
being a 'defender of faiths' rather than the present oath which makes the monarch the
'Defender of the Faith'—Christianity. ... He has also told senior staff he would want
his coronation to be a 'multi-faith' experience in contrast to the heavily Christian
service of his mother's coronation in 1952. 'We want to make the argument that the
monarchy needs to be seen as a modern institution there for all of the people of Britain,
whether they are Christians or non Christians,' said one source close to [the Fabian
Society] commission [on the Future of the Monarchy]. 'It is no longer appropriate for
the monarch to be so closely allied with one religion.'[16]

This is obviously going to become even more of an issue with Muslims in the future. It is interesting that one former Prime Minister of England, John Major, questioned the ability of Prince Charles becoming 'defender of faiths' when he is not a member.

Prince Charles is defender of the faith because he becomes head of the Church of England and he is a practising member of the Church of England. ... I think we would want as a government and as a country to defend the integrity of all faiths whatever they may be. They are equally important to the people who hold that particular faith, but I think it would be a little odd if Prince Charles was defender of faiths. ... he will defend faiths, he will defend all faiths. He is an open-minded man.[17]

How Muslims react to the Christian gospel is an entirely different matter. That depends on the grace of God touching their hearts, which we must always bear in mind.

Demographic information

The fact that Muslims consolidate together in localities has been mentioned. However, you will also find Muslims scattered everywhere. This may be by reason of occupation, such as restaurants, pharmacies, hospitals, etc.

Some of the figures given earlier were from the 2001 census. The ethnic origins of the 1.6 million Muslims in Britain can also be gleaned from it. The oldest Muslim group is the Arab Yemenis who mainly settled in the ports of England, and which now totals some 80,000, but the majority of Muslims are found among the ethnic Pakistani and Bangladeshi populations. Other ethnic groups are also present, such as Algerians, Bosnians, Jordanians, Kurds, Lebanese, Mauritanians, Somalis, Sudanese, Syrians and Tunisians. British Muslims number around 5,000, many of whom are of Afro-Caribbean origin. It is perhaps the more experiential aspects of Sufism that appeals to converts from ethnically white British inhabitants, though some claim that it is the more logical aspects of Islamic teaching.

Greater London has a much larger proportion of Muslims than the rest of the country, for more than half of the Bangladeshi community live there. Some 41% of Middle Eastern Muslims can also be found in the capital, but the remainder are scattered in various places. Pakistanis are concentrated further north in the industrial West Midlands, the Lancashire mill towns and West Yorkshire. In the south-east of England they can also be found in north and west London, Slough and Oxford.

Scotland has about 68,000 Muslims, most of whom are Pakistanis, but there are also small numbers of Arabs, Turks and Iranians in the larger cities. In Northern Ireland there are around 4,000 Muslims. Wales has about 50,000 Muslims, mostly Pakistani and Bangladeshi, but also Arabs, Turks and Iranians are to be found in Cardiff and Newport.

The following chart shows the ethnic Muslim distribution throughout England and Wales. Muslims of Arab, Turkish and Persian ethnicity are probably included in the 'Other' category. Scotland and Northern Ireland are excluded. The figures are all rounded to the nearest thousand.

Ethnic Group	Population in England and Wales (thousands)		Percentage of total	
Indian (subcontinent)		1,090		69
Pakistani	679		43	
Bangladeshi	269		17	
Indian	142		9	
Black African/Caribbean, etc.		95		6
White British		63		4
Other		332		21
Other Asian	33		2	
Irish and other white	92		6	
Mixed—White/Asian	119		8	
Mixed—rest	30		2	
Chinese or other ethnic group	58		4	
TOTAL		1,580		100

As London is the capital of Britain, more than half the Muslim immigrants settled there. The following shows the differing ethnic proportion of Muslims in London. The table shows the ethnic breakdown of Muslims in London.

The distribution of Muslim populations in the UK

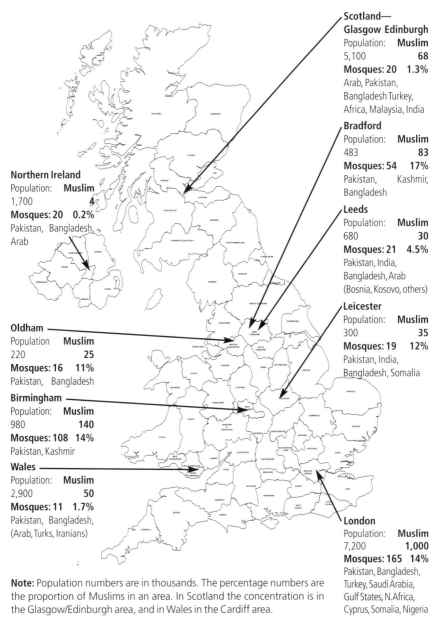

**Scotland—
Glasgow Edinburgh**
Population: **Muslim**
5,100   **68**
Mosques: 20   1.3%
Arab, Pakistan,
Bangladesh Turkey,
Africa, Malaysia, India

Bradford
Population: **Muslim**
483   **83**
Mosques: 54   17%
Pakistan,   Kashmir,
Bangladesh

Leeds
Population: **Muslim**
680   **30**
Mosques: 21   4.5%
Pakistan, India,
Bangladesh, Arab
(Bosnia, Kosovo, others)

Leicester
Population: **Muslim**
300   **35**
Mosques: 19   12%
Pakistan, India,
Bangladesh, Somalia

Northern Ireland
Population: **Muslim**
1,700   **4**
Mosques: 20   0.2%
Pakistan, Bangladesh,
Arab

Oldham
Population   **Muslim**
220   **25**
Mosques: 16   11%
Pakistan,   Bangladesh

Birmingham
Population: **Muslim**
980   **140**
Mosques: 108 14%
Pakistan, Kashmir

Wales
Population: **Muslim**
2,900   **50**
Mosques: 11   1.7%
Pakistan, Bangladesh,
(Arab, Turks, Iranians)

London
Population: **Muslim**
7,200   **1,000**
Mosques: 165 14%
Pakistan, Bangladesh,
Turkey, Saudi Arabia,
Gulf States, N.Africa,
Cyprus, Somalia, Nigeria

Note: Population numbers are in thousands. The percentage numbers are the proportion of Muslims in an area. In Scotland the concentration is in the Glasgow/Edinburgh area, and in Wales in the Cardiff area.

Ethnic Group		Population in London (thousands)	Percentage of total
Indian (subcontinent)		322	53
	Pakistani	134	22
	Bangladeshi	146	24
	Indian	42	7
Black African/Caribbean, etc.		79	13
White British		24	4
Other		182	30
	Other Asian	36	6
	Irish and other white	85	14
	Mixed—White/Asian	12	2
	Mixed—rest	18	3
	Chinese or other ethnic group	30	5
TOTAL		607	100

Notes

1 **Christopher Catherwood**, *Christians, Muslims and Islamic Rage* (Grand Rapids: Zondervan 2003), p.44.

2 John 18:36.

3 *Muslimedia International*: www.muslimedia.com/archives/world98/islapho.htm. Report on Islamophobia.

4 A survey that was taken for the Asian magazine, *Eastern Eyes* 'to counter myths surrounding the Afghan crisis': reported by British newspaper, *The Guardian*: hmedia.guardian.co.uk/attack/story/0,1301,604081,00.html.

5 *The Guardian*: Report: http://www.guardian.co.uk/business/story/0,,642715,00.html. Article: '5,000 Muslims make millions', 1st February 2002.

6 **Humayun Ansari**, *Muslims in Britain*, Report: Minority Rights Group International, August 2002, p.16. Available in pdf format: www.minorityrights.org/admin/ Download/pdf/muslimsinbritain.pdf.

7 *The Muslim News*: www.muslimnews.co.uk/paper/index.php?article=209 for a further breakdown of these figures.

8 ICIT: www.islamicthought.org/mp-intro.html. Article: 'The Muslim Parliament of Great Britain 1992–1998', ¶8.

9 **Humayun Ansari,** 'Muslims in Britain', Report: Minority Rights Group International, August 2002, p.20. Available in pdf format: www.minorityrights.org/admin/Download/pdf/muslimsinbritain.pdf.

10 *Ibid.,* p.22.

11 *Ibid.,* p.22, citing *The Muslim Manifesto—A Strategy for Survival* (London, The Muslim Institute, June 1990).

12 *Ibid.,* p.31.

13 United Kingdom National Profiles: www.statistics.gov.uk/census2001/profiles/uk.asp. The page of the official website of National Statistics.

14 **N. Smart,** 'Church, Party and State', in **P. Badham,** ed. *Religion, State And Society in Modern Britain* (The Edwin Press, 1989), p.390.

15 **T. Modood,** 'Establishment, Multiculturalism and British Citizenship', *The Political Quarterly,* Vol.65, No.1, January-March 1994, p.56.

16 **Kamal Ahmed,** http://politics.guardian.co.uk/print/0,3858,4691601–108685,00.html. Report: 'Call for Queen to lose title as head of Church', *The Observer* Newspaper, Sunday 15 June 2003. Also http://observer.guardian.co.uk/uk_news/story/0,6903,977846,00.html?=rss.

17 **Andrew Alderson,**
www.naqshbandi.net/haqqani/features/HRH%20Prince%20Charles/prince/Prince_Major.html, Article: 'Major warns Charles of "empty gesture" on faiths', *The Sunday Times,* May 26th 1996, ¶9–10.

Reaching out

It is always important, when reaching out to any unbeliever, to start where he is. This is therefore true of Islam. Muslims have already been shown to differ widely. There is no simple formula.

The book of Acts highlights this situation. On the day of Pentecost, it was wholly by the prompting of the Holy Spirit that Peter was able to give that masterly sermon of which we have a summary in Acts 2. Peter applied familiar Old Testament truths to the Lord Jesus Christ, so recently crucified, but now raised from the dead. He explained to them that the man Jesus whom they had known walking among them until so very recently, had the hand of his heavenly Father upon him. Even though so many of them felt they were doing God's will in putting him to death, they were in fact doing so in a way they could never have realized. Yet they were personally responsible for what they had done. Read Acts 2:22–41 carefully. It is a familiar passage, but vital to our understanding.

There was a positive response to Peter's explanation and applying of the Word of God. The Holy Spirit worked in the hearts of his hearers, and they were convicted of their sin. They recognized that God the Father was holding them responsible for what they had done to his Son in crucifying him, and they needed to do something about it. Peter told them to repent and their sins would be forgiven. Three thousand were baptized, and the church was born that day.

In Acts we discover many different situations in which the gospel was preached, and we find that that there were many and differing responses to that gospel. People who believed came from many different backgrounds, from many different experiences of life, and no one believer is stereotypical.

The same must be said of our desire to share the gospel of the Lord Jesus Christ with Muslims today. There could be many wise ways of presenting the gospel message, and things to avoid at the beginning. We can apply all the correct principles, but none of this guarantees that we will ever win one Muslim.

Thus if you are looking for procedure, you will be disappointed. God is sovereign, and we must recognize this. He will work in the hearts of men and women according to his gracious will. We may not be able to discern that until later, perhaps not even in our lifetime, but his sovereign power and wisdom are supreme.

However there are certain principles that are worth considering, of which the need for personal and private prayer is paramount.

Where are the Muslims? Nearer than most of us think—neighbours, fellow employees and parents on the 'school run', for instance. This being the case, we must seek to make friends with them. This can mean simply chatting and getting to know them. It will involve hospitality—you could invite them to have coffee with you. Perhaps you would like to invite them for a meal, but that will be a more difficult move, and probably best left to a later stage in your friendship. The reason for this is that your Muslim friends will be very hesitant, as they do not know you—probably fearful that you may try to feed them pork (after all, you're a Christian aren't you!). Anyway, there is the issue of *halal* meat which is a requirement for them. Maybe when they have learnt to trust you, having seen your genuine interest in them, they will invite you for a meal. That will be a big positive step in your relationship with them. Do not hesitate to accept the invitation. Any indecision will show that you do not trust them, and could spoil your friendship.

Do not rush to share the gospel—you need to gain their trust and respect first. They may question you about your faith, and given the opportunity you will be happy to share with them that you trust the Lord Jesus Christ as your Saviour. Let them see how important this is to you—that you are a regular church-goer, that you believe prayer is important, and also to know that your sins are forgiven. Your Muslim friends will be interested in what you believe.

Ask your Muslim friends questions about what they believe. Listen, and do not assume anything. Ask questions to make sure you understand what they are saying—but if at this time you express anything to suggest that you cannot believe what they are saying, you could damage the relationship you are seeking to build up.

Eventually you will get an opportunity to tell them more about the Saviour, and be able to share the gospel message with them more openly.

The danger will be that you will want to tell them too much on any one occasion. I know a believer who had the ear of Muslims and always shared only one truth with them. Often the first stage was getting them to understand what sin is, and that all men and women are sinners before God, including himself and them. Then he would leave and return another time to what he had shared. This had the advantage of helping to ascertain whether they had really understood him on the previous occasion. Therefore, encourage interest in a truth, leave at that point, and then they may be willing to hear you next time.

Use appropriate literature. If it is written with Muslims in mind, it will be more useful. Muslims have various misconceptions about Christian faith and truth. Seek to avoid using literature that appears to focus on difficult areas, so that their misunderstanding and prejudice is not perpetuated.

Language is an area to be cautious about. It may seem to be a good idea to find literature in the ethnic language of your Muslim friends, but they may not see it that way! Sometimes ethnic Muslims who have left their own country may want to forget everything to do with their previous existence, including turning their back on their home language. Others may feel they are educated people, and therefore to speak with them in their mother tongue would be considered a put-down, and not appreciated. Therefore we need to be sensitive to this issue of language, and seek to know their preferences.[1] The type of literature to use will again depend on the situation. Sometimes simply worded tracts are useful. Other times, booklets with colourful illustrations,[2] or even something more substantial[3] will be more appropriate. They may even ask for a copy of the *Injil* (Arabic for 'gospel'). If appropriate, offer a gospel portion, such as John's Gospel, for them to read. (Be aware of the start of Mark's Gospel—its opening words may not be helpful for an introduction to the gospel for Muslims.) Maybe you will discover editions of the New Testament especially translated with Muslims in mind, or in a language used among Muslims, that are called the Holy Injil, or similar.[4] Cassettes and CDs in different languages are available from various Christian organizations. They may include appropriate ethnic singing as well as a message. You will have to assess the situation for yourself, in the particular circumstances you face, as to what your best approach may be. It is difficult to give more specific guidelines—except to reiterate the need to bathe all you do with prayer, and exercise the spiritual wisdom for which you have prayed.

You may feel called of the Lord specifically to go and seek out Muslims in the inner cities and larger towns. To find yourself among Muslims living in such an area, perhaps one in which you do not live, can be very daunting. You need to find some point of contact, but it could be quite expensive going for a meal at the same restaurant regularly just to meet the staff! Some other way must be found.

One possibility is to set up a bookstall in a market. Avoid using a church foyer because that would be a big put-off. On your bookstall have things of general interest, but also ensuring that you have materials, perhaps in different languages, that could be taken, or sold for a nominal price. In this case having literature in ethnic languages does not matter, as here it is a personal choice for the visitor to take something in his (or her) language. What we are looking for is that initial contact and encouragement of interest.

How one may appropriately proceed after the initial contact will depend on the circumstances and type of interest. Much the same applies here as previously mentioned with personal contacts.

Some situations, however, are best avoided. If a Muslim begins to try to argue with you, carefully and politely refuse to take up the challenge. Perhaps suggest that he might find something of interest to read among the books or pamphlets that you have on offer. If a crowd of Muslims approach you, again avoid in-depth discussion. Speaking with a Muslim individually is no threat to either you or him.

It is not a good idea to preach in the open air. This may (or may not) attract a crowd, and you can find yourself in a dangerous situation if a group of Muslims decides it does not like what they hear.

If you make a number of contacts in a district, you may well find that the local *imam* gets to hear and visits the same people, and interest may suddenly diminish. Wisdom is needed in these circumstances, to know how to proceed. It is probably the wisest thing to try to keep open the contact, but to give them space, and not visit regularly. Perhaps encourage them to revisit you where they first spoke with you (at the bookstall?).

Another approach might be to pay regular visits to a coffee place or tea house that Muslims frequent. Do not evangelize outside, or in the vicinity, of a mosque: that could be asking for trouble. Simply look for opportunities of meeting Muslims, but preferably not where you are confronted with a group. Maybe a local organization of some sort might be appropriate, where you could discreetly meet and make personal contacts.

Another important point to bear in mind is that such sharing must be done strictly using the wise strategy of men talking with men and women talking with women. To do otherwise brings other unhelpful factors into play. It gives the wrong impression among Muslims.

Be careful also of focussing on young people in a Muslim community. Yes, they may be more accessible. Some may be more open to consider what you want to say than their parents. But you are in danger of the community reacting against you and putting pressure on you to abandon what you are doing. On the other hand, you may find that younger people are more antagonistic than their parents. Some are finding a deeper identity within Islam. Everything must be done with great sensitivity.

There is another issue that is worth considering. Ethnic white Britons may not be readily accepted into a suspicious Muslim community. The local *imam* may well encourage their suspicion. Of course, we believe that all barriers can be broken down, and we trust the Lord to that end. Therefore it may prove useful encouraging Bible-believing Christians from a similar ethnic background to be involved in such outreach. Your local church may wish to support such a venture, if you live in, or near, a Muslim community. This has the distinct advantage that such a believer will be accepted without prejudice because, to all intents and purposes, he is 'one of us'.

No doubt many other things could be said, but there are those who are better acquainted with such outreach than I am. I have made these recommendations from my own observations over a number of years. Having listened to a good number of those already involved in such work, I have tried carefully to weigh up the things heard. This is not an attempt to give any definitive strategy, but simply pointers to what may be done.

Those wanting to try such outreach should listen to those already doing this work. Contact appropriate Christian organizations that can offer support and encouragement. Pray that the Lord will help us in our weakness to be useful to him who is able to save to the uttermost.[5] This means we do not work alone, and sharing the gospel will be effective, for every one of his elect children. We must always remember that he has already won the victory. And remembering who he is will be our encouragement to continue the work, however hard it may prove to be.[6]

Let us make sure that we always keep our hearts and minds focussed on the Saviour, recognizing that he has promised that he will build his church, and include those from every language and nation.[7] His is the victory. He will bring those whom he promises to save to heaven, where he is the central figure.[8]

Notes

1   Usually in good mission strategy it is argued that we ought to use a person's mother-tongue wherever possible, because this reflects their 'heart-language'—and issues of faith are centred in the heart, where they are deeply seated. Thus to move them in matters of faith, one has to move their heart. But there will be 'exceptions that prove the rule'.

2   **Gerard Chrispin**, *How can God accept me?* and *How can I find God?* (Day One Publications).

3   **John Blanchard**, *Ultimate Questions* (Darlington: Evangelical Press).

4   Note the *Holy Injil*, Gospel of Matthew, by IBS, using the New International Readers Version adapted to Muslim vocabulary. Mentioning this doesn't necessarily endorse its use. Check it out for yourself.

5   Hebrews 7:25.

6   Hebrews 8:1,6.

7   Revelation 7:9.

8   Revelation 21:22–27.

Women in Islam
Introduction

There is a tremendous feeling in the western world about Muslim women, especially among evangelical Christians. The place of Christian women is itself a very hot issue. In recent years the attitude towards women in the Christian family and in the life of the church has been given more balance than in years past. There is, however, a strong tendency to tip that balance into a non-biblical position. We inevitably see the status of women in Islam through our western eyes, especially in the light of what many consider to have been the inexcusable way Christian women were treated in the past.

Hence we need to look at this subject by putting aside our own cultural bias. We must not impose on Islam what we may think the place of women in *our* society ought to be. It would be much more profitable to consider the Muslim view of women in the light of the Scriptures. We need to address Muslim attitudes towards women by first considering biblical teaching.

Chapter 17

A biblical foundation

In Christian thought, women are equal to men in person and character. Both men and women have a parallel identity and equality before God. We recognize, however, that men and women have different roles and different responsibilities in Christian society. The creation ordinance points to the responsibility and privilege of a woman to be a helpmeet to a man—to complement him, and bring a balance to his life.[1]

There is another important matter. God gave to women the particular responsibility of child-bearing. This was made more difficult and painful because of the entrance of sin into the world, and its judgement.[2] The scriptural view of a woman is that she has an important role in the family and in society—both of which would suffer if she did not fulfil her God-given responsibility. It is a role that is different from that of a man, but it must never be considered inferior. A woman is not a second-class person before God, and certainly should not be so in human society.

Another truth is clearly seen in Genesis. Man has a distinct authority to exercise. Adam demonstrated it as he fulfilled God's command in naming 'Woman', emphasizing the fact that both man and woman are equally created in the image of God.[3]

This gives us a biblical foundation concerning the Christian view of women. An important passage in the New Testament on this subject comes from Paul in Ephesians 5:22–33. Under the guidance of the Holy Spirit, he expressed powerful truth concerning the rightful place of women. Paul is specifically addressing the distinctive roles within the family. He is seeking to redress the balance between husband and wife, based on biological differences and spiritual principles. Can there be any greater incentive to make sure that the role of men and women is kept in a right and noble balance? He shows respect, acceptance and special regard for the various and differing roles of men and women.

Do we see this truly transcendent view of the relationship between men and women in the western expression of the evangelical Christian church? If we are to answer truthfully, we surely have to admit that we easily fail.

So often we fall short of our own biblical standard. To consider the place of women in Islam, we ought to take our Lord's example when he was faced with a specific moral question.4 Therefore let us turn to consider the subject of the place of women in Islam in a sensitive, caring and compassionate manner. We need to think of the situation they face in the light of God's word and truth, and not with the limitations and attitudes of personal prejudice.

Notes

1 Genesis 2:22–24.
2 Genesis 3:16.
3 Genesis 1:27–28; 2:19–20, 23.
4 John 8:7.

Mohammed's women

Mohammed's own personal attitude to women has been, for Christians, something approaching a scandal. While in no way wishing to explain away the problem, we need to consider it with some degree of impartiality.

His faithfulness to Khadijah is emphasized a great deal in Muslim literature relating to Mohammed's life. His marriage was considered a happy one. They had six children: two boys, who died during childhood, and four girls.

Muslims are deeply sensitive about their prophet's private life and his attitude to women in his later years. Many historians tend to gloss over, or even ignore, some of these problems. They seek to emphasize his numerous 'political' exploits, and attempt to show that he exerted all his energies in the establishing of the Muslim community in troublesome circumstances.

Commentators also maintain that Mohammed saw in Sawdah a spiritual companion to replace the encouragement and support his beloved Khadijah had brought to him. It has also been suggested that this marriage may have been more of a political expedient. As Mohammed was leader of what was then a small band of Muslims, he might have considered marriage with Sawdah as a prudent measure for her own protection and security, avoiding the necessity of her having to marry someone outside the group. Remember that in Arab society a woman had no security outside marriage, and, as a widow, may well be left destitute. One supporting statement for this view argues for Mohammed's mature years and heavy burden of responsibility: 'As for Mohammed himself there are signs that deepening religious experiences were taking the place of human companionship.'[1]

In his next marriage to Aisha it is argued that a relationship between a fifty-three year old man and a girl of nine years of age must necessarily have been more like that of father and daughter.[2]

It is not appropriate for us to enter into an in-depth study of Mohammed's marriages. However, we must be clear about what we are being asked to believe, namely that most of Mohammed's marriages, as well as those of his daughters and close Muslim associates, 'are found to have political reasons of one kind or another'.[3]

A Muslim author appeals quite forcefully that Mohammed's motives should not be misunderstood. He sets forth the argument that a fifty-year-old man who was establishing political ideals does not get married for the same pleasure that one would expect that a twenty-five year old would.

Even if the Prophet had married a number of women, as a normal Arab of his day did, there would be nothing morally repugnant about this providing a sense of proportion was kept. ... Given the right conditions monogamy is certainly the ideal form. ... The Qur'an, therefore, laid down monogamy as the moral law for long-term achievement, but permitted polygamy immediately as a legal solution of the situation.[4]

Whatever one feels about the validity of the argument, we must bear in mind the prevailing conditions of Mohammed's day. However, the actions of Mohammed are questionable.[5]

This leads us on to consider the teaching of the Qur'an on the place and status of women. Curiously, the Qur'an has more to say about the standing of women in society than on any other social question. The condition of women in the Arabia of Mohammed's day had been very low indeed, but Mohammed sought to make amends for their degradation and dishonour. To that end he established new principles on how women were to be considered and treated. It is claimed that his reforms enhanced the status of women in Arabia to a considerable degree.

However, the Qur'an still maintains the superiority of both father and husband over a woman in the matter of marriage and divorce. Commentators have emphasized that divorce was personally disapproved of by Mohammed. He maintained that divorce was something 'odious in the sight of God'. The following observation underlines the problem:

[Mohammed's] own family life at Medina and his numerous marriages have been the subject of much insinuating comment on the one side and of heated and disingenuous apology on the other. The traditions make no secret of the attraction which he felt towards women, or of the fact that it was combined with a peculiarly strict regard for the proprieties. But critics have tended to overlook the almost unfailing patience which he displayed even under provocation and the gentleness with which he attended to the griefs of all sorts of women and comforted them, even at times to the extent of revising his legislation.[6]

Because of Mohammed's influence and example, a woman was now being accepted as an individual in her own right, instead of being considered merely an object to be used. This was a real improvement.

On the other hand, some Muslims try to solve their dilemma over the status of women in Islam with a deliberate whitewash.

... the most important legal enactments and general reform pronouncements of the Qur'an have been on the subjects of women and slavery. The Qur'an immensely improved the status of the woman in several directions but the most basic is the fact that the woman was given a fully-fledged personality. The spouses are declared to be each other's 'garments': the woman has been granted the same rights over man as man has over his wife, except that man, being the earning partner, is a degree higher. Unlimited polygamy was strictly regulated and the number of wives was limited to four, with the rider that if a husband feared that he could not do justice among several wives, he must marry only one wife. ... The overall logical consequence of these pronouncements is a banning of polygamy under normal circumstances. Yet as an already existing institution polygamy was accepted on a legal plane ... [but] when gradually social circumstances became more favourable, monogamy might be introduced. This is because no reformer who means to be effective can neglect the real situation and simply issue visionary statements. But the later Muslims did not watch the guiding lines of the Qur'an and, in fact, thwarted its intentions.[7]

These comments need to be considered in the light of Qur'anic teaching.

Notes

1 **Montgomery Watt**, *Muhammad: Prophet and Statesman* (Oxford University Press, 1980, 1961), p.79.
2 *Ibid.*, p.102.
3 *Ibid.*, p.102–3.
4 **Fazlur Rahman**, *Islam* (University of Chicago Press, 1979, 1966), p. 29.

5 See **Ergun Mehmet Caner and Emir Fehi Caner**, *Unveiling Islam*, (Monarch Books, 2003), pp.56–60.

6 **H.A.R Gibb**, *Islam* (Hyderabad: Henry Martyn Institute of Islamic Studies, 1979; London: Oxford University Press, 1969), p. 23.

7 **Fazlur Rahman**, *Islam* (University of Chicago Press, 1979, 1966), p.38.

The Qur'anic and Sunnah witness

hen we refer back to the teaching of the Qur'an on the place of
women, we quickly discover that there are some very strong
sentiments expressed: 'Women are your fields; go, then, into your
fields as you please.'[1]

Professor Fatima Mernessi is a Moroccan Muslim feminist writer
seeking to challenge the present situation in Islam:

> In western culture, sexual inequality is based on the belief in the biological inferiority
> of woman. In Islam, it is the contrary: the whole system is based on the assumption that
> woman is a powerful and dangerous being. All sexual institutions (polygamy,
> repudiation, sexual segregation, etc.) can be perceived as a strategy for constraining her
> power.[2]

This gives a wholly different complexion to what we normally might
perceive of Islam. We find here a picture of the Muslim man
endeavouring to carry out the commands of Allah, but challenged and
distracted by the power of women! The Muslim world thus faces two
threats: the infidel without and the woman within. Women have a
powerful attractiveness to men which distracts men from serving Allah.
Such distractions are evil. This expresses the antagonism between Allah
and women.

Consider that Allah has given *ruh*, *nafs* and *aqal* (spirit, passion and
rationality) to humanity. Women have strong *nafs* and weak *aqal*. So in a
marriage relationship, the husband, who represents reason and piety,
unavoidably embraces the woman's irrationality, disorder, and everything
that is polluting to his piety. Therefore even his wife is a threat to the pious
Muslim. There is thus an Arabic term for her: *hbel al-shaitan*, 'the devil's
leash', and Muslims have to protect *themselves*.

Professor Mernessi presents the picture of the woman as a kind of trespasser among Muslim men. She is upsetting the order of things that Allah has established. Worst of all, it is the man who has everything to lose: social prestige, self-determination, peace of mind and allegiance to Allah.

For this reason, Islamic society down the ages has developed various mechanisms for repressing women and keeping them away from men. Two of these are obvious:

(1) Minimum education of girls, or even none at all.

(2) The veil, expressing the invisibility of women outside the home.

In these ways, Muslim men are doing their best to lessen the evil influence of women on their Muslim duties.

So even within the home, though the wife (or her mother-in-law, if she is present) appears to be absolutely in charge, she has no personal choice. The division of Islamic duty imposed by men establishes the *status quo*, and the woman's only option is to fulfil her allotted role. She can neither do anything, nor believe anything different, without her husband's express permission.

The relationship between men and women in Islam is summed up by a respected Muslim commentator: 'The woman is absolutely the greatest affliction in a man's life.'[3] To find out the reasons for this, it is needful to consider the teaching of the Qur'an, and to note what its well-known interpreters have to say.

The defining chapter in the Qur'an is Sura 4, called *Al Nissa* (The Women). It has 176 verses dealing with the rights of women and orphans, and clearly legitimizes gender inequality. We will consider what is said on the position of women in Islam.

i. Sura 4:24

You are also forbidden to take in marriage married women, except captives whom you own as slaves. Such is the decree of Allah. All women other than these are lawful to you, provided you seek them with your wealth in modest conduct, not in fornication. Give them their dowry for the enjoyment you have had of them as a duty; but it shall be no offence for you to make any other agreement among yourselves after you have fulfilled your duty.

Seven hundred years ago the great Muslim scholar Al Ghazali wrote:

The most satisfying and final word on the matter is that marriage is a form of slavery. The woman is man's slave and her duty therefore is absolute obedience to the husband in all that he asks of her person. A woman, who at the moment of death enjoys the full approval of her husband, will find her place in Paradise.[4]

A Muslim scholar, 1980:

The institution of marriage in Islam is very different for men as compared with women, the rights accorded to husbands being distinct from those accorded to wives. Above all, Muslim marriage is a contract with all the benefits belonging to the man. The dowry is therefore essential to the legality of the marriage since it purchases rights over the woman. Thus she has the right of support as long as she does nothing without her husband's agreement. ... In fact it is probably not accurate to use the term 'rights of the woman' since a woman under the Islamic system of marriage has no human rights unless we consider that a slave has rights under a slave system. Marriage, in so far as women are concerned, is just like slavery to the slave, or the chains of serfdom to the serf.[5]

More recently, in 1990: 'Women must perform their duties with perfection for their husbands to please Allah.'[6]

ii. Sura 4:11

Allah has thus enjoined you concerning your children: A male shall inherit twice as much as a female. If there be more than two girls, they shall have two-thirds of the inheritance; but if there be one only, she shall inherit the half. Parents shall inherit a sixth each, if the deceased have a child; but if he leave no children and his parents be his heirs, his mother shall have a third. If he have two brothers, his mother shall have a sixth after payments of his debts and any legacies he may have bequeathed. You may wonder whether your parents or your children are more beneficial to you. But this is the law of Allah; He is wise and all-knowing.

There is no avoiding the implication that women have a much more raw deal, and do not enjoy the same status as men. Both the ancient Islamic commentators Zamakhshari (AD 1070–1143) and Tabari (AD 835–870) concur with the *hadith* statement:

In this verse Allah says that the man is the leader over the woman and is the one who disciplines her if she does wrong. This is because *men are superior to women, and a man is better than a woman*. ... Here Allah refers to the dowry and expenses, which Allah prescribed in the Qur'an and *sunnah*; and *given a man is better than a woman*, it is appropriate that he be her protector and maintainer, as Allah says (Sura 2:228).[7] (Italics added for emphasis.)

Then also note what Mohammad Ibn Zakariya Al-Razi (AD 864–930) wrote commenting on Sura 4:11:

Man is more perfect than the woman in creation, and intelligence, and in the religious sphere, such as the suitability to be a judge, and a leader in worship. Also, the testimony of the man is twice that of the woman. So that whoever is given great responsibilities must be given correspondingly great privileges. *As the woman is deficient in intelligence and of great lust*, if she is given much money, much corruption will be the result.[8] (Italics added for emphasis.)

It is clear that the early Islamic commentators certainly didn't hold women in very high esteem.

iii. Sura 4:19–20

Believers, it is unlawful for you to inherit the women of your deceased kinsman against their will, or to bar them from re-marrying, in order that you may force them to give up a part of what you have given them, unless they be guilty of a proven crime. Treat them with kindness; for even if you do not love them, it may well be that you may dislike a thing which Allah has meant for your own good.

If you wish to divorce a woman in order to wed another, do not take from her the dowry you have given her even if it be a talent of gold. That would be improper and grossly unjust.

We note here that there is a degree of consideration for the woman who is caught up in a difficult situation. Men are not to treat women as they will, but with certain respect and human dignity. Men are not to treat women harshly or inconsiderately, but there is a clear expectation of a wife's absolute obedience to her husband. Indeed, a wife's disobedience represents an unlawful and irrational act. Her obedience to her husband is for her the key to paradise, as in the following al-Masabih *hadith*:

There are three (persons) whose prayer will not be accepted, nor their virtues be taken above: The runaway slave until he returns back to his master, the woman with whom her husband is dissatisfied, and the drunk until he becomes sober.[9]

Whosoever female dies while her husband is pleased with her, will enter Paradise.[10]

From this *hadith*, a wife's response to her husband is understood as resembling worship. The general drift is that it is a noble sacrifice for a man to share his life with a woman, she being so deficient in mind, religion and gratitude.

It is claimed that Mohammed said, 'If I were to order anyone to prostrate before another, I would have ordered a woman to prostrate before her husband.'[11]

Commentators point out that this cannot be true because in Islam it is not allowed that anyone should prostrate themselves before any other than Allah, but the words portray the attitude of Muslims to women.

iv. Sura 4:4:34

Men have authority over women because Allah has made the one superior to the others, and because they spend their wealth to maintain them. Good women are obedient. They guard their unseen parts because Allah has guarded them. As for those from whom you fear disobedience, admonish them and send them to beds apart and beat them. Then if they obey you, take no further action against them. Allah is high, supreme.

So men are the protectors of women because Allah created man before woman. That is the grounds for their obedience. If they do not obey, then grind them down until they do. A report concerning a ruling of Muslim lawyers (1996) states: 'A husband has the duty to educate his wife and therefore has the right to punish her as he wishes.'[12]

The Federation of Islamic Councils holds the same opinion.

Women's rebelliousness (*nushuz*) is a medical condition. It is of two kinds: The first is the condition *when the woman delights to be the submissive partner who finds pleasure in being beaten and tortured*. This is what is called Masochism. The second is when the woman loves to hurt and master and dominate the other partner. This is what is called Sadism. Such woman has no remedy except removing her spikes and destroying her weapon by which she dominates. This weapon of the woman is her femininity. *But the other woman who delights in submission and being beaten, then beating is her remedy*. So the Qur'anic command: 'banish them to their couches, and beat them' agrees with the latest psychological findings in understanding the rebellious woman. This is one of the scientific miracles of the Qur'an because it sums up volumes of the science of psychology about rebellious women.[13] (Italics added for emphasis.)

In other words, the 'the woman who delights to be the submissive partner' feels pleasure in being beaten because it makes her feel valued!

But Sahih al-Bukhari states in his *hadith*: 'Narrated Abu Huraira: Allah's Apostle said, "The woman is like a rib; if you try to straighten her, she will break. So if you want to get benefit from her, do so while she still has some crookedness."'[14]

The inference is that a woman is like a crooked rib, something incurable. Another *hadith* certainly does not encourage any better view.

[Mohammed] passed by the women and said, '*O women! Give alms, as I have seen that the majority of the dwellers of Hell-fire were you (women)*.' They asked, 'Why is it so, O Allah's Apostle?' He replied, 'You curse frequently and are ungrateful to your husbands. I have not seen anyone more deficient in intelligence and religion than you. A cautious sensible man could be led astray by some of you.'[15] (Italics added for emphasis.)

The picture presented in the Qur'an and in various *hadith* does not give women a very good status. The Arabic word *nisa* is straightforwardly translated as 'woman', sometimes as 'wife'. But also in Islam woman is designated as *awrah*. The Encyclopaedia of Islam defines *awrah* as the Latin word *pudendum*, that is 'the external genitals, especially of the female (Latin *pudendum*, literally, a thing to be ashamed of).' According to the *hadith*, a woman actually has ten *awrat*. 'Ali reported the Prophet saying: "Women have ten (*awrat*). When she gets married, the husband covers one, and when she dies the grave covers the ten."'[16]

The implication is that a wife has something to be ashamed of, and going outside the house is perceived as a form of exposure of the *awrah*—a thing that is said to delight the devil. 'A woman is closest to God's face, if she is found in the core of her house. And the prayer of the woman in the house is better than her prayer in the mosque.'[17]

Thus from what al-Ghazali said, a woman is found closest to Allah in her home. When she goes out the devil welcomes her—an action that exposes the shameful, and thus causes men to fall. This principle of *awrah* is a support for the concept of *purdah* (literally, curtain) where women are kept in a separate place in the home. The seriousness of this matter can be gauged from a statement made in 1991 by the Iranian Prosecutor-General: 'Anyone who rejects the principle of the *hijab* (dress code) is an apostate and the punishment for an apostate under Islamic law is death. ... The dress code, which also applies to women of the Christian and other minority faiths, violates the right of all Iranian women to freedom of conscience and belief.'[18]

More recently a commercial bank in Bangladesh was proposing to lend money to women to start small businesses, but this was immediately attacked by Muslim leaders. Afghanistan's Mohammed Hassan, Taliban governor of Kandahar, said: 'The motive of the bank was to lead Moslems away from Islam and promote shamelessness among women.'[19]

Al-Ghazali speaks of women quite harshly, but then he puts on a softening rider, with Sura 30:21 in mind:

By one of [Allah's] signs He created you from dust; you became men and multiplied throughout the earth. By another sign He gave you wives from among yourselves, that you might live in joy with them, and planted love and kindness in your hearts. Surely these are signs in this for thinking men.[20]

Other relevant Qur'anic references
Further observations that support this position are given in the Qur'an.

If any of your women commit fornication, call in four witnesses from among yourselves against them; if they testify of their guilt confine them to their houses till death overtakes them or till Allah finds another way for them.[21]

If you wish to divorce a woman in order to wed another, do not take from her the dowry you have given her even if it be a talent of gold. That would be improper and grossly unjust; for how can you take it back when you have lain with each other and entered into a firm contract? Henceforth you shall not marry the women who were married to your fathers. This was an evil practice, indecent and abominable. (There follows a lengthy statement forbidding incest in various forms.)[22]

If you fear a breach between a man and his wife, appoint an arbiter from his people and another from hers. If they wish to be reconciled Allah will bring them together again.[23]

Lawful to you are the believing women and the free women from among those who were given the Scriptures before you, provided that you give them their dowries and live in honour with them, neither committing fornication nor taking them as mistresses.[24]

Enjoin believing women to turn their eyes away from temptation and to preserve their chastity; to cover their adornments (except such as are normally displayed); to draw their veils over their bosoms and not to reveal their finery except to their [family and its servants]. And let them not stamp their feet in walking so as to reveal their hidden trinkets.[25]

In spite of earlier statements, we see here a genuine concern for propriety at the time of Mohammed. It is coloured by the prevailing situation. In spite of the general observations he made, Mohammed was also very aware of the abuse of women. He genuinely sought to bring about changes that would enhance their role and command more respect for them. His position on this was certainly a reaction against the prevailing spirit of his times, and is balanced by a desire to ensure that women knew their place and lived respectfully without vaunting themselves. The discerning Christian is surely reminded here of the teaching of Paul on the way women, whether young, older or widowed, ought to adopt modest and appropriate conduct.[26] Remember also his balancing instructions to men.

This is not to gloss over the fact that we see a number of major problems with the way Muslims treat women. They are not considered to have equal rights. The expressions used in the Qur'an give legitimacy to real abuse. The harshness and the injustice that we so readily associate with the Muslim view of women is justified by the Qur'an.

We also have to face the difficulty that on religious grounds Muslims are allowed to have up to four wives at one time. However, the Qur'an clearly affirms that wives must be treated with deference, kindness and strict impartiality, and that if a man cannot treat all alike then he must keep to one. That is quite an admonition. In reality, a man often only takes one wife for economic reasons. This helps to alleviate some of the abuses, but we have to say that the Qur'an is ambivalent on the matter.

Notes

1 Sura 2:223.

2 **Fatima Mernessi**, *Beyond the Veil* (New York: John Wiley and Sons, 1975), p.16. Quoted at: www.iran-bulletin.org/Islamic_Feminism.html.

3 **Sa'id al Buti**, through a personal communication from **Paul Simpson**.

4 **al Ghazali**, Dar al-Kotob al-'Elmeyah, *Ihy'a 'Uloum ed-Din'* Beirut, Kitab Adab al-Nikah. Website reference: http://debate.domini.org/newton/womeng.html. *Hadith:* Vol.2, p.64.

5 **Nawal al Sa'dawi**, *The Hidden Face of Eve* (London: Zed Press, 1980), pp. 139–140.

6 **Abdur Rehman al Jiziri**, in 1990. From a personal communication from Paul Simpson.

7 **Tafsir ibn Kathir**, Part 5, Surah An-Nisa' (Women), ayat 24–147, abridged by Sheikh Muhammad Nasib Ar-Rifa'i, p.50 (commenting on Qur'an: Sura 4:34).

8 **Abu Bakr Mohammad Ibn Zakariya Al Razi**, *At-Tafsir al-Kabir*, quoted at website: http://debate.domini.org/newton/womeng.html#sup. Article: 'The Place of Women in Pure Islam': Men's Superiority. Quoting **al-Razi**, (commenting on Qur'an: Sura 4:11), ¶5.

9 **Mishkat al-Masabih**, English translation, Book 1, Section: 'Duties of husband and wife', (Hadith reported by Abu Dawood, Ahmad, Tirmizi, Ibn Magah and Ibn Haban). *Hadith* no ii, 74.

10 *Ibid., Hadith* no ii, 60.

11 **al-Tirmidhi** (Narrated by Hadhrat Aisha) Hadith 3270. Book of Suckling, Chapter: 'The right of a husband over his wife'. Hadith: 3270.

12 Quoted from a personal communication from **Paul Simpson**.

13 *The Australian Minaret,* published by the Australian Federation of the Islamic Councils, November 1980, p.10. quoted at http://debate.domini.org/newton/womeng.html. Article: 'The Place of Women in Pure Islam: Men's prerogatives' (Abu Bakr Mohammad Ibn Zakariya, *At-Tafsir al-Kabir*), ¶17.

14 **al-Bukhari**. *Hadith*: www.usc.edu/dept/MSA/fundamentals/hadithsunnah/bukhari/, Book 62 Nos. 113. These *hadith* are considered to be among the most trustworthy and authoritative. Also at: www.lahoretown.com/bukhari/, www.agnatemoslem.com/data/hadiths/hadsahb/iindex.html. Each site includes the 93 books of *hadith*.

15 *Ibid., Hadith* Book 6, no. 301.

16 **Kanz al-Ummal,** *Hadith*. See also Ihy'a Uloum ed-Din by Ghazali, Dar al-Kotob al-'Elmeyah, Beirut, Vol. II, Kitab Adab al-Nikah. Vol. 22, Hadith No.858; Ghazali: Ihy'a 'Uloum ed-Din, Dar al-Kotob al-'Elmeyah, Beirut, Vol. II, Kitab Adab al-Nikah, p.65. Cited http://debate.domini.org/newton/womeng.html.

17 **Dr Mohammad Sa'id Ramadan al-Buti,** *Ela kul Fataten Tu'min be-Allah* (Mu'asasat ar Risalah, Beirut, 1987, Eighth edition), pp.41–42, cited at http://debate.domini.org/newton/womeng.html.

18 *Women, Islam & Equality* (National Council of Resistance of Iran, Foreign Affairs Committee, 1995), p.28.

19 *Dispatch,* an East London daily paper, 6 October 1997, p.4: www.dispatch.co.za/1997/10/06/page%204.htm.

20 Sura 30:21.

21 Sura 4:15.

22 Sura 4:20–22.

23 Sura 4:35.

24 Sura 5:5.

25 Sura 24:31.

26 1 Timothy 5:3–16; Titus 2:3–5.

More areas of difficulty

This chapter highlights three interdependent topics: women's role in society, women's role in marriage and women's rights in divorce.

i. Women's role in society

Above all, in Islam, women are considered as home-makers and the bearers of children. Traditionally, education for women has been considered superfluous. This view has changed somewhat in recent years. For a daughter to have the opportunity to receive a good education, including university, is now often regarded as a considerable advantage. This raises her status, acceptability, and attractiveness as a prospective wife, leading to a good dowry on marriage.

Her place in society varies considerably, depending on where she lives. She has far more opportunities to go to work in a country such as Turkey, but in more fundamentalist countries such a 'liberal and dangerous' practice is out of place. As there is no simple pattern, we must take each situation we meet on its own merits. Generally, of course, there is the problem of *purdah*, also referred to as *hijab*. Both words literally mean screen, veil, curtain, partition and concealment. The general rule of *hijab* is total seclusion and segregation between males and females.

Hijab refers to the way that women in the home are to keep themselves restricted to their area of the dwelling—in Arabic terms, behind the dividing curtain of the Bedouin tent. Today very few Muslims live in a Bedouin style, but this principle is extended to more substantial properties. Muslim propriety demands that women may not be seen by any man who could legally marry them.

In most orthodox Muslim communities this principle is maintained with some variation. Basically, the concept is one of restriction for women—with respect to their movement—and, in practice, means confinement to home life.

Seclusion for Muslim women is not absolute in the sense in which we understand it for a western woman in the family house. Muslims often live within an extended family unit. On the Indian subcontinent, for example, the family home might well consist of several houses together in one compound. In that situation a wife is often freely allowed to move among the separate dwelling places within the family compound, so long as no male stranger is present. To move outside means that she must put on the *burqa* or *chador*. The *chador* is a black veil that covers her from head to toe, having slits for the eyes, or a net sewn into the veil through which to view the world. The *burqa* is merely a cloth used as a head covering, like a veil or a shawl, but does not fully cover the face, though it may be brought across as desired. All this is justified in the Qur'an, as mentioned earlier.

The veil is often considered by Christians as demonstrating the bondage of Muslim women, who are thus thought to be utterly repressed.

Why is such a custom so strenuously maintained? There are reasons for it. The fundamental intention of *hijab* is for protection—from the lustful stares of men. Insistence on the *burqa/chador* being worn is considered to be an expression of love and respect by the husband. No self-respecting man would ever allow his wife to be degraded by the carnal and lascivious looks of other men. The veil is a symbol of her protection, security and good reputation.

Many Muslim women today do not wear a full face veil. It is more common to see women in loose clothing topped by a type of scarf worn around the head and under the chin. For many it shows that they are following God's commandments, dressing modestly, or simply they are wearing the type of traditional clothes they feel comfortable in.

It must also be recognized that a Muslim woman herself would consider that she had sinned if she had ever caused a man to look upon her in such a way that would sexually attract him. She is ever seeking to be modest. On the whole, Muslim women accept this. They quite happily exercise the role of a submissive wife and mother. A Muslim wife believes that her duty is towards her home, and she sees that her responsibility lies within it. Recently, in places that have experienced a fundamentalist Islamic revolution there have been indications that many women have gone back to wearing the *hijab* voluntarily.

Generally, our outlook as western Christians has been to accuse Islam of imposing an extreme and unwarranted modesty and subjection upon women, which has been achieved by setting aside their rights.

However, we need to ask: 'How do Muslim women view western women?' It appears that in general they are totally shocked at how western, so-called Christian, women behave. They believe that western men cannot possibly value, respect or love their wives. They consider the way western women dress in public is a form of obscene and open immorality!

We would do well to reflect on this. There are some good and valid reasons why Muslim women live as they do, and we have much to lament about how Christian women are treated in our own culture.

In Pakistan men still are, as you call it, 'the boss.' And these men prefer to guard their women from the covetous eyes of the world. You may have the idea that the Pakistani woman leads a frightful life. … subservient, … humble. … In public she appears to be all these things. But in the home she is revered. … Because she works hard to please only her family, her husband does everything within his emotional and economic power to please her. He has pride in her. … And she is precious because she is all his. Here is … a much easier life than that of the Western woman. Her position is crystal clear. Her husband is the boss, but in a very real spiritual way she rules.[1]

A Muslim woman does not feel as put down and under such 'bondage' as western women might want to project. It also seems that many Muslim women strongly object to what they perceive of as the stereotypical western view of wearing the *hijab*.

The assumption that western culture is inherently superior to all other cultures is the vantage point from which all social and religious philosophies are judged by the west. Muslim societies are, thus, regarded with special interest, fear and ignorance. Hostility, however, is the west's most prevalent attitude towards Muslims. … When, in the nineteenth century, .,. the major European nations began making inroads into the Middle East, they came armed not only with technology and a belief in racial superiority, but with a predetermined set of ideas and prejudices about Islamic society and Muslims. The Middle East is perceived as the west's cultural and spiritual opposite. …

Only a small proportion of families—almost all urban upper-class—practised strict seclusion and few do so today. …

Muslim women's lives are viewed by the west in several ways: the life of the upper-class harem is indolent, boring, idle and without occupation; the rest are ignorant, enslaving and degrading. Either way, Muslim women are seen as passive victims. What is interesting is that upper-class western women, too, have little to do except relax, attend social functions and administer the running of their home, including the servants—much like upper-class women worldwide. The remaining women are overworked and underpaid, often uneducated.[2]

Every individual Muslim woman must be considered in her own circumstances—and we must listen to her own views. To do otherwise is not only the height of folly, but will also alienate. A Muslim woman usually delights to conform to that pattern of life which will please her husband.

Such is the modern Muslim woman; not a feminist but submissive to the teaching of Islam. It surprises us that those who show a desire to wear the *hijab* often live in more open Muslim countries such as Turkey, but especially in the West.

However, there will also be those who hold to a more controversial view within Islam: wishing to discard *hijab* altogether. Therefore we are concerned about those who seemingly all too readily take the *hijab*, but we ought to be equally concerned about those who reject it. For we discover that those who wish to discard the *hijab* often live in the more repressive Muslim regimes, under the strong influence if Islam, in countries such as Afghanistan and Iran.

So in spite of much western prejudice, if we are seeking to understand the Muslim man or woman with a view to sharing the gospel, we must respect their practices, even that of *hijab*.

ii. Women's role in marriage

We have already referred to the Muslim understanding of this aspect of the life of a Muslim woman in the previous section. She is to be submissive to her husband, to work faithfully in the home, seeking to bring up the children to the best of her ability.

Officially permitted polygamy is a great problem where it is encountered, but the majority of marriages are monogamous. Many

Muslim marriages are happy, and there is mutual respect and a deepening love relationship.

As is the common custom in the East, marriages are usually arranged, but this factor alone does not diminish the prospects of their being successful. We as Christians must remember that this was the usual practice in biblical times.

We must also acknowledge that marriage has to be worked at to make it successful in any culture. Children of an arranged marriage can equally be born in love, as in the West. Sadly, we do not have all the answers with respect to successful marriage. This is evidenced on one hand by the high divorce rate today, and on the other hand by the growing trend of couples living together in 'trial marriages'. Many couples express the view that they do not want the commitment of marriage, seeing it as an institution that holds oppressive financial obligations and curtails individual freedom. These ideas are sadly affecting the Christian view of marriage.

The extended family, found in most if not all Muslim cultures, is also a very important factor. The wife is not left on her own, but the grandparents' role, and especially that of mother-in-law, is very important, by alleviating excessive pressures in keeping a home together. There is often a greater measure of security, and a deeper sense of solidarity.

Muslims are criticized, for very good reason, as Islam gives a woman a very low status. Against this there must be a recognition of the strengths of the Muslim viewpoint. We can note four specific areas where there are real benefits for Muslim women:

a. All Muslim women have the opportunity to be married.

b. Ideally, these marriages are arranged by concerned and understanding parents or other relatives.

c. The divorce rate, in most Muslim countries, is extremely low. There is security in marriage.

d. The family becomes a supportive unit that acts as a refuge from the harsh realities of life.[3]

It is also right to observe that there are some very bad attitudes among Muslim men regarding women and marriage. We know, for instance, of many recorded occasions of wife-beating, wife-tormenting, and much worse, in many Muslim countries.

More areas of difficulty

As Christians we may not be quite so ready to confess with shame that there are also some very bad attitudes among western men regarding women and marriage. There are many publicized court cases of severe wife-beating, as well as of a more general abuse of women in western households—actions which we certainly do not condone, and would wish to see change dramatically. However, this is also happening in western society, and we know that the more the Christian ethic is discarded as irrelevant for today, the more problems we shall face in relationships.

iii. Women's rights in divorce

Muslim divorce governs, and replaces, secular legislation in a Muslim country, and is a religious affair. It is a comparatively easy thing. All the husband has to do is to say '*talaq, talaq, talaq*', which is the Arabic for 'divorce' three times over. There should then be a three-month waiting period (to check that the wife is not pregnant) before the divorce becomes final. Although the marital bond can be so easily broken by the husband, the wife has no similar right. However, Islam teaches that divorce is the most hateful to Allah of all the things that he permits. It is therefore something that is not to be undertaken rashly. The rationale of this somewhat questionable state of affairs is presented in a statement supporting the Qur'anic view.

Since the man is sounder in judgement, and more capable of self-control and the one who has to pay the alimony, Islam has given him the right to dissolve marriage. Yet he is admonished not to divorce unless it is absolutely necessary, for that is hateful to Allah … The woman is liable to abuse such a right since she is temperamental and emotionally unstable. … Yet Islam has permitted the woman, on concluding wedlock, to ask that the matter of divorce be the same for her as for the man. Furthermore the woman is permitted to seek a *qadi* to help her divorce, if the man has mistreated her or been too miserly.[4]

Not every Muslim would agree with this analysis, but the good news is that family solidarity checks the ease with which divorce can be obtained. Family pressure is often brought to bear on marital problems, and a

Chapter 20

solution found, given tact and common sense. Divorce can be a real disgrace and bring shame to the family name.

The current situation among those who would claim to be within the evangelical Christian community should also make many of us consider carefully before we are too ready to condemn others. Both the acceptability and the seeking of divorce have dramatically increased and so has the acceptability of non-marriage. We must remind ourselves of the instructions that are clearly given us in Scripture on the matter of making judgements.[5]

Nor must we ignore another important matter that has wider implications: the way we conduct ourselves in mixed company. Our Muslim friends see great danger in our free and easy approach to relationships.

Notes

1 Quoted in *Bangladesh at a Glance* (Chittagong: A.B.W.E., 1980), p.57.
2 **Laila Hasib**: http://www.muslimedia.com/archives/special98/women.htm. Article: 'Exotic Western of Muslim Women', ¶1,5,6.
3 **Phil Parshall,** *New Paths in Muslim Evangelism* (Grand Rapids: Baker Book House, 1980), p.69.
4 **Kenneth Cragg,** *The Call of the Minaret* (New York: Oxford University Press, 1956), p.168.
5 Romans 2:1–4.

Our concern to reach women

Thiswill always be a sensitive issue because of all the factors already
outlined. There are some vital points to consider. In seeking to share
Christ with Muslims

i. We must take care that we witness only to members of our own sex

This is true both for men and women. A man may feel flattered by the
attentions of a woman, and will have mixed motives in responding. I
strongly advocate that men only seek to witness to Muslim men, and that
similarly, only Christian women should seek the opportunity to speak to
Muslim women, who may often have to remain in the confines of their
home. Such Christian women can be readily invited into the veiled area of a
Muslim home. Women should therefore take great care how they approach
a Muslim man they may perhaps meet at the door of a house at which they
are calling, not to enter into discussion with him, but respectfully request
that they may speak to the ladies of that house.

ii. We must be careful in our personal attitude about Muslim cultural norms

We must take great care to show deference and respect to the way
relationships are being treated in any particular household. Any hint of
criticism or disrespect will alienate you from the male members of that
house, and maybe even the women too, the very women that you want to
relate to. It may even have further repercussions within the rest of that
Muslim community. We must consider the family as a whole, and seek to
reach the elders or heads of the family wherever possible, but this is the
responsibility of Christian men. The possibility of such a head of family
coming to faith in Christ would be, in human terms, a tremendous
advantage. This advantage would be seen in being able to share Christ with

the other members of that particular family, without causing offence or suspicion. It would alleviate the exceedingly grievous threat of one who comes to believe in Christ as Saviour being unceremoniously thrown out of the family—or even, in some cases, coming under the threat of murder. Our Lord told us to 'be wise as serpents and harmless as doves'.[1]

Another factor we should bear in mind in reaching Muslim wives is the degree to which they feel responsible to their own families. A wife may take her example in religious teaching and understanding from her father, not her husband. In some circumstances it has been known for the woman's father to cause a fuss on his daughter's behalf when the family considers that she is being neglected, mistreated or misled, or even if her husband comes to faith in the Lord Jesus Christ. Thus to discover that the husband has turned away from Islam and has come to faith in the Lord Jesus Christ is enough for a wife's father to make a strong protest, and seek to protect his daughter from 'being led astray'. This has important implications for our understanding of a Muslim wife's allegiance in the domain of religious belief.

We must never think only in simplistic terms of witness on a one-to-one basis with a Muslim woman as having no significant repercussions on the rest of the family. The very opposite is true, and therefore we would do well to make progress very carefully, thoughtfully, and with the wisdom that can only be given to us by the Holy Spirit.

iii. Assess the situation that the Muslim woman herself actually faces

Here in the western world a number of factors may have already altered the circumstances of a Muslim woman. Secularization of immigrant families often takes place in Britain, which gives the women of some Muslim families a far greater freedom of movement and expression.

The conditions under which many Muslim women live may not be as bad as cultural prejudices may have led you to believe.

iv. Befriend the ladies of the household and share your life with them as far as possible

Common interests and practical skills such as cooking and sewing can be a great asset to share (this is being practical, not sexist). Maybe when dealing with immigrant families in a western country, offering to help in language learning will be a useful way of becoming a friend. These things help to bridge the natural reserve of Muslim women, and give you a platform on which to base your friendship. Through mutual respect and trust you may find that the Lord gives you the opportunity to ask about their faith and to share with them something of yours. These principles of sharing Christ are covered more fully in chapters 24 and 25.

Notes

1 Matthew 10:16.

Part 3

Conclusion

The subject of the family is also of great interest and relevance, but outside the scope of this study. However, one other important issue needs comment. Some are suggesting that as the children of Muslim families are more open to our western cultural influences we should try to reach them rather than their parents, because children would be more readily influenced by the gospel message and more likely to challenge their family cultural norms. This approach does not respect the family, and this would become a major cause of anger among the Muslim community. We must respect Muslim views, beliefs and practices, especially at family level.

On the other hand, to respect Muslim culture and practice does not mean that we condone or agree with them, but we ought to avoid doing anything that may alienate Muslims from us. Approaching children could do just that. Rather we must come to the Muslim family with the love of the Lord Jesus Christ, a love which was expressed in respect, concern, compassion and tenderness.[1]

May the Lord grant us the wisdom we need in order to carry forward the great commission, and see souls saved and brought into his kingdom, that he will receive all the honour and glory.

Notes

1 1 John 3:16, 18, 23.

Presenting the Gospel
Introduction

The first question we have to ask ourselves is, how can we do what appears impossible to us?

Our primary concern must be to get our own foundation right. We need to look for a valid *biblical approach* to the Muslim. The Word of God is where we need to go.

As we tackle the problem of how Christians should view Islam and approach Muslims with the gospel there is a fundamental premise we have to make. However, we must start by making it clear that we do not accept the conclusions Muslims arrive at with their particular world view. We believe that Islam is a false religion, for the Lord Jesus Christ is the ultimate revelation of God to us.

If any other name is put forward and claimed to bring a revelation of God to the world, especially one that comes after Christ, it is false. The New Testament writers often warn of those who will seek to divert men and women away from the true gospel.

Islam must therefore be a deception from Satan. You may have thought Part 1 of this treatise was perhaps a little pro-Islam; that it was not critical enough. This was deliberate. There is so much anti-Islamic and uninformed criticism among western Christians, originating purely from prejudice. Many tragic events of recent history have not done anything to alleviate the tendency.

This has resulted in a situation where we not only rightly hate Islam as a satanic deception, but we also come to hate Muslims. However, we must make a distinction. We need to extend love to Muslims because they are in subjection to the Islamic way of thinking, the framework in which they are trapped. In this way we may bring down the strongholds of Satan, and we can do it with the Word of God.

One of the most prevalent of Satan's schemes has been to convince the world that Christians and Muslims all worship the same God. But the Word of God shows us very clearly this cannot be the case. We must be able to discern the difference, and to apply the Word of God carefully.

A biblical background to Islam?

Islam is a post-Christian phenomenon. Historically this cannot be doubted, arising as it did in the 7th century AD. It is clear that the Bible does not address itself specifically to the problem of Islam, even though Muslims claim to see references which anticipate the coming of Mohammed (e.g. John 14:16). There is no place in the Bible that even prophetically speaks of the teaching of Islam.

Yet nothing is outside the scope of the Word of God—not even Islam. The message of the Bible is always that human nature does not radically change, except in its outward manifestation. The principles taught by Islam, therefore, were not new in themselves, not even in Mohammed's day.

Islam has a pre-Christian philosophy and ethos. There is a substantial amount of Old Testament thought and history embodied within the Qur'an. Satan's strategy is to mix truth with error so craftily that the confusion is not readily discernible. Some of the ideas he presents do have a basis of truth, and it is this subtlety that makes Islam appear attractive, and consequently so difficult to deal with, but much of the teaching, people and situations referred to are factually incorrect.

Islam is a religion that is based on law. It holds to a doctrine of works which includes a system of worship and sacrifice that possesses similarities to the Old Testament. There were identifiable periods in Mohammed's life in which he was deeply interested in Jewish teaching. Therefore, as we note the ingredients that make up the basic principles of Islam, we begin to see that there are parallels, but please bear in mind that parallels in teaching are *not* the same as identical truth.

A biblical understanding of Islam begins to emerge when we note that the Muslim faith originated among Arabs who claimed to be descendants of Ishmael. The story of Ishmael is extremely relevant to understanding the Muslim. We need to make note of the specific promises that God gave with respect to Ishmael. His mother, Hagar, was given the first promise.[1]

Abraham loved Ishmael deeply. We find him pleading on Ishmael's behalf[2] and God responded to Abraham's intercession by giving a promise.[3]

The promise that Ishmael would become a great nation is fulfilled today, as the Arabs hold power and riches because of oil, but Islam is, sadly, the spiritual heritage of Ishmael, Abraham's son of a bondwoman.

Also, we need to face Islam from a New Testament perspective. Islam is a system of works based on law that demands absolute and unquestioning obedience in order to obtain merit and gain acceptance with God. The Pharisees had similar views, and the Lord Jesus spoke plainly of their pride and hypocrisy.[4] He also condemned the Pharisees' practices which are common in Islam, even speaking a parable which reflects this.[5] Finally, and by contrast, consider the case of the Pharisee named Nicodemas and take encouragement from his story.[6]

Notes

1 Genesis 16:10–12; 21:8–21; 25:9, 13–17; 28:9; 36:3, 10.
2 Genesis 17:18.
3 Genesis 17:20.
4 Matthew 23:2–5, 16–29.
5 Luke 18:11–12.
6 John 3:1–21; 19:39.

A biblical approach to Islam

To prepare ourselves for the task that lies before us, we need first to consider our own attitude as Christians towards Muslims. We may understand much that Islam teaches, but we must also ensure that our tactics are not hindering our efforts to draw Muslims to Christ. The following points are important.

i. We need to recognize that we cannot reach Muslims in our own strength

It is the Holy Spirit who applies the truth of God's Word to a person's heart. Muslims are entrenched in the stronghold of Satan, and this surely requires us to take careful stock of the situation. Knowing that only the Holy Spirit can open blind eyes and overcome the problems of misunderstanding is an incentive for us to pray for ourselves, as well as for the Muslim. Let us not underestimate Satan's ability to retaliate.

ii. We need to be totally committed to God and conscientiously obedient to the two great commandments[1]

Without such dedication and close fellowship with the Lord, all attempts to witness to the Muslim will fail. We must learn what it means to love our Muslim neighbour as ourselves. A life of total commitment and love for the Lord speaks volumes to Muslims. Having a spirit of humility as we seek to establish a basis of trust will show them that we wish to meet them with compassion and concern. We have to come with the same passion that was in the heart of Paul.[2] He showed us by his own example that we must come 'as under the law'. This is not to take on the identity of being Muslim, but going as far as we can to meet them on their own ground.

We must do all we can to get alongside Muslims to present the message of God's grace in terms they can understand, being willing to deny ourselves things we normally accept in our own lives. In our desire to share the gospel we must be willing to lay aside anything that could offend Muslims. The 'offence' should be the gospel itself, not us. Therefore, it is wise for us to consider what we need to change in our way of life, and how we need to change our thinking, in order to bring them into submission to our desire of leading Muslims to Christ.

iii. We need to use language appropriately

Paul changed from one language to another to address different groups of people appropriately.[3] His use of language was effective.[4] He recognized the importance of distinguishing between personal language ('heart language') and cultural language ('trade language') of the people with whom he was speaking. Paul was looking for a personal response from the people to whom he spoke.

Even if speaking English is appropriate, we must use vocabulary that is both understandable and pertinent to Muslims. However, if we are in a situation where another language is spoken by Muslims, we must learn the language that reaches their heart.

We need to be careful to avoid being misunderstood and giving the wrong impression when we are speaking to Muslims about eternal issues. It is a biblical principle to start where the people are, even if their understanding of a particular word or idea is inadequate or incomplete, and to apply the truth appropriately. We must seek to establish a correct knowledge of the truth of God, while being very sensitive to any weakness in Muslim understanding. Muslims think we believe certain things we would not recognize at all, for their understanding of the Christian faith is different from what the Bible teaches. There are going to be clashes in both culture and understanding, so we must seek to share with Muslims in a loving manner, while being aware that we will meet with miscommunication and misgivings. We must cautiously seek to change their wrong beliefs, so that they may come to know truths they have never understood or appreciated before. Language is the cradle of understanding, so let us use it sensitively and carefully, while appreciating the difficulties of good communication.

iv. We need to have a biblical attitude to culture

Some Christians find it difficult to accept any aspect of Muslim culture, because religious beliefs strongly influence cultural values. However, we must not reject Muslim culture out of hand because that is seen as rejecting the people. Peter learnt this principle, as he came to see his own cultural inhibitions in their true light.[5] He had been deeply influenced by rituals and laws centred on the Old Covenant, but Christ had now fulfilled all the legal requirements. However, because of culturally preconceived notions resulting in a deep-seated prejudice against the Gentiles, Peter found it difficult to apply this truth. The Gentiles were not covered by God's covenant, for they were excluded by their ungodliness. Yet it was in the will of God that the Gentiles should be blessed through the privileges granted to the Jews.[6] Therefore the gospel will cross cultural boundaries as well as religious, and men and women from all backgrounds will be saved.[7]

As Peter overcame his prejudice by recognizing the cause, so also we must recognize our own culturally conditioned prejudices against any way of life that differs from ours. We can have negative responses to anything that is different from our own personal experience. Applying the same principle that Peter learned, we must consider Muslims 'where they are', and 'as they are', and learn to accept them with their cultural norms and practices, for that is where they are at the moment. As we accept Muslims for who they are, they will respond to us. We must first work at befriending Muslims, before we can hope to win confidences, and then we shall earn the right to speak on spiritual matters and be able to present the gospel of grace in a relevant way.

The practical application of the gospel will bring about significant cultural changes, dealing with those elements that are positively sinful. We need to apply biblical truth in appropriate and sensitive ways so that the gospel message might be effective, not trying to do the work of the gospel in our own strength and wisdom.

The gospel will also change things that are culturally indifferent. As the Holy Spirit convicts of sin and applies the Word of God, bringing sinners to salvation, everything belonging to culture will necessarily be brought under the authority of God. It is the gospel that will change culture; it is not our direct responsibility to bring about such radical change.

Paul also develops this theme,[8] and we can apply it to the eating of pork. We must make every effort not to give unnecessary offence. Eating pork offends Muslims. We see no problem, and consider it our liberty to eat pork. But in reality we are as much at liberty not to eat pork; it is not an issue. Yet facing this problem we immediately want to defend ourselves, claiming our right to eat pork. We are free to eat pork if we so wish, for Christ brings that freedom. But he also gives us freedom to say, 'No' to the things that are indifferent. For the sake of reaching Muslims for Christ, we do not need to eat pork, and it is wise not to do so. As we want to befriend Muslims for the sake of the gospel we must be willing to give up anything that offends, especially those things that don't really matter to us, as it significantly affects our witness to Muslims.

Certain other practical considerations must also be considered. When you greet a Muslim never shake hands with the left hand, or offer anything with the left hand, for the left hand is used for personal hygiene. Befriend a Muslim but do not refer to him as your 'brother', because as a Christian you are not accepted by him as a brother. When a Muslim offers you hospitality, it is a personal affront to decline. Eat whatever is given you without question, and show appreciation for the food and thank him for it. Giving hospitality is more difficult, as you need to know the dietary norms of Muslim society: no pork, or lard-based cooking, and no shell fish. Tell them that you give thanks before a meal, and do so simply, referring to God only by the name 'Lord'.

We must think about the ways we may need to adapt, so that we do not offend those with whom we are sharing the gospel. We must bring everything into submission to our purpose of leading Muslims to Christ. As far as it is possible and legitimate for us to do so, we must seek to do everything we can to achieve our aim, as expressed by the apostle Paul: 'that I might by all means save some.'[9] Our Christian liberty includes the freedom to abstain from anything that may give offence.[10]

v. We need to understand the Muslim thought patterns

How do Muslims think? Why do they express themselves in the particular way that they do? How does their thought pattern subsequently affect their lives? It is necessary to work this out for ourselves: to know the Muslim mind, so that we may proclaim the gospel message in terms that they will understand and find acceptable. Not that we have any wish to change the gospel to suit our purpose. That is not the issue—and nothing is further from our mind. For it is our longing to be able to present the true gospel—the true Word of God, his true revelation—in a meaningful and purposeful way to the Muslim. And we underline the fact that this is not to suggest that we are thinking of compromising the truth in any way whatsoever. Rather, we should ensure its absolute integrity as the Word that God has revealed.

Although the gospel contains truths that offend the Muslim mind, we may present the gospel in terms that Muslims will find reasonable and acceptable. Take the biblical example of Paul in Athens. The altar inscribed 'To the unknown God' was a point of contact. Paul addressed the philosophers of Athens and told them about the living God, whom they confessed they did not know, who had revealed himself in Christ. Paul appealed to one of their own respected advocates of their philosophy, and was thus able to make a theological truth appropriate and meaningful. 'For in Him we live and move and have our being, as also some of your own poets have said, "For we are also His offspring."'[11] By this use of their own sources, Paul moves them inoffensively to where they need to be for a right and true appreciation of the gospel message. We should learn from this, and start with the Muslim's own comprehension of the nature of God, and seek to build on it.

It has been common practice to dismiss the Muslim perception of Allah, but this will cause a Muslim to shut his mind to what we teach about God. But there is good reason for the approach we propose, for a Muslim will perceive our rejection of his beliefs as a rejection of himself. We need to pray that the Holy Spirit will give us wisdom in our seeking to share Christ, that he will enable us to set forth the glories of Christ in a way that may be understood—and that he will apply his saving grace to the Muslim heart. Pray that the Holy Spirit will over-rule all our weakness, that his power may be made evident to the saving of souls.

Notes

1 Mark 12:30–31.
2 1 Corinthians 9:19–23.
3 Acts 21:37–40.

Chapter 23

4 Acts 21:37; 22:2.

5 Acts 10:12–15.

6 Isaiah 60:3,5,9

7 Isaiah 49:6.

8 Romans 14:14–15, 20.

9 1 Corinthians 9:22.

10 Romans 14:21.

11 Acts 17:28–29.

Potential problems

M uslims perceive various doctrines of the Christian faith to be a major stumbling-block, for they fail to understand our religious terminology as we do. When we use various words to describe the gospel of God's grace, Muslims do not always hear what we are saying, but will comprehend something else.[1] Therefore we must understand what Muslims *think* we are saying, in order to avoid putting up communication barriers.

The following are a selection of potential problems where we will find some difficulty in communicating the truth.

i. God ... or Allah?

Muslims worship Allah. They may speak of 'God' to us, but we must recognize that as they do so, they have the full content of 'Allah' in their minds. It is all too easy for us to assume our own understanding of God as he reveals himself in Jesus Christ when we hear a Muslim speak his name. But if we do so we shall find ourselves in a difficulty.

Note this observation by a Muslim author:

It is important to note that 'Allah' is the same word that Arabic-speaking Christians and Jews use for God. If you pick up an Arabic Bible, you will see the word 'Allah' being used where 'God' is used in English. This is because 'Allah' is the only word in the Arabic language equivalent to the English word 'God' with a capital 'G'. Additionally, the word 'Allah' cannot be made plural or given gender (i.e. masculine or feminine), which goes hand-in-hand with the Islamic concept of God. Because of this, and also because the Qur'an, which is the holy scripture of Muslims, was revealed in the Arabic language, some Muslims use the word 'Allah' for 'God' even when they are speaking other languages. ... It is interesting to note that the Aramaic word 'El', which is the word for God in the language that Jesus spoke, is certainly more similar in sound to the word 'Allah' than the English word 'God'. This also holds true for the various Hebrew words for God, which are 'El' and 'Elah', and the plural form 'Elohim'. The reason for these similarities is that Aramaic, Hebrew and Arabic are all Semitic languages with common origins. It should also be noted that in translating the Bible into English, the Hebrew word 'El' is translated variously as 'God', 'god' and 'angel'. This imprecise language allows different translators, based on their preconceived notions, to translate the word to fit their own views. The Arabic word 'Allah' presents no such difficulty or ambiguity, since it is only used for Almighty God alone. Additionally, in English, the only difference between 'god', meaning a false god, and 'God', meaning the One True God, is the capital 'G'. In the Arabic alphabet, since it does not have capital letters, the word for God (i.e. Allah) is formed by adding the equivalent to the English word 'the' (Al-) to the Arabic word for 'God/God' (ilah). So the Arabic word 'Allah' literally means 'The God'—the 'Al-' in Arabic basically serving the same function as the capital 'G' in English. Due to the above mentioned facts, a more accurate translation of the word 'Allah' into English might be 'The One-and-Only God' or 'The One True God'.[2]

Thus we see that the Muslim puts his own meaning into our word 'God', and so we have to stress the truth of his revealed sovereignty and transcendence, but also add that he is personal and knowable. We must do this before we can be sure that our Muslim friend's understanding of 'God' is what we intend it to be. Islam does not know the loving fatherhood of God, for such an intimate relationship with God is foreign to Islam. It is even explicitly condemned by the Qur'an.

The Jews and the Christians say, 'We are the children of Allah and His loved ones [or, His beloved].' Say: 'Why then does he punish you for your sins? Surely you are mortals of His own creation. He forgives whom He will and punishes whom He pleases. His is the kingdom of the heavens and the earth and all that lies between them. All shall return to Him.[3]

For Christians, the concept of God being our heavenly Father lies at the very centre of the Christian faith. To the Muslim such an idea is anathema. Allah is unknowable, and so he cannot have a personal relationship with those whom he created. Muslims do not have a real concept of men and women being created in God's image, as does the Christian. The concept of *tauhid* is so very strong, that Allah cannot be personal, and so it is extremely difficult for a Muslim to conceive of God as being our heavenly Father.

ii. The person of Jesus

Jesus the Messiah is greatly respected by Muslims as the penultimate prophet. But they despise the cult of Christianity (as they see it) that has arisen around him. Muslims usually deny his crucifixion and consequent resurrection. However, the Qur'anic verse on which they base this is an ambiguous one, which allows various possible interpretations. It is common for Muslims to argue that another person took his place on the cross (for it is not denied that there was a crucifixion)—Jesus himself being taken directly into heaven.

Muslims consider Jesus to be a man just like Adam,[4] that the birth of Jesus parallels that of Adam, and so Jesus is a mere man. He is *ibn Maryam* (Son of Mary),[5] *al Masih* (Messiah), the 'anointed one', *rasul* (the Messenger) but not God. Jesus was a 'prophet' as Allah gave revelation through him.[6] As he has not died, Muslims expect Jesus to return. Then he will fight and defeat the Antichrist, confess Islam, break all crosses, kill all pigs, abolish *jizya*, and establish 1,000 years of righteousness. This is not the Jesus of the Bible.

The Qur'an contains many traditional beliefs about Jesus, but we must never assume that the Muslim is rejecting the Jesus of our faith—he is not doing that. He simply does not understand him. As Bishop Stephen Neill has stated: 'It is not the case that the Muslim has seen Jesus of Nazareth and rejected him; he has never seen him, and the veil of misunderstanding and prejudice is still over his face.'[7]

It is important to understand that Muslims have not rejected the gospel. They have not understood its message.

iii. The Scriptures

In the Muslim view of revelation the word of God is first written in heaven. Allah gives his word to men—the final and complete revelation being the Qur'an, transmitted by the archangel Gabriel to Mohammed. The Qur'an is believed to be a perfect replica of the eternal word. The claims for its perfection lie in the idea that there was no human interference in its transmission. They maintain that Mohammed only received it by dictation. This assertion has resulted in two assumptions:

(i). Mohammed was illiterate, therefore incapable of personal involvement in forming the text;

(ii). As any translation of the Qur'an from the Arabic is impossible it becomes an interpretation, and no longer a replica of Allah's word.

Another problem lies in what a Muslim perceives of the *Injil*—our gospels. We are used to the fact that they have been written by the evangelists. The description given of each Gospel is therefore 'The Gospel according to …', but the Muslim looks for the actual gospel that was with God in heaven and which was revealed through Jesus. He does not want any man's account of Jesus. The Muslim therefore deduces from this that the Christians have lost the original gospel, and have corrupted the Scriptures. Muslims find it difficult to accept the Gospels as they are. Therefore they find it equally hard to accept the gospel message as we present it, because they believe that we do not have the original word of God.

Muslims believe that Christians have knowledge of the truth in the Bible but have interpreted it wrongly.[8] But the Qur'an also witnesses to the truth of the Bible: 'If you doubt what We have revealed to you, ask those who have read the Scriptures before you. The truth has come to you from your Lord: therefore do not doubt it.'[9] Is this is not a testimony to the authenticity and authority of the Bible? It ought to be noted that the Bible is the Word of God according to the Qur'an,[10] and if the Word of God it cannot be corrupted.

This problem is further enhanced when the Muslim picks up and examines a reference Bible and sees alternative readings given. Again, the Muslim is looking for the actual words which God revealed—but the Christian is unable to produce what he demands. The problem is compounded by the factor of so many Bible versions today, especially in English. There is apparently no one authoritative original text which we can produce. Furthermore, there are contradictions between the Qur'an and the New Testament. The result is that we have to face what seems an insurmountable difficulty.

As Christians, we confirm our Scriptures are the full revelation of God, confidently asserting that they do not merely contain the word of God but that they are God's authoritative Word. Therefore they are not to be argued about, but used! The Scriptures witness to having been given by the sovereign power of the Holy Spirit who, working in the hearts of godly men, applies them to the heart of man, where they prove to be 'sharper than any two-edged sword'.[11] We must recognize our own personal weakness, but that the Holy Spirit and the Word of God are strong. Our Lord Jesus Christ, the living Word, asserted, 'without Me you can do nothing.'[12]

The Scriptures themselves witness to the truth that all things are possible to him who believes. The glory will never be ours—it must always and necessarily be his!

iv. The Word of God

As Christians we interpret the 'Word of God' to mean 'the revelation of God'. This is the true knowledge of God which thus carries his complete authority. The Muslim understands the concept of 'the Word of God' in the same way. He contends that the Qur'an fits that description, for it is uncreated and eternally with Allah in heaven.

Interestingly, this title—Word of God—is applied to Jesus the Messiah in the Qur'an. As Christians we recognize Jesus as the Word of God. He, in himself, is the complete, authoritative revelation of God to man.

Muslims believe that the complete will of God is revealed in the Qur'an, and that it is the 'living word of God'. We believe Jesus is the living Word of God. We also assert that the Bible is God's Word, in the sense that it is God's revealed will and purpose for mankind. We believe it is the written account of the life and ministry of Jesus, faithfully recorded, and revealing him fully, given by inspiration of God,[13] revealing his will for mankind. The focus of the Scriptures is the Lord Jesus Christ as the complete revelation of Almighty God to all mankind.[14]

If we are to compare Christian faith and Islamic beliefs, we must take care how we do so. We need to ask what the Qur'an really means to the Muslim:

It is essential to realize that the Qur'an is to the Muslim what Jesus is to the Christian. It is a mistake to make a direct comparison between the role of Jesus in Christianity and the role of Muhammad in Islam, or between the place of the Bible in Christianity and the place of the Qur'an in Islam.[15]

We cannot equate Mohammed with Jesus, or the Qur'an with the Bible. The true parallel is found in the claim concerning the revelation of God, and the comparison is thus between Jesus and the Qur'an. Mohammed's message to his people was the Qur'an, but the message of Christianity is the person of Christ. This is an important distinction which must not be misunderstood.

That Jesus is also called 'Son of God' is another important consideration.[16]

v. The Trinity

This is the paramount stumbling-block. 'Allah is One' asserts the Muslim. None can be associated with him, and he certainly cannot have a Son. The Muslim also adds, 'He is *totally other*'—that is, so very different from anything man can imagine. He cannot be described, nor can anyone show him to us.

In his lifetime Mohammed had only spoken with heretical Christians, was totally misled, and his wrong ideas have been perpetuated. Muslims are taught from a very young age that Christians believe in three gods: the Father, Mary the Mother, and the Son. The sonship of Jesus is only understood in terms of gross materialism—that Jesus was the offspring of Mary through a purely physical relationship. Mohammed was aware of the results of the fifth century Nestorian-Monophysite controversy over the title 'Mother of God' as applied to Mary. This has not helped. That title had become widely used instead of 'Mother of Christ'. There is consequently an explicit assertion to be found in the Qur'an concerning this heresy: 'Unbelievers are those that say: "Allah is one of three." There is but one God. ... Allah will say: "Jesus, son of Mary, did you ever say to mankind: 'Worship me and my mother as gods beside Allah'?"'[17]

The Qur'an portrays Jesus as having denied this indignity. The biblical Christian must also agree—for the concept of three gods is just as offensive in Christianity as it is in Islam. Interestingly, the Qur'an speaks of the virgin birth of Jesus through the mediation of the Holy Spirit almost in opposition to this blasphemous idea.

Muslims emphatically deny the Holy Spirit is the third person of the Trinity, often identifying the 'Holy Spirit' as the Angel Gabriel.[18] Though Christians understand the reference to 'the comforter' (Greek: *parakletos*) in John 14:26 as a reference to the Holy Spirit, Muslims emphatically deny this and argue that it is a prophetic reference to Mohammed. What Christians would consider to be the work of the Holy Spirit is often attributed to angels.

In opposition to the concept that God can ever be referred to as the Father and Jesus the Messiah as the Son, the following quotation is an interesting observation, that shows where the Muslim misunderstanding lies.

The Christian Scriptures characterized Jesus as *ibn'u'llah* or the Son of God, where God is depicted as the Heavenly Father. Such a characterization is a rather interesting one if one is to divorce oneself from the dogmatic interpretation of various Churches which have historically understood this 'Sonhood' in a literal sense, implicating incarnation of God in the person of Jesus which is clearly rejected by the Qur'an.

NOTE: if the term 'Son of God' was to be understood in the same spiritual sense as Jews being 'sons of God' then there would have been no theological contradiction between the Qur'an and Christian dogma. I am making a distinction here between the teachings of Jesus as reflected in the Gospels and Churches' understanding of those teachings (i.e. dogma) which the Qur'an rejects.[19]

Muslims reject the idea of Trinity. God cannot be three persons if he is one. For Allah to descend to the level of his creation is perceived of as an *imperfection*. Allah cannot be imperfect, and so it is impossible for him to live on earth. So our claim that Jesus is God is a problem to the Muslim mind.

We have to handle the Muslim misconception of the idea of the Trinity with great care, if we are to break through Muslim prejudice which is based purely on a misunderstanding of what they *think* we believe.[20]

vi. Faith

Muslims identify faith as being identical with obedience and conformity to God's revealed law. For Muslims 'Faith is the devoting of the heart unto God by man and his acceptance of what God has revealed to His Prophets, his belief in His determination and His will … so that he reverences Him in his prayers and is obedient in His almsgiving'.[21]

Acts of obedience are not merely the expression of faith: the Muslim mind conceives of the works themselves as faith. Faith is commitment to a system of works. It is not expressed by Muslims in love to God, but in doing what is expected, according to the rules laid down. Muslims view faith as the means of earning salvation: the way to merit God's mercy. In fact, to use the word faith with respect to Islam is really to describe the unity observed in the rituals of Islam. Faith is conformity to Islam and uniformity in the ritual observance of the requirements. Therefore, Muslim faith can only be understood 'as an unreasoned and mechanical observance of the laws of Islam'.

In practice it is exceedingly difficult to hold these distinctions. However, we must be careful. When we use the term 'faith', or hear a Muslim use it, we must never assume that we are talking about precisely the same concept as they are.

vii. Sin

Muslims teach that man was created good, but being made of clay he was inherently weak and fallible by nature. Thus sin is merely making a mistake. Muslims have no concept of 'original sin'. They maintain that man is intrinsically good. When he contradicts and disobeys God's commandments or his will, then he commits sins, but he is not inherently a sinner. Sin is a deliberate act against the will of Allah. Blasphemy is understood to be rebellion against the will of Allah and his revelation.

A few examples of blasphemy are: believing that Allah has a son, worshipping an idol, and saying that Allah does not know everything. Some examples of sins less than blasphemy are: killing a person unjustly, adultery, drinking alcohol, and stealing. When a Muslim makes sincere repentance as was described, it is as if he did not sin, in that he will not be punished for what he repented of, for Allah is ever-merciful to the Muslims. Also, when a person becomes a Muslim for the first time, Allah forgives all his past sins.[22]

Therefore Muslims hold to a high view of mankind and his ability. They teach that we have the ability to live in and by God's will—thus equally we have the ability to ignore his will or to deliberately oppose it, for Allah has given us that freedom. But it is a freedom that has limits because Allah is greater than man. Muslims are deeply aware of human weakness, and yet they deny that human beings are prone to sin. In this superficial understanding of sin, sinful actions become insignificant, and of little or no consequence. Muslims will focus on unbelief as sinning against Allah because of the failure to accept Allah and his revelation. It is the unwillingness of unbelievers to submit themselves to Allah that designates them as infidels (*kafir*). They are rejecting the final revelation of Allah. Thus infidels sin against Allah. Christians refuse to submit to Allah, and hence they are infidels, therefore Christians are 'sinners'. Sin is therefore defined in terms of non-submission to Allah.

Muslims will focus on the penalty of sin, rather than admit responsibility for the 'mistake'. Being caught out and exposed as having committed a 'wrong' action is a matter of shame and embarrassment rather than of feeling and admitting guilt. In the case of stealing, the sin is in being found out, rather than the action. This concept of non-responsibility must be understood in terms of the absolute will of Allah which decrees how a man will act.[23] However, if found out, then Muslim teaching is that of restitution:

For a sin less than blasphemy, one must stop doing the sin, regret having done it, and have the intention not to commit the same sin again. If the sin is stealing from a person, for example, then the stolen goods must be returned in addition. Allah is ever-merciful to the Muslim and no matter how many times he sins in his life, if he stops it, regrets having done it, and intends not to do it again, he will be forgiven by Allah. But for those who are non-Muslim, no matter what good things they do, those deeds are not to their credit in the Hereafter; they must first become Muslim.[24]

viii. Salvation

This concept for the Muslim is only understood in terms of submission to Allah's will through obedience. One is 'saved' solely through doing good works—but even then it is entirely at the discretion of God.

The ultimate question is always, 'How do I get to heaven?' For a Muslim, the answer to this question is shrouded in mystery. There is no straight answer. All that Muslims can do, and all that they are encouraged to do, is to make every effort to please Allah in the hope that they will enter heaven. But ultimately it is a matter of fate (*kismet*); it is something that is in the hands of an all-powerful Allah. There is no guarantee.

The Muslim concept of 'salvation' is an achievement, a sense of fulfilment, the feeling of realization, the fulfilment of human potentials. So through obedience, seeking to obtain more merit before Allah, believers progress through stages of improvement.

Man must discover in what direction his self can develop and then he must create the conditions, physical as well as social, which favour the development. His main task in this life is to develop his self by conquering the forces of nature and employing them for the development of mankind.[25]

Thus salvation depends on merit achieved, and the will of Allah.

ix. Sanctification

Any concept of the holy life that the Muslim may hold to, of being made holy, is in terms of obedience to the law. He must seek to gain the approval of God by all means available. This is the natural extension of the Muslim concept of salvation.

We must take great care to distinguish between the biblical concepts of sanctification and justification, in the light of Muslim thought. The Christian cannot become righteous in God's sight by any obedience to the law of God; here again there is much ground for confusion in the Muslim mind. Christians should study the Scriptures so that we are clear in our own minds before discussing these things with Muslims.

x. Love

In Islam there is no appreciation of Allah as the God of love, for Muslims believe that he is unknowable and remote, and no one is capable of having a relationship with Allah. To suggest such a relationship is akin to associating with Allah (the Muslim concept of *shirk*). Such an idea is both wrong and unforgivable. Intriguingly, one discovers that Muslims more readily speak of having a love for Islam, whatever that may mean.

The above considerations, though neither detailed nor comprehensive, show us something of the magnitude of the challenge that we have in confronting Muslims with the claims of Christ. We are limited in what we can achieve, humanly speaking, but we have the encouragement that, in the face of the seemingly impossible, the Lord has power to save.

Notes

1 Information sheet 10, *Comparison of Muslim and Christian world views,* is an appraisal of Muslim and Christian differences of understanding.
2 eMuslim: www.emuslim.com/WhoIsAllah.asp. Article: 'Who is Allah?', ¶1.
3 Sura 5:18.
4 Sura 3:59.
5 Sura 34:45. This title is used 23 times in the Qur'an to stress his humanity and mortality.
6 Sura 19:30.
7 Quoted in **Martin Goldsmith**, *Islam and Christian Witness* (Hodder and Stoughton, 1982), p.60.
8 Sura 3:70–71, 78.
9 Sura 10:94.
10 Sura 2:75; 15:9.
11 Hebrews 4:12.
12 John 15:5.
13 2 Timothy 3:15–17; 2 Peter 1:19–21.
14 Hebrews 1:3.
15 **C. Chapman**, *You Go And Do The Same* (Church Missionary Society/BMMF International, 1983), p.31.
16 See Chapter 26, p.200–201, discussion on the Son of God.
17 Sura 5:73,116.
18 **M. Nader,** http://www.submission.org/jesus/holy_spirit.html Article: 'The Holy Spirit in the Quran'.
19 **Kamran Hakim**, http://www.bci.org/prophecy-fulfilled/pmmg.htm. Article: 'Prophets, Messengers and Manifestations of God', ¶ 4–5.
20 See also Chapter 26, x. God gave his Spirit to the disciples who acknowledged Jesus as God's Messiah and God's Word, p.209.
21 Quoted in **Kenneth Cragg**, *The Call of the Minaret* (New York: Oxford University Press, 1956), p.127–128.

22 Anwarul-Islam: www.anwarul-islam.com/html/religion.html. Article: 'Islam The Only True Religion: Sins', ¶4.

23 See chapter 6: vi. Belief in predestination, p.64.

24 Anwarul-Islam: www.anwarul-islam.com/html/religion.html. Article: 'Islam The Only True Religion: Sins', ¶3.

25 Salvation in Islam, www.geocities.com/WestHollywood/Park/6443/Salvation/salvation.html. Article: 'Islam–A Challenge to Religion'. A Muslim essay, ¶6.

Practical considerations

A s we come now to our central concern—sharing the gospel—we need to consider how we may approach the Muslim with the gospel in a sensible and godly way.

i. Evaluate our personal attitude

Prayer needs to be our priority in Muslim evangelism. We have to recognize our own weakness and cry out to him who alone is able. All our efforts will result in failure if we go forward in our own strength. We need the power and wisdom of God.

We also need to ask that the Holy Spirit will prepare the heart of the Muslim, and pray for wisdom to speak to him in a relevant and sensitive way. The Lord knows the heart of the Muslim and his situation: we do not. We need, through prayer, to know the Lord's guidance in our thoughts and in our speech.

Respect Muslim beliefs. Read again in Acts 17 how Paul spoke to the Athenians. He disarmed their natural antagonism to him, and he attracted their attention. The apostle did not attempt to ridicule his hearers by showing up the false basis of their thinking. Instead, he addressed, and built upon, their inadequate understanding, and we must do the same.

Consider Muslim feelings. Any direct, frontal attack on Muslim beliefs will immediately damage your avenue of communication. How much better to show love and genuine concern.

Understand Muslim problems. You must realize that even though they may have many misconceptions about the Christian faith, Muslims have been taught them from early childhood. As a result, their prejudices are very deep-seated, and therefore change will be at great cost to their personal feelings. You need to sympathetically understand what change would mean to a Muslim.

Be sensitive to the possibility of communicating the wrong thing. You must be careful in choosing your words, and explain the meaning of such terms that can be misunderstood. It is wise to consider using only those expressions that will be helpful to the Muslim listener, depending on his understanding at the time.

Take only one step at a time. We are not required to present the whole gospel all at once. Do not rush what you are doing, and be patient. Consider one important truth at a time, and ensure that it is understood. You can draw out the implications of that truth another time. We are more likely to fail if we attempt to do too much.

Encourage a basis of friendship and trust before overtly sharing gospel truth. We should find that our Muslim friend will be able to accept what we are saying far more readily if he feels that we are not a threat to him. He will be less antagonistic, and more ready to listen to what we are actually saying.

ii. Consider legitimate points of contact

Our Muslim friend would be very happy for us to pray with him. Sadly, this is often the last thing a Christian will think about in his relationship with a Muslim. But it should be the first! It would be good for our Muslim friend to be able to see how natural our relationship with God is, and how meaningful prayer is to us. It is extremely wise for us to be aware that a Muslim usually considers a Christian to be a person who does not pray! Let us establish the fact that we consider prayer important, and that we believe in the power of prayer.

A Muslim will appreciate the praise of God, and giving thanks for his many blessings. But if you pray particularly for him and his family he will be deeply touched and grateful. We can pray that they may be blessed of God. We can pray that they may receive his mercy, and his healing power (in the case of ill-health). Appropriate and applied prayer will speak volumes to a Muslim. It is also fitting to remember in prayer that God knows us and our weaknesses, and that we are all like sheep that have gone astray. Our Muslim friend will appreciate all this. We may include all these concepts without offending him—and we can pray in the name of Jesus as we ought.

Posture in prayer could well be important to consider. Many of the various positions used by the Muslim in prayer may seem strange to us, but they can all be identified in Scripture. As Christians we are free to worship God in whatever way seems right as long as it is reverent. Nothing ought to stop us praying in a manner which is meaningful to our Muslim friend.

Muslims often engage in prayer by raising their hands in front of them, with their palms upward. Many Christians have understandably become suspicious of this particular action because of its misuse by some people. Yet we ought to recognize that this is a biblical way of coming into the presence of God. Hands raised to the lower chest level as a Muslim prays can be a demonstration of real humility of our true submission to God. It appears that Moses prayed in a very similar manner.[1]

We may have further opportunities to show our Muslim friend that we have even more common areas of understanding, in which we can freely participate without fear of compromise. We too believe that God is one, that he is the sovereign Creator, that he reveals his will to his people, etc. Let us pray for sanctified wisdom to know how to reach out in love as we seek to win our Muslim brother or sister.

iii. Establish our own guidelines from Scripture

Are all Muslim beliefs entirely false? To answer this question we need to break down the beliefs of Muslims into their constituent parts and compare them with the Word of God. It is not impossible to point to aspects of our Scriptures that have a distinct parallel to what is believed in Islam. As a whole, Islam leads a person in a misguided direction, but many of the constituent parts are close to what we believe, and they may be pointers to a basis on which to build. Let us look at one or two of these.

We need to be surrendered to God. To the Muslim, this is a basic understanding and requirement. He cannot be a Muslim without considering his life in this way. He demonstrates submission by his ritual practices. We ought to remember that this submission is what God requires of the believer in Christ. Our Scriptures plainly teach that the Christian life is one of total commitment through faith.[2]

We have a simple creedal statement. The Muslims have the s*hahada*. We are used to the idea of the need for confessions of faith to guide our thinking. However, these are usually relatively long declarations. But do we have anything to compare with the short and pithy Muslim statement? Paul's declaration is one we could use: 'God … has highly exalted Him and given Him the name which is above every name, that at the name of Jesus

every knee should bow … and that every tongue should confess that Jesus Christ is Lord, to the glory of God the Father.'[3]
To be able to say with meaning and conviction that 'Jesus Christ is Lord', as other New Testament writers explain, is the privilege that Christians possess.[4]

Our Lord himself gave us another concise statement of faith: 'this is eternal life, that they may know You, the only true God, and Jesus Christ whom You have sent.'[5] Here we have an explicit declaration concerning the oneness of God, Jesus his 'Apostle' or 'Sent One'—and that eternal life is 'knowing God'. Notice the similarity of style to that of the Muslim *shahada*.

We believe in the perfect revelation of God's will to mankind. The revealed will of God shows us all that is necessary for us to live for God in every aspect of life. This is made completely clear in the Bible with many appropriate references.[6]

We are convinced that our Scriptures are perfectly adequate and fully suited to meet the Muslim need. The Muslim system is one of legal requirement, but as Christians we understand that salvation is a free and sovereign gift of God. There is a great gulf between these two views. It is beyond question that to bridge the gap is a major but not insurmountable problem. We read that the law is from Moses, and grace comes through Jesus Christ.[7]

iv. Make use of the Scriptures

By now, we are aware that our Muslim friends have problems of one sort or another in connection with our Scriptures, the Holy Bible. We must not be intimidated by this. Consider these points:

• Handle the Bible carefully. It is a holy book, and holds a special place in our lives. We must ensure that we take care to handle our copy of the Bible appropriately before the Muslim onlooker. We will not, of course, go to the lengths that he does with the Qur'an;[8] but we ought to show a deferential respect with our personal copy of the Bible. Therefore, in the presence of Muslims, we should not put it on the floor, nor place it on our laps. To do these things is offensive to the Muslim, for then he thinks that you have no respect for the Word of God. But show that you *do* respect the fact that it is

God's written Word, and that you recognize that it is no ordinary book. You will also find it helpful to refrain from using a marked and underlined Bible. It must not be thought that we are tampering with God's Word in any way. Handle your Bible reverently.

• Treat the Bible lovingly. It *is* the Word of God, and it means a great deal to us. If God gave his Word to us by his love then we ought to show our Muslim friend that it means as much to us. Let him see for himself, by the way we speak of it, that the Bible is the word of life to us.

• Employ the Bible authoritatively. We must not, in any sense, be apologetic about the Bible, or give that impression. We do not need to argue its case, or defend it. Nor do we give the impression that we merely think that it is God's Word. Rather, we must show that we know, and are convinced, that it is God's Word and that he is speaking to us through its written pages.

• Utilize the Bible prayerfully. We need to know which aspects of teaching within the Scriptures are those that the Holy Spirit wants us to use on any particular occasion. Even if we have carefully planned our discussion material beforehand, we still need to be sensitive to the guidance of the Holy Spirit. We may be led not to use what we have prepared at all, for he may direct our thoughts to even more applicable Scriptures with these truths.

• Use the Qur'an only with extreme caution. While the emphasis is on how we must use the Scriptures with boldness and upon its own authority, the question is raised as to how we should use the Qur'an as the Muslim scriptures. Caution is the best approach here. It is tempting to use certain statements from the Qur'an as perhaps being advantageous in a discussion. To do so could seem to lend authority to what we say. We might think that a Muslim would appreciate us using their book, but there are two problems. The first is that by using the Qur'an you may give the impression that you are accepting these writings on an equal footing with the Bible. A Muslim would indeed be very happy with that! The second is that as the Qur'an is said to be only reliable in Arabic presupposes that we are able to quote it in Arabic as the *imams* do. For us this is a problem, but in Muslim countries, the Qur'an in Arabic is taught from a young age, and children repeat it by rote. They do not understand it, but they learn it as the real Qur'an. Any translation of it into a vernacular language is only an interpretation of the Qur'an, and thus does not carry the same weight when quoted.

Observation and experience indicate that the only people who can use the Qur'an in such a way are those who themselves have come to Christ out of such a background. They have first-hand understanding of how it is used, what it says, and how its words are interpreted. They are much more able to quote from the Qur'an (and other Muslim books, such as the *hadith*). Even such ethnic background Christians need to handle this issue with great care, for Christians do not accept the authoritative status that Muslims give to the Qur'an.

Our prayer must be, as we consider the practical implications of sharing the gospel in an appropriate manner, that all we do and say will be prompted by the Holy Spirit.[9]

Notes

1 Exodus 17:11.
2 Psalm 37:5; Proverbs 3:5–6; Romans 12:1.
3 Philippians 2:9–11.
4 1 John 4:15.
5 John 17:3.
6 2 Timothy 3:15–17; 2 Peter 1:21; Deuteronomy 4:29–31; 1 John 2:3, 5; 3:22–23; 5:2–3.
7 John 1:17.
8 Muslims keep a copy of the Qur'an wrapped in cloth. They will ritually wash before touching it, and when they take it out to use, they will kiss it.
9 Colossians 1:9–11.

Making known the Gospel message

Having prepared our own hearts and understanding, we now look at presenting the truths of the Gospel so that Muslims may understand and come to know the Lord Jesus Christ.

i. Using the Word of God

How can we show the Muslim the glory of Christ? This is surely one of the basic requirements of declaring the gospel message. Muslims are antagonistic before we start, but our task is not impossible.[1] God can overcome obstacles.[2]

So we may go forward with confidence. We do not need to be aggressive. We can take a more indirect route to overcome those inbuilt prejudices wisely. We may approach the gospel by way of the Old Testament Scriptures. We have much in common with our Muslim friend here. He will discover that he has a great affinity for what he finds there—and it may generate a remarkable curiosity and an inclination to discover what he believes is reiterated in the Qur'an.

We may look first at the Pentateuch (Jewish *Torah*, Muslims *Taurat*), the five books of Moses. According to a Qur'anic injunction every Muslim ought to accept and know them. They demonstrate God's sovereign power and authority. From the very first verses they show the God who reveals himself as the Almighty who is the Creator, Guide and Protector of his people.[3]

After relating God's dealings with Adam and Noah (two recognized Muslim prophets), this continues with Abraham and his family and shows how they were called by God to become the people of God. The Law is given as instruction to God's people, to show them how to relate to him and how to live appropriately before him.[4]

The Psalms (the Muslim *Zabur*) are a wellspring of teaching on the godly life. They clearly show many elements of the life that is pleasing to

God. For example, Psalm 1 is very suitable to use with a Muslim because it shows the contrast between the godly and ungodly life.

The Book of Proverbs is a valuable repository of faithful and wise sayings that have a great appeal to the Muslim mind. They are a collection of psychologically and spiritually sound, practical advice on relationships. They address our relationship with God, working it out in the family, and in the community at large.

Also apply the Books of the Prophets. Our Muslim friend believes in the prophets, so we may show how God spoke through them, and highlight the disobedience of God's chosen people and how impossible it was for them to keep the Law. Also, the prophets are messengers of hope, for they speak of One whom God would send—his anointed Servant, the Messiah. God has explained through the prophets that the Messiah would be a Son, who would come to save his people, and give them a glorious future in his kingdom.

There is no single guaranteed method of convincing a Muslim that the Bible is true. We must continually trust in the leading of the Holy Spirit to give us wisdom in this matter. We must recognize that the Holy Spirit may well be inspiring the particular line of questioning that comes from our Muslim enquirer when it comes with sincerity of heart. We must take great care not to be drawn into controversy. An argument will effectively demonstrate that there is no basis of mutual trust or respect. For this reason, the debate that many Muslims look for is unprofitable.[5]

We are now at the point of introducing the Lord Jesus Christ to our Muslim enquirer. When talking with Muslims, it is not wise to speak merely of 'Jesus', for that is not reverent to Muslim ears. We ought rather to speak of the Lord Jesus, Jesus the Messiah, Jesus the Word, the Lord Jesus Christ. There are also other biblical titles that we are at liberty to use with great effect. By doing so we can present all the truth that there is behind the name 'Son of God'.

The Bible reveals the Lord Jesus Christ as the Son of God, and we need to convey this truth. Yet it is wise not to use the term, for it immediately offends. So we need to develop some understanding of what it really means. The Muslim already has in mind what *he* thinks we mean by it. If we listen to him, we will discover that his idea of what it means to be 'Son of God' is blasphemous. But does that mean we might be undermining Scripture if we avoid using this expression? Many Christians suspect that we undermine Christ's true position and authority if we avoid using this title. It is a fundamental doctrine, and any attempt to avoid using this term 'Son of God' must surely mean that we are detracting from both his person and work. But is this really the case? When challenged by the high priest at his trial, the Lord did not use this term.[6] He affirmed it by saying, 'It is as you said.' Nevertheless, as so often elsewhere in the Gospels, Jesus prefers to use the title 'Son of Man' when speaking of himself.[7] We therefore have the example of our Lord to follow. Consider the balance in the Gospels between the truth that Jesus is the 'Son of God' and his speaking of himself in other ways to a people who would be greatly offended at that term. It is not dishonest, misleading, or even a compromise to try to find alternative inoffensive ways of speaking about our Lord Jesus Christ to Muslims. The way the Lord Jesus is presented to us in John's Gospel is very instructive.[8] The person of the Lord Jesus Christ is introduced without mentioning the fact that he is the Son of God. Instead, we are given another name that indicates his eternal standing, and that he has a common identity and shares the same nature with God. We are also told that he was 'in the beginning' indicating before time began, and that he was the agency of creation.[9] John is underlining the truth that he who is named 'the Word of God' has a common identity with him who is introduced in Genesis 1:1. That he is called 'the Word of God' indicates an important truth. In human experience, for a word to be expressed requires the thought that inspires it, the means of producing it (the larynx and vocal cords), and the breath that passes through causing vibrations in the air, enabling us to hear the word. So to apply the analogy, 'the Word of God' is the expression of God's mind, will and thought, the means by which the Word of God is known and applied to our hearts and minds by the work of the Holy Spirit.[10] The writer to the Hebrews explains that God has 'in these days spoken to us by his Son'.[11] Thus we understand Jesus the Messiah is 'the Word of God', in that he is the exact representation of the Father in terms we can understand, being fully human as well as fully God. Remember that nowhere in the Bible is this relationship explained, but we understand it through the Holy Spirit working in our hearts.

So it is biblically quite legitimate to explain the person of the Lord Jesus

Christ as 'the Word of God' to Muslims in order to bring them to an understanding of who he is, avoiding the misunderstanding of the controversial term 'Son of God'.

This is not a 'cop out', or an excuse—or a watering down of theology. For in no sense do we advocate never using the term 'Son of God': it can be used freely after we have explained who he is. There is also another reason why it is useful to emphasize the name 'the Word of God (*kalimat'u'llah*). This term is also used in the Qur'an to refer to Jesus; thus it is a name that the Muslim is already extremely familiar with. All we have to do is explain the biblical meaning of the name.

This brings us to consider the concept of the Trinity. The word is not biblical, but has been coined as being a helpful word to use in order to describe the relationship between the one true God, who reveals himself as Father, Son and Holy Spirit. It is not essential to use the term. The best way for us to teach the doctrine is in the same terms the New Testament uses. To try to address the subject philosophically will only confuse and aggravate the situation.

At creation, 'the Spirit of God was hovering (brooding) over the face of the waters.' Thus by using the word 'Spirit' (Hebrew: *ru'ah*, meaning 'wind', 'breath'), we have a manifestation of God's power and presence described to us.

In all this God remains one in essence, transcendent, and far greater than we can ever imagine. In describing the Father, Son and Holy Spirit we do not divide God into three, but merely speak of how Almighty God in his written Word, the Bible, reveals himself to us. This is not something we can explain—but we do not divide God—he remains one. In the end, all we can appeal to is that this is God's revelation of himself to us. We cannot fully understand. We have to be careful of applying analogies, for they can so easily end up destroying the concept we are trying to explain. Some have usefully applied the analogy of water, manifesting itself in three forms: solid (ice), liquid, vapour (steam), yet always being water (H_2O). However, the Almighty God is always far greater than we can ever think him to be, or imagine him to be.

ii. Applying the teaching of Jesus the Messiah

When we turn to the New Testament we should be able to use the Gospel parables systematically to great effect. The parables are not merely illustrations of truths; they must be thought of as much more. They constitute a cultural method of teaching. The Lord Jesus used parables to teach truths that were difficult to assimilate, presenting them in a positive form, so that they become more understandable and acceptable. His listeners heard what the Lord Jesus had to say, before realizing the truth he was teaching applied to them. If Jesus had spoken the truth more openly, they would have been offended before fully hearing what he had to say.

We must bear in mind that these parables were spoken to Jewish audiences. They may need some exposition to make them relevant to Muslim thinking and experience. However, we do have a great advantage in the fact that they were originally spoken in a Middle Eastern context, and are therefore already appropriate to the Muslim outlook.

Bearing all this in mind, we must conclude that we may legitimately use the parables to teach the fundamental truths of the gospel to Muslim people. Here is a suggestion as to how they may be used to illustrate gospel truth.

Concerning sin:

Luke 18:9–14	The Pharisee and the tax collector.
Luke 12:16–21	The rich fool.
Matthew 15:1–20	Ceremonial and real defilement compared.

Concerning God's love and mercy, together with our need for repentance:

Luke 15:3–7	The lost sheep.
Luke 15:8–10	The lost coin.
Luke 15:11–32	The lost son.

Concerning the judgement of God:

Matthew 13:24–30	The wheat and the weeds.
Matthew 13:47–50	The fishing net.

Concerning God's plan for man's salvation:

Matthew 22:1–14	The wedding banquet (emphasizing the need for righteousness).
Luke 20:9–18	The vineyard tenants (showing how God sent his Son and how he was rejected).

Concerning the cost of discipleship in following Christ:

Matthew 13:44	Hidden treasure.
Matthew 13:45–46	A precious pearl.
Luke 6:48–49	The wise and foolish builders.

Concerning Christian living and stewardship:

Matthew 18:23–35	The unmerciful servant (on forgiveness).
Luke 7:41–43	The two debtors (on forgiving others).
Luke 12:42–48	The faithful servant (on serving God).
Luke 19:11–27	The gold coins (talents) (on serving God).
Luke 5:36–39	New cloth, new wine (on the fact that the way of Christ is completely new).
Luke 10:25–37	The good Samaritan (on love).

Of course there are various other ways of applying the teaching of the Lord Jesus Christ. What I have not done is present the method that will bring results. It is only given as an aid to thought.

If we do have the opportunity to meet with a Muslim enquirer on a regular basis, and he has the desire to examine Christian teaching in a serious way, then we need to consider a programme that will present the gospel message systematically. We ought to devise our own scheme, starting with less controversial subjects on which we have some common ground of contact, but which are very important doctrinally.

iii. A suggested themed scheme

Some ten subjects are suggested which would be valuable in such a scheme.[12] Many of the biblical references are put as endnotes, but it is intended that these Scriptures are used to teach these themes.

I. GOD IS ONE, AND HAS CREATED MAN TO SERVE AND LOVE HIM

The Ten Commandments begin with an outright condemnation of idolatry: Exodus 20:3–5. This identifies with the Muslim concept of *shirk*, the sin of associating anything created with God the Creator. Muslims take this command quite literally.[13] A strong emphasis also needs to be put on complete personal commitment to God.[14]

The apostle Paul is often accused by Muslims of corrupting the pure teaching of the real gospel, thereby causing Christians to associate others with the one God. This is clearly not true, as he declares that 'there is no other God but one'.[15] Paul is consistent in his teaching on the Lord Jesus Christ and states there is 'one God and one mediator between God and men, the man Christ Jesus'.[16] Paul condemns idolatry.[17] The Psalms give a call to worship the one creator God.[18] We can also note the prayers of worship which express the believer's joy, and his confidence in him as a personal God.[19]

II. GOD HAS GIVEN HIS LAWS TO MAN

Having first established that God is eternal and transcendent, and that man was created in God's image,[20] establishes the necessary foundation of all that follows. God desires a meaningful relationship with those whom he created. Relating to him is not *shirk*, as the Muslim sees it.

We may then refer specifically to the Ten Commandments to show the standards that God has set mankind.[21] When we know what God requires we then know what sin is.

As we examine God's commandments and apply them to our lives, we are able to show the various ways in which Jesus the Messiah based his teaching on these revealed laws: loving God and loving our neighbour.[22] Our Lord demonstrates that the Law of God not only applies to outward actions but also to our inner thoughts and motives.[23] A look at the whole of the Sermon on the Mount is useful.[24] Psalm 119 points out how the basic desire of the true believer is to surrender himself completely and utterly to God, and to a dedicated obedience of his revealed will. It also shows how important and precious his commandments are.

III. GOD WARNS MAN OF THE CONSEQUENCES OF FAILURE TO KEEP HIS LAWS

Genesis shows how God related to Adam and Eve personally, and gave them a commandment to obey, and chapter 3 demonstrates how Adam and Eve doubted God, disbelieved God, disobeyed God, and describes the punishment that God gave them. This punishment has affected the souls of all mankind through the curse of sin. This leaves mankind with a proneness to sin. Sin brings a sense of shame. We must teach that every man and woman is responsible before God for all their actions.[25] Sin is rebellion against God, not just making mistakes through inherent moral weakness. The need is to acknowledge and confess sin and to repent.[26]

IV. GOD IS MERCIFUL AND FORGIVES

We may now be able to introduce the concept of the Fatherhood of God in terms of Psalm 103:8–14. This doctrine is foreign to the Muslim, yet it should not present any major problem as we take care to explain that God is the one who is the origin of all life, and that he gives us life.

God has decreed that he will deal with man's sin by means of sacrifice. This sacrifice must be understood as the giving of a perfect life in place of the sinful life. God cannot look upon sin, and therefore cannot accept the sinner without his sin being atoned for. By means of a just atonement God's anger against sin can be turned away from the sinner.[27] Forgiveness is not a matter of mere words: there is a tremendous price to pay. The prophets show how God forgives, and point to the need for atonement.[28] Then turn to the Psalms, and witness the joy there is in knowing that one's sins are truly forgiven.[29]

V. GOD REVEALED TO THE PROPHETS THAT HE WOULD COME AMONG MEN

There are many references in the Old Testament to the incarnation, and how the Tabernacle foreshadows it.

The doctrine of the incarnation may be introduced through relevant Old Testament passages which speak of how God reveals himself in his word,[30] dwells among his people,[31] and how he personally declares that he is coming to make himself known in truth, and to proclaim his covenant.[32] The believer, who recognizes that God is coming to establish justice and his kingdom on earth, finds real joy and boldness through confidence in God.[33] In Isaiah 64:1–9 we have a prayer that God will come as he has promised to reveal himself and show mercy to sinful and rebellious man.

VI. GOD SENT JESUS THE MESSIAH AS HIS WORD BY MEANS OF A MIRACULOUS BIRTH, AND GAVE HIM MIRACULOUS POWERS

We look first at the accounts of the birth of Jesus the Messiah.[34] Muslims accept the virgin birth in principle, but the Bible gives the detailed historical account of how it all happened. We have to admit that most details of his childhood and earlier life have not been recorded—but we have a great deal of evidence to show the uniqueness of his life in the record of his ministry. Three particular miracles are helpful to point this out, from differing angles. The stilling of the storm, showing the reaction of his disciples, demonstrates that their faith in him increased gradually.[35] The feeding of the five thousand is helpful in the light of the Qur'anic passage, in which Jesus the Messiah is asked: 'Is thy Lord able to send down for us a table spread with food from Heaven?'[36] The casting out of the unclean spirit shows the power that the Lord exercised over all forces of evil.[37]

VII. GOD GAVE JESUS THE MESSIAH THE MESSAGE OF THE INJIL (GOSPEL) TO PROCLAIM

We are given brief summaries of the gospel message in the words of Jesus himself.[38] Bear in mind that although the Qur'an indicates that the *Injil* was granted to Jesus the Messiah, no content is given to it in the Qur'an, and consequently it becomes a nebulous entity. This is our opportunity to share its real message. The particular value of the passage in Luke is that it draws attention to what Jesus actually did. He healed the sick man and declared his sins to be forgiven. Do not be surprised if our Muslim friend reacts as the Pharisees did. However, we may point out that our understanding of this truth is not drawn from the later apostolic writings. We can assert that this is not merely an interpretation of what happened, but is a true account of what Jesus did and said.

The parable of the lost son[39] emphasizes that God's forgiveness is based on his love for the sinner. Note that the relationship of the one forgiven is not the status of a slave, as the Muslim maintains, but rather it is that of a son. The Lord's Prayer[40] shows how Jesus encouraged his disciples to pray to God as sons addressing a loving Father. This is an invaluable and necessary aspect of teaching to introduce to a Muslim, but we must do so carefully.

VIII. GOD DEMONSTRATES HIS LOVE FOR SINNERS THROUGH THE DEATH OF JESUS THE MESSIAH

This subject is one of the most difficult to discuss with a Muslim. He is prejudiced deeply against the concept of God's love requiring such a payment for sin, and against the idea that God should require the death of Jesus the Messiah. The Muslim denial that Jesus the Messiah is the Son of God is fundamental to this. Nevertheless, we need to place the death of Jesus the Messiah within the context of the love and wisdom of God. It is probably prudent to consider the reasons why God expressed his love in this way, before considering the details of the event itself. Bear in mind that the Muslim does not deny that the Jews wanted to kill Jesus, nor that Jesus was willing to be killed. He denies only that God should allow Jesus the Messiah to be crucified, or even that it was God's will.[41]

Appropriate parts of the Gospel narrative ought to be pointed out very carefully. We must show something of the hostility of the Jews against Jesus the Messiah.[42] Point out his willingness to be captured and killed;[43] that he laid down his own life voluntarily: he was not forced to do so. He knew that the Father in heaven could have rescued him from death if that had been his will.[44] Show how the Jews finally decided to kill Jesus.[45] We need to be aware that the Muslim is likely to react in a very similar way to the Jews: that this is blasphemy.

We may then go on to look at a straightforward account of the actual crucifixion.[46] In this context the prayer of the psalmist is very meaningful:[47] it is the prayer of one who feels that God has rejected and abandoned him. His utterances become the very words Jesus used on the cross. Jesus' prayer was heard and answered. He was not rescued before his death, but after. Through his death Jesus broke the power of death and cancelled the debt of sin. The death of Jesus the Messiah was a substitute for sinners.[48]

IX. GOD RAISED JESUS THE MESSIAH FROM DEATH TO LIFE

We now come to consider the empty tomb and the appearances of the risen Messiah.[49] The record of the two disciples on the Emmaus road is particularly helpful, and other further appearances to his disciples consolidate the eye-witness account. There are many references in the epistles which explain the purpose of the resurrection.[50]

The Gospel record shows Jesus the Messiah was raised up from the grave and given resurrection life. Consequently, his resurrection brings hope to every believer, that like him, we too will be raised to the same resurrection life.

The psalmist expressed his confidence in life beyond death.[51] It is a resurrection life in which we have the ultimate joy of being in the actual presence of God himself. How different this is from the Muslim concept of paradise as portrayed in the Qur'an.[52]

X. GOD GAVE HIS SPIRIT TO THE DISCIPLES WHO ACKNOWLEDGED JESUS AS GOD'S MESSIAH AND GOD'S WORD

Peter's sermon in Acts 2 expresses the relationship between God, the Lord Jesus, and the Holy Spirit, in the simple terms in which the early church was to understand it.

The work of the Holy Spirit is particularly described in Romans 8:1–17, and clearly establishes that man is unable to help himself spiritually although he thinks he can, a notion that is in line with Muslim optimism. The Holy Spirit has been given to enable believers to obey God's law. It is here that our discussion about Jesus being the Son of God may be taken out of the area of controversy and placed in the context of our experience of God.

David's prayer of penitence is the confession of a heart that is overwhelmed by shame; humbled and broken by guilt.[53] It is also a clear statement of faith, confidence and hope in the mercy of God. It is surely our prayer that our Muslim friend may show such true repentance and faith in the Lord Jesus Christ.

We must present a clear message of the gospel as the grace of God that brings forgiveness for sin, through the debt being paid. We proclaim a message of freedom from works which cannot save, and the fear of a life held in the balances. It is a message of love from a loving God. Allah may be as 'close as your jugular vein'[54] but his presence is a threat of judgement. Through the grace of God in the Lord Jesus Christ we have a glorious message of a personal God who loves the sinner, and whose desire it is to bring even sinners into an intimate and personal relationship with a merciful God, who is full of love and compassion. Such transcendent love, centred on a cross on which Christ died to redeem us, is wonderful and amazing news in the light of the fear and hopelessness that is experienced through the teaching of the Qur'an.

**

Please note that all the suggestions made in this chapter are only meant to be a guide. Other helpful material is available. The author worked on a foreign language Bible correspondence school programme which divided the curriculum into four sections, as follows:

(i) a general course on the contents of the Books of Moses, the Psalms and the Prophets, following the progressive revelation of God's plan for salvation in the Old Testament.

(ii) 'Jesus the Messiah': a course specifically on the life of Christ as narrated through the Gospels.

(iii) 'God's way': this was compiled from a set of papers written by a born-again Muslim national, which discussed (not argued) various theological topics of particular interest to Muslims that were covered in the previous two courses. It sought to consolidate the truths presented in the first two courses, and considered their implications.

(iv) *The Way of Salvation* was a translation of *Right with God* by John Blanchard (published by Banner of Truth Trust). This volume, it was believed, presented the gospel in terms that might be acceptable to a Muslim. Chapter 1 was not used, as that deals with arguments for the Bible being the Word of God. It was felt that it was right to begin with that assumption, as the students had already been using Scripture with this understanding. The rest of the book presented the gospel message and employed very appropriate Scriptures for use with Muslims. The last chapter ('The Way Ahead') was expanded with helpful material to encourage the new believer, and give him practical help to know how to live sensitively as a Christian in a Muslim environment.

A published course that takes a similar approach is one produced in Africa. It is in the form of four booklets with the following titles:

(i) 'The Beginning of People': 'Lessons from the First Book of the Taurat of the Prophet Moses';

(ii) 'God's Covenant with the People of Israel': 'Lessons from the Second Book of the Taurat of the Prophet Moses, Zabur of the Prophet David, and Other Prophets of God';

(iii) 'God Loves People': 'Lessons from The Injil of Jesus the Messiah';

(iv) 'The People of God': 'More Lessons from The Holy Scriptures.' This last booklet deals with the church as portrayed in Acts and discusses aspects of the practical Christian life, quoting from Matthew through to Revelation.

This course is published by Evangel Publishing House, P.O. Box 1015, Kisumu, Kenya. It is a very appropriate approach, sharing with a Muslim the teaching of the Holy Bible very simply. It is also available in Bengali.

This general review of approaches to Muslim enquirers and contacts is presented in the hope that it might be of assistance in showing the sort of direction it is profitable to take in thinking through a faithful presentation of the truths of the Word of God. It is our prayerful concern that the gospel may be shared as appropriate opportunities arise, and that this may be done in a helpful and relevant manner—addressing the particular problems that are presented by our Muslim friend.

**

Many modern Muslims demand debates with Christians. The idea is that they should be able to demonstrate the superiority of the Qur'an. One Muslim name that is well known in this area is that of Ahmad Deedat, who is based in Durban, South Africa. The tapes and videos of many of his public debates are used by many Muslims worldwide, of whatever Islamic distinction they may be. The reason is that Muslims like the diatribes that Deedat makes against Christians, seeking to belittle them. That so many Muslims accept and use Deedat's debates is interesting, for very few accept his position as a leader in the Ahmadiyya movement. This is an illustration of how *ummah* works in practice.

There have been other notable high profile public debates over the years, with Muslims trumpeting the claim of victory, whatever is said. It is the Muslim *ummah* standing against a Christian spokesman, and their own internal divisions are forgotten.

It is tempting to debate with Muslims, but Christians should be very cautious. There is only one debate sanctioned in Scripture. It is the Lord who calls for this debate, and he alone. The subject is 'Sin and its remedy'.[55] It is recorded in the prophecy of Isaiah. It is the Lord who is reasoning with sinners, and calling them to repent; a 'reasoning' in the light of God's truth. Seen from this perspective we have nothing to debate with God!

Debate is a seemingly attractive way of sharing with Muslims, and learning where they are coming from, and what they believe. Many Christian leaders and others have felt it right to undertake debate with Muslims. Their motives are highly honourable. However, as interesting as this medium appears to be, it does not achieve very much in terms of enlightenment of truth.[56]

How then do we share Christ with Muslims? It necessarily must be on a personal basis. The local Muslim *mullah* (or *moulavi*) is concerned that the *ummah* is at risk when Christians approach a Muslim. This is something we must be aware of, and we must take care how we speak with him. Therefore the best option is to try to find neutral ground on which to meet with him: not in his home, or in yours.

Notes

1 Genesis 18:14.

2 Isaiah 40:4, 5.

3 Genesis 1:1.

4 Deuteronomy 6:4–9.

5 Debate demands a crowd, and that gives Muslims the power base they need, for then the Muslim *ummah* comes into its own—the support of the oneness of community. We need to meet Muslims on a personal basis to share Christ in a personal way—for it is a personal relationship through the gospel that we are wishing to share. See further comment on debate on p. 211.

6 Matthew 26:63–64.

7 Mark 8:31.

8 John 1:1–3.

9 Genesis 1:1, John 1:1–8.

10 John 3:1–8. It is interesting to bear in mind that the biblical words for Spirit, *ru'ah* (Hebrew), *pneuma* (Greek) also mean 'breath' or 'wind'.

11 Hebrews 1:2–3.

12 The subsequent outline is based on a series of passages of Scripture that have been published as a pamphlet by the Bible Society in Lebanon (in English, French and Arabic) entitled *The*

Message of the Tawrat, the Zabur and the Injil—selected Passages from the Holy Bible. In his book *You Go and Do the Same* (Church Missionary Society/BMMF International, 1983), **Colin Chapman** gives a very helpful study based on the same source, and it is recommended for consideration.

13 Some Christians are happy to use illustrations that depict the Lord Jesus Christ. The *Jesus Film*, set up by Campus Crusade as an independent project, is now universally shown in Muslim and non-Muslim countries. Muslims will have no such depiction of Mohammed in pictures, let alone in film. Therefore I do wonder how wise it is to use this film among Muslims, in the light of the second commandment (Exodus 20:4). When is a depiction of Jesus Christ not idolatry? When is a depiction of Jesus Christ ever a true or adequate representation that is not misleading?

14 Deuteronomy 6:1–7.

15 1 Corinthians 8:4–6.

16 1 Timothy 2:5.

17 Galatians 5:19–21; also note Revelation 21:8.

18 Psalm 33:1, 4–9; 105:1–6.

19 Psalm 95:1–7; 139:1–6, 13–14.

20 Genesis 1:27–30; 2:7.

21 Exodus 20:1–17.

22 Matthew 22:34–40.

23 Matthew 5:21–24, 27–28.

24 Matthew 5–7.

25 Ezekiel 18:1–4, 30–32.

26 Psalm 51:1–9.

27 Leviticus 9:7; 16:5–10, 21–22.

28 Jeremiah 5:7, 9; Hosea 11:8–9.

29 Psalm 32:1–7.

30 Isaiah 55:10–11.

31 Exodus 29:44–45; Leviticus 26:1–2, 11–12; Ezekiel 37:26–27.

32 Isaiah 40:3–5.

33 Psalm 96:1–10.

34 Matthew 1:18–25; Luke 2:1–20.

35 Luke 8:22–25.

36 Sura 5:112–115.

37 Luke 4:31–37.

Chapter 26

38 Mark 1:14, 15; Luke 5:17–26.

39 Luke 15:11–32.

40 Matthew 6:9–13.

41 The Ahmadiyya (whom most Muslims do not accept as true Muslims) assert that Jesus was indeed crucified, but that he resuscitated and was eventually buried in Kashmir when he died (see the Ahmadiyya Community Website: www.alislam.org/library/jesus).

42 John 5:15–18.

43 Luke 22:41–44.

44 Matthew 26:51–54.

45 Luke 22:66–23:2.

46 Luke 23:20–26, consider in the light of the prophecy concerning the Suffering Servant (Isaiah 53:4–6).

47 Psalm 22:1–9.

48 Luke 24:36–47; John 11:50; Galatians 1:4; 2:20; 1 Timothy 2:6; 1 Peter 1:18, etc.

49 Luke 23:50–24:49.

50 Ephesians 1:20–21; Romans 1:4; Colossians 2:12; Hebrews 2:17–18.

51 Psalm 16:1–11.

52 See Chapter 6, v. Belief in the day of Judgement.

53 Psalm 51:10–17.

54 Sura 50:16.

55 Isaiah 1:18.

56 Answering Islam: http://answering-islam.org/Debates/. Article: Debates: 'Muslim Christian dialogs and debates', ¶1.

Conclusion

The first *sura* of the Qur'an is a prayer the Muslim recites every time he comes formally to pray on many occasions. The words are very meaningful to him, and he says them very fervently:

Praise be to God, the Lord of Creation,
The Compassionate, the Merciful, King of Judgement Day!
You alone we worship, and to You alone we pray for help.
Guide us to (show us) the straight path,
The path of those whom You have favoured (blessed),
Not of those who have incurred Your wrath,
Nor of those who have gone astray.

This is the cry from a Muslim heart, but there is an answer to it in the Bible. 'Jesus said, "I am the way, the truth, and the life. No one comes to the Father except through Me".'[1]

It is not an easy task to reach Muslims for Christ. The history of missions is testimony to that. But we trust that we have demonstrated from Scripture that it is not impossible. Muslims have a very high view of God, though it is misplaced and misdirected. We have an even higher view of the sovereignty of God—of the one true God who reaches down in love and mercy in the person of the Lord Jesus Christ to save sinners who are unable to help themselves. When all the misunderstandings are removed the Muslim is wonderfully open to the gospel message. After all, he is a sinner just like us all, who is seeking the Saviour.

You will find that a Muslim is usually very willing to talk with you about the gospel. Let us take every opportunity that is presented to us.

In closing it may be good to consider the following astute assessment of the task:

There is, of course, the biblical command to shake the dust from our feet and go elsewhere when a people reject the gospel. *Nevertheless, most Muslims have never explicitly rejected the gospel.* Their apparent resistance is usually related to the fact that they have never understood its message. An apparently resistant people are not necessarily a people who have rejected. In fact I have seldom interacted with any other people who seem as open to hearing the gospel as Muslims. Nevertheless, the misperceptions run deep, the theological issues are profound, and community pressures are tremendous. It takes time. *Patience is required*, the kind of patience which does not fit the categories of any forms of cost effectiveness and analysis. It is patience born out of commitment to Jesus Christ who also lived among a people who often painfully misunderstood his ministry.[2]

We approach Muslims with understanding, with care, with concern, and with compassion. What Paul said of Jews may also be said of Muslims: 'For I bear them witness that they have a zeal for God, but not according to knowledge.'[3] We need to pray that they come to the truth through the grace of God.

Let us therefore consider a thorough-going and well thought-through biblical presentation of the gospel of Christ that we may take to the Muslim. He is not outside the scope of our understanding, nor beyond an appropriate application of the glorious gospel of the sovereign grace of God. There is an open door before us … (see Acts 24:27; 1 Corinthians 16:9; 2 Corinthians 2:12; Colossians 4:3).

Notes

1 John 14:6. Note also Psalm 23:1–3; Proverbs 14:12; Isaiah 53:6; Matthew 7:13–14; John 10:11.

2 **David W. Shenk,** 'The Muslim Umma and the Growth of the Church', *Exploring Church Growth,* **Wilbert R. Shenk,** ed. (Chicago: Wm. B. Eerdmans Publishing Company, 1983), p.153.

3 Romans 10:2.

Information sheets

T he following items are short statements to give further information of interest to those who would like to know more details about Islamic thinking and practices.

The Qur'an

The Qur'an is considered by scholars to be the earliest and by far the finest work of classical Arabic prose. It constitutes the foundation of Islam. Islam cannot be truly known without an adequate understanding of the Qur'an.

Mohammed's revelations cover a period of twenty-three years. After his death, his followers realized that they needed to gather together all the scattered pieces of his revelations and put them into one collective book, for the use of the Muslim community. They had relied on the fact that when Mohammed was alive he acted as Allah's mouthpiece, and there was then no urgent need to gather the revelations together. So, on his death, that concern became apparent, and they collated all the material, putting it into one book.

They also realized that they needed practical guidelines on many issues, and so they also gathered together several collections of the sayings of Mohammed. These sayings, over and above the revelations, gave answers to questions concerning the how and when of situations. Many of them were incidents from Mohammed's life, and the response he gave as he dealt with different circumstances. These were collected together, from several sources of those who were close to Mohammed, and became known as the *hadith*. The *hadith*—the traditions—are not on a par with the Qur'an, but they are used authoritatively to support the 'revelations'.

In collecting the 'revelations' of Mohammed, they were not compiled together in any chronological manner. There were distinct periods in Mohammed's life, and there was a notable difference in his ministry in the later Medina period, after he had been expelled from Mecca. The revelations of this period take on a distinctly different emphasis—one difference being seen in a change in attitude to Jews and Christians who did not accept his revelations. Although they cannot be dated accurately, it is usually considered that eighty-six chapters were revealed in the Meccan period and twenty-eight in Medina, though some are mixed.

The Qur'an was arranged roughly in order of the length of the revelations, the longest coming first, and the shortest last. For those who are interested, the Qur'an is said to require twelve hours to read right through. There are 114 chapters (*sura*), and 6,226 verses (*ayat*), containing 99,464 words. The longest chapter is s*ura* 2, with 286 verses, and the shortest *sura* is 108 with 4 verses (*sura* 103 and 100 also compete). Every *sura* begins with the *Bismillah—bismillahir rahmanir rahim*: 'In the name of Allah, the Compassionate, the Merciful', except *sura* 9. Each of the *sura* are given names, derived from an important or distinguishing word from the text itself, or from the first few words of the *sura*, though they do not indicate the theme of the whole chapter. There are those who see a great miracle in the compiling of the Qur'an, and claim a mathematical foundation for it, based on the number 19 (the *Bismillah* consists of 19 Arabic letters, and the figures quoted above are divisible by this number!).

The names of prophets in the Qur'an

Qur'anic Name	Biblical Name
Adam	Adam
Idris	Enoch
Nuh	Noah
Hud	——
Salih	——
Ibrahim	Abraham
Isma'il	Ishmael
Ishaq	Isaac
Lut	Lot
Ya'qub	Jacob
Yusuf	Joseph
Shu'aib	——
Ayyub	Job
Musa	Moses
Harun	Aaron
Dawud	David
Sulaiman	Solomon
Ilias	Elijah
Al-Yusa	Elisha
Yunus	Jonah
Zakariyya	Zechariah
Dhu-Al-Kifl	——
Yahya	John the Baptist
'Isa	Jesus
Mohammed (The Final Prophet)	——

There is also an unnamed prophet in the Qur'an (Sura 2:246–248), and because of the obvious reference to King Saul in the context it is assumed this is Samuel.

Another personality by the name of Uzair is also believed to be a prophet, but not spoken of as such. His importance is emphasized as having collected the Torah, 'the book revealed to Moses' after it was lost during the captivity of Israel in Babylon. His Old Testament name is Ezra.

The Ninety-nine names of Allah

The following list of names are the revealed names of Allah, most of which appear in the Qur'an. Sometimes an alternative meaning is given, which indicates difficulty of translation from the Arabic. Usually, only one example reference from the Qur'an is given. Also be careful not to interpret the meaning of a name from a Christian perspective, for this is often misleading.[1]

	Arabic Name	The Meaning	Qur'anic Reference (example only)
1.	Ar Rahman	The Compassionate, The Beneficent, The Gracious	1:1
2.	Ar Rahim	The Merciful	1:1
3.	Al Malik	The King	20:114
4.	Al Quddus	The Holy One	62:1
5.	As Salam	The Peace, The Flawless	59:23
6.	Al Mu'min	The Faithful One, The Giver of Faith	59:23
7.	Al Muhaimin	The Protector, The Guardian	59:23
8.	Al 'Aziz	The Mighty, The Incomparable	59:23
9.	Al Jabbar	The Almighty, The Compeller	59:23
10.	Al Mutakabbir	The Great One, The Proud	59:23
11.	Al Khaliq	The Creator	59:24
12.	Al Bari	The Maker (of Perfect Harmony)	59:24
13.	Al Musawwir	The Fashioner	59:24
14.	Al Ghaffar	The Forgiver	40:42
15.	Al Qahhar	The Dominant, The Subduer	40:16
16.	Al Wahhab	The Bestower	3:8
17.	Ar Razzaq	The Provider,	51:58
18.	Al Fattah	The Opener	34:26
19.	Al 'Alim	The All-knowing	2:29
20.	Al Qabiz	The Restrainer, The Constricter	2:245

21.	Al Basic	The Expander	2:245
22.	Al Khafiz	The One Who Humbles, The Abaser	56:1–3
23.	Ar Rafi'	The One Who Exalts, The Exalter	56:1–3
24.	Al Mu'izz	The One Who Honours	3:26
25.	Al Muzil	The Destroyer, The One who Dishonours	3:26
26.	As Sami'	The One Who Hears	3:35
27.	Al Basir	The One Who Sees	4:58
28.	Al Hakam	The Ruler/Judge, The Arbiter	6:62
29.	Al 'Ad!	The Just	16:92
30.	Al Latif	The Gracious	6:103
31.	Al Khabir	The Aware	35:14
32.	Al Halim	The Merciful, The Forbearer	64:17
33.	Al 'Adhim	The Great One, The Magnificent	2:105
34.	Al Ghafur	The One Who Pardons, The Concealer of Faults	2:173
35.	Ash Shakur	The Rewarder of Thankfulness	35:30
36.	Al 'Mi	The Most High, The Highest	87:1
37.	Al Kabir	The Great	13:9
38.	Al Hafiz	The Guardian, The Preserver	34:21
39.	Al Muqit	The Giver of Strength, The Maintainer	4:85
40.	Al Hasib	The Reckoner	4:6
41.	Al Jail	The Majestic, The All-glorious	—
		(This is understood to summarize many positive attributes of Allah)	
42.	Al Karim	The Bountiful, The Generous	23:116
43.	Ar Raqib	The Watcher, The Vigilant	4:1
44.	Al Mujib	One Who Hears Prayer, The Responder to Prayer	11:61
45.	Al Wasi'	The Comprehensive, The Vast	2:115
46.	Al Hakim	The Wise	2:32
47.	Al Wudud	The All-loving	11:90
48.	Al Majid	The Glorious	—
		Combines The Majestic, The Bestower and The Generous	
49.	Al Raith	The Awakener, The Resurrector	22:7
50.	Ash Shahid	The Witness, Applied attribute of The Knower	(6:73)
51.	Al Haqq	The Truth	22:6
52.	Al Wakil	The Guardian, The Trustee	3:173

53.	Al Qawi	The Powerful, The Strong	11:66
54.	Al Matin	The Firm	51:58
55.	Al Wall	The Friend	2:107,
			2:257,
			47:11
56.	Al Hamid	The Praiseworthy, The Praised	22:64
57.	Al Muhsi	The Enumerator, The Appraiser	58:6
58.	Al Mubdi	The First Cause, The Beginner	85:13
59.	Al Mu'id	The Restorer	85:13
60.	Al Muhyl	The Life-Giver	2:28
61.	Al Mumit	The Death-Giver, The Slayer	2:28
62.	Al Haiy	The Living	2:255
63.	Al Qaiyum	The Self-existing	2:255
64.	Al Wajid	The Resourceful, Allah's quality of lacking nothing	—
65.	Al Majid	The Magnificent	85:15
66.	Al Wahid	The One (Unique)	13:16
67.	Al Samad	The Eternal	112:2
68.	Al Qadir	The Able	18:45
69.	Al Muqtadir	The Prevailing, The Powerful	18:45
70.	Al Muqaddim	The One Who Brings Forward, The Promoter	50:28
71.	Al Mu'akhkhir	The One Who Delays, The Postponer	11:8
72.	Al Awwal	The First	57:3
73.	Al Akhir	The Last	57:3
74.	Al Dhahir	The Evident, The Manifest	57:3
75.	Al Batin	The Hidden	57:3
76.	Al Wali	The Governor	42:9
77.	Al Muta'ali	The Exalted	13:9
78.	Al Barr	The Source of All Goodness	52:28
79.	At Tauwab	The Accepter of Repentance	2:37
80.	Al Muntaqim	The Avenger	32:22
81.	Al 'Afuw	The Pardoner	22:60
82.	Ar Ra'uf	The Clement, The Most Kind	2:207
83.	Malik al Mulk	The Ruler of the Kingdom (The King of Kingdoms)	3:26
84.	Dhu 'l Jalal wa'l Ikram	The Lord of Majesty and Generosity	55:27
85.	Al Muqsit	The Impartial One, The Equitable	3:18

86.	Al Jami'	The Assembler, The Gatherer	3:9
87.	Al Ghani	The Rich, The All-sufficient	47:38
88.	Al Mughni	The Enricher	9:28
89.	Al Mu'ti	The Giver	—
90.	Al Mani'	The Withholder, The Protector	—
91.	Adh Dharr	The Afflicter, The Punisher	—
92.	An Nafi'	The Benefactor, The Benefiter	—
93.	An Nur	The Light	24:35
94.	Al Hadi	The Guide	25:31
95.	Al Badi'	The Originator	2:117
96.	Al Baqi	The One Who Remains, The Everlasting	6:101
97.	Al Warith	The Inheritor	15:23
98.	Al Rashid	The Director, The Guide	11:87
99.	Al Sabur	The Patient One	8:46

The above list is a composite one derived from various sources and varies from some lists. Some authorities mention the possibility of a hundredth name, but 'Allah' is not given as that name. The greater majority of Muslim sources believe that this name is hidden with Allah—that only he knows it, and can reveal it. It is often referred to as *Isma al A'zam*, 'the Exalted Name' which no human being knows.

The names are commonly classified by dividing them into two groups that define the attributes: (i) *Isma ul-Jalaliyah*, the 'terrible' attributes; and (ii) *Asma ul-Jamaliyah*, the 'glorious' attributes. Bevan Jones[2] gives a more detailed summary analysis of the names used:

i. Seven describe Allah's Oneness and Absolute Being.

ii. Five speak of him as Creator, or Originator of all nature.

iii. Twenty-four show him as merciful and gracious (i.e., to believers!). These are also called 'beautiful' names and are some of the most often used in the Qur'an.

iv. Thirty-six emphasize Allah's power and pride and absolute sovereignty: the 'terrible' attributes.

v. Five reveal him as hurting and avenging. In Muslim terms, he is a God who leads astray, avenges, withholds his mercies, and does harm (cf. *sura* 6:39, 32:21, 13:32, 45:23).

vi. Four refer particularly to the moral qualities in Allah.

The Muslim Rosary

The rosary is commonly used in Islam, as an act of piety reciting the 99 names of Allah. The word for 'rosary' in the Arabic language is *sibha* or *masbaha*, which is derived from *subhana Allah* (God be praised). The number of beads in the Muslim rosary varies: there is a 33 bead rosary which requires three turns around the circle of beads. Each bead represents one of the names of God mentioned in the Qur'an, the total being 99. Another variant is divided into three parts, each made up of 33 beads. These may be used at the end of each of the five daily prayers. Other variants include 100 bead rosary used in accordance with *sunnah*, and there is even a 1,000 bead rosary used for funerals. There are differing opinions as to the origin of the Muslim rosary. One view is that 'the idea of praising God using a string of beads originated with *Al Sahabah* (companions of Prophet Mohamed). For instance, Abu Horaiyra used to practise this religious exercise using a knotted thread daily before sleeping. Wives of the Prophet, such as Fatemah Bint Al-Hussein Bin Ali and Safiya Bint Hoyayi, used to praise God using a group of stones. Hence, praising God using a string of beads or rosary is a *sunnah* from the early days of Islam. Using a rosary helps people to remember to praise God most of the time.'[3] Another opinion is that using a rosary to praise God was not part of the rituals of early Islam. At the time it was said that all living creatures on earth praise God and hence there was no need for the use of the small beads. However, the claim is made that the practice was borrowed from various faiths that preceded Islam. The use of the rosary is, for some, an indication of their devoutness.

Notes

1   See **Ergun Mehmet Caner, and Emir Fethi Caner,** *Unveiling Islam* (London: Monarch Books, 2003), pp.110–118.

2   **L. Bevan Jones,** *The People of the Mosque* (Delhi: ISPCK Madras: Christian Literature Society, 1980 (First edition 1932)), pp.87–88.

3   Quoted from *Al Ahram Weekly Online,* article dated 27th Feb–5th March 2003, edition No. 627. http://weekly.ahram.org.eg/2003/627/fe2.htm. Accessed 5 May 2005.

Muslim prayer

The formal prayer (*namaz*) of Muslims is called *salat*. First there is the call to prayer, the *adhan*, then Muslims must do a ritual washing, *wudu*, as outlined in the Qur'an:

Believers, when you rise to pray, wash your faces and your hands as far as the elbow, and wipe your heads and your feet to the ankle.[1]

The ritual involves (1) washing the hands up to the wrists three times; (2) rinsing out the mouth three times; (3) cleaning the nostrils by sniffing water three times; (4) washing the face from forehead to chin and from ear to ear; (5) washing the forearms up to the elbows three timers; (6) passing a wet hand over the whole of the head; and finally (7) washing the feet up to the ankles three times, first the right foot, then the left.

Muslim prayer is an act of obedience. It is not petition as Christians think of it. The repetition of prayer is like a mantra. It invokes the power of Allah and his blessing, but does not request anything. There is, however, an opportunity for personal prayer, called *du'a*, at the end of ritual cycles. This is almost afterthought recognition that individual Muslims do have personal needs, yet there is no assurance that Allah hears personal prayer. Prayer for Muslims is an act of submission, demonstrated by their prostrations.

The purpose of prayer for Muslims is to reassure faith (*iman*), to remove evil and obtain rewards.[2]

Prayers are recited facing the *qibla*, the direction of Mecca. There are many *qibla* calculators to show the correct direction in which to pray in whatever country a Muslim may be.

The prayers consist of a cycle of positions and recitation. *Sura* 2:37 says that Allah gives the words by which contact is established with him: *Sura* 1 is often referred to as 'the Key'. It is said that the Arabic sounds of the 'the Key' represent a 'numerical combination that opens the treasure'. Thus prayer in this precise manner is the way to Allah and his blessing. We list the main points of the *adhan* (prayer times) and explain the basic *rak'ah* procedure. Prayers are translated into English, but the rule is that these must be said in Arabic!

(1) The *adhan,* the call to prayer, is as follows:

Allahu akbar—Allah is the greatest (four times).

Ashadu an la ilaha illa llah—I testify that there is no other god but Allah (twice).

Ashadu anna Muhammada rasul u llah—I testify that Muhammad is Allah's messenger (twice).

Haya ala-a-salat—Come to prayer (twice).

Haya alal falah—Come to success (twice).

Allahu akbar—Allah is the greatest (twice).

La ilaha illa llah—There is no god but Allah (once).

One further sentence is added to the call to dawn prayer:

As-salat khair min in nawm—prayer is better than sleep.

(2) Each of the five times of prayer include a different number of *rak'ah.*

1. *Salat al Fajr*—at dawn, before sunrise
   —two compulsory and two optional *rak'ah.*
2. *Salat al Zuhr*—after noon
   —four compulsory and eight optional *rak'ah.*
3. *Salat al Asr*—in the late afternoon, one and half hours before sunset
   —four compulsory and four optional *rak'ah.*
4. *Salat al Maghrib*—immediately after sunset
   —three compulsory and four optional *rak'ah.*
5. *Salat al Isha*—After sunset but before midnight
   —four compulsory, three obligatory, and ten optional *rak'ah.*

(3) A *rak'ah* is a prayer sequence that follows eight consecutive positions:

i. *Takbeerat*

   Allahu Akbar: 'Allah is the greatest'

ii. *Qiyam*

Thana: 'Oh Allah, glorified, praiseworthy, and blessed is your name and exalted your majesty, and there is no deity worthy of worship except you.

Ta'awaz: 'I seek Allah's shelter from Satan, the condemned'

Tasmia: 'In the name of Allah, the Beneficent, the Merciful.'

Al-Fatiha
(Sura 1):   'Praise be to Allah, Lord of the Creation,
The Compassionate, the Merciful,
The King of Judgement Day!
You alone we worship,
and to you alone we pray for help.
Guide us to the straight path
The path of those whom you have favoured,
Not of those who have incurred your wrath,
Nor of those who have gone astray.'

On the second *rak'ah* another *sura* of choice is recited:
'Say he is Allah: the one and the only.
Allah, the Eternal, the Absolute
He begets none, nor is he begotten
and there is none like unto him.'

Moving to next position:
'Allah is the greatest.'

iii. *Ruku*

'Glory be to my Lord, the Greatest.'
(three times)

Moving to next position:
'Allah is the greatest.'

iv. *Qiyam*

'Allah listens to him who praises him.
Our Lord, praise be to you only.'

Moving to next position: 'Allah is the greatest.'

v. *Sajda*

'Glory to my Lord, the Most High (Exalted).'
(three times)

Moving to next position: 'Allah is the greatest.'

vi. *Tashahud*

'O my Lord forgive me and have mercy on me.'

Moving to next position: 'Allah is the greatest.'

vii. *Sajda*

'Glory to my Lord, the Most High (Exalted).'
(three times)

This completes one *rak'ah*. For two *rak'ah* return to position i. *Qiyam* repeating through to vii. *Sajda*.

Then, to finish:

viii. *Quood*   (1) *Tashahud:*

'All prayers and worship through
words, action and
sanctity are for Allah only

Peace be on you, O Prophet,
and mercy of Allah and
his blessings
Peace be on us
and on those who are righteous
servants of Allah.

I bear witness to the fact that there is no

      deity but Allah.

I bear witness that Mohammed is his slave

      and messenger.'

Here the third/fourth *rak'ah* would begin by returning to i. *Qiyam*.

The following are said at the close of a two or three or four *rak'ah* cycle, this time omitting *Quood* (1):

    (2) *Salat Alan-nabi:*

      'O Allah, bless Mohammed and his followers as
        you blessed Ibrahim
        (Abraham) and his followers.

      You are the Praised, the Glorious.'

      'O Lord! Make me one who
      establishes regular prayer, and also
      (raise such) among my offspring.

      O our Lord! Accept my prayer.

      O Lord! Cover (us) with your
      forgiveness

          —me, my parents and all
          believers—

          on the Day that the reckoning will be
          established.'

ix. *Salam*   In this position but looking first to the right,

              'peace and mercy of Allah be on
              you',

      then looking to the left

              'peace and mercy of Allah be on
              you'.

After the performance of the requisite rak'ah, now is the time for personal prayer (*du'a*).

Notes

1 Sura 5:6.
2 See Sura 2:3–4; 11:114; 20:14–15.

A day of rest?

For Muslims, Friday is a very special day. It is compulsory for Muslim men to attend worship at the mosque on a Friday. Fridays are often marked red on a Muslim calendar. In most Muslim countries Friday is a holiday, rather than Sunday. However, Friday is not prescribed as a day of rest but rather an emphasis is laid upon the obligation to meet together for worship. In fact, work and business transactions are permitted as usual before and after the time of the Friday noon-prayer.

But why is Friday such an important day for Muslims? That question is not easy to answer. We would like to be able to say that the reason is made clear in the Qur'an, but there is only one reference to Friday.

Believers, when you are summoned to Friday prayers hasten to remembrance of Allah and cease your trading. That would be best for you, if you but knew it. Then, when your prayers are ended, disperse and go in quest of Allah's bounty. Remember Allah always, so that you may prosper.[1]

This quotation comes from a *sura* entitled *al-Jum'a*, 'Friday, or the Day of Congregation'. Rather than being an explanation of the importance of Friday, it portrays Allah as being 'the Sovereign Lord, the Holy One, the Almighty, the All-knowing' (62:1). It then speaks of Allah sending his revelations, and how those given by Mohammed are superior to those of the Jewish *Torah*, which the Jews would not obey. Then the above summons is given, with the promise of Allah's blessing.

However, in the *hadith* there are many references to Friday. Here are some relevant quotations from the *hadith* of Sahih Muslim:

The best day on which the sun has risen is Friday; on it Adam was created, on it he was made to enter Paradise, on it he was expelled from it, and the last hour will take place on no day other than Friday.[2]

It was this day which Allah prescribed for us and guided us to it and the people came after us with regard to it, the Jews observing the next day and the Christians the day following that.[3]

We were guided aright to Friday (as a day of prayer and meditation), but Allah diverted those who were before us from it. The rest of the hadith is the same.[4]

The tradition of Friday being a special day for Muslims is based (1) on their understanding of the days of creation, (2) that Allah prescribed it, and (3) that it was designed to be a day for prayer and mediation. Muslims maintain that Mohammed said this was the best day to meet together to worship Allah.

There is an interesting article by Imam Ibn ul Qayyim al Jawziyyah entitled 'The Excellence of Friday', which quoted the above *hadith* extracts. It adds statements which are interesting.

With regard to Friday, the Holy Prophet was also reported as saying: 'There is no time on Friday at which no [*sic*] Muslim would stand, pray and beg Allah for what is good but He would give it to him' and he pointed with his hand that (this time) is short and narrow.[5] There is a good deal of difference of opinion among the scholars as to what exactly is that fortunate hour on Friday. ... The best course is that this hour should be treated as hidden, and the whole day should be spent in supplication and glorification of Allah. It was the Holy Prophet's practice to attach special significance and honour to Friday ... [by] going to Friday's congregational prayer early, listening to the sermon, wearing one's best clothes and remembering Allah all the time. When the Holy Prophet stood on the pulpit delivering Friday speech (sermon), his eyes would redden and his voice rise sharply with extreme anger. He, however, used to shorten the speech but prolong the prayer following it.[6]

Another *hadith* describes the days of creation in which Friday features.

[Mohammed said:] Allah the Exalted and Glorious, created the clay on Saturday and He created the mountains on Sunday and He created the trees on Monday and He created the things entailing labour on Tuesday and created light on Wednesday and He caused animals to spread on Thursday and created Adam ... on Friday; the last creation at the last hour of the hours of Friday, i.e., between afternoon and night.[7]

Although Islam holds to a six-day creation, we see that the actual days of creation are significantly changed from the biblical account. Friday is important because it is the last day of creation and the day on which Adam was created, was put into the Garden of Eden, and the day he was expelled from it. This begs a question. Why was Adam expelled from the Garden of Eden?

The Muslim conception of Adam and Eve differs from what the Bible teaches. The Qur'an states that Adam and Eve were directed by God to reside in the Garden of Eden and enjoy its produce as they pleased, assured of bountiful supplies and comfort. But the Garden exists in Heaven (Paradise), and is not an earthly creation. Adam and Eve were warned not to approach a particular tree so that they would not run into harm and injustice. But Satan tempted them and caused them to lose their joyful state. They were then immediately expelled from the Garden and brought down to earth to live, die, and to be taken out again for the Final Judgment. But having realized what they had done, they felt shame, guilt and remorse. Note that in Muslim teaching Adam and Eve did not understand they had sinned (in the sense of rebellion and defiance of God's command), but they prayed for God's mercy and were forgiven.[8]

For these reasons, Friday is understood to be the vital day for coming together to commemorate the *ummah* and to pray for God's forgiveness and blessing. Friday holds special powers in this respect.

The following is a more detailed explanation of the Muslim creation account.

We have stated before that time is but hours of night and day and that the hours are but traversal by the sun and the moon of the degrees of the sphere. ... The Jews came to the Prophet and asked him about the creation of the heavens and the earth. He said: God created the earth on Sunday and Monday. He created the mountains and the uses they possess on Tuesday. On Wednesday, He created trees, water, cities and the cultivated barren land. These are four (days). ... On Thursday, He created heaven. On Friday, He created the stars, the sun, the moon, and the angels, until three hours remained. In the first of these three hours He created the terms (of human life), who would live and who would die. In the second, He cast harm upon everything that is useful for mankind. And in the third, (He created) Adam and had him dwell in Paradise. He commanded Iblis

(Satan) to prostrate himself before Adam, and He drove Adam out of Paradise at the end of the hour.⁹

There are differing accounts of creation among the *hadith*, and there are conflicts within these accounts. This is not the place to discuss these in depth, but note this quotation from the same source.

The Jews asked the Prophet: What about Sunday? The Messenger of God replied: On it, God created the earth and spread it out. They asked about Monday, and he replied: On it, He created Adam. They asked about Tuesday, and he replied: On it, He created the mountains, water, and so on. They asked about Wednesday, and he replied: Food. They asked about Thursday, and he replied: He created the heavens. They asked about Friday, and he replied: God created night and day. Then, when they asked about Saturday and mentioned God's rest(ing on it), he exclaimed: God be praised! God then revealed: 'We have created the heavens and the earth and what is between them in six days, and fatigue did not touch Us.'¹⁰

Such is the essence of the *hadith!* However, from these quotations we rightly conclude that Muslims do not see Friday as a day of rest. It is a 'holy' day for Muslims, considered to be sacred (set apart) and is commemorated because they believe the Day of Judgement will take place on Friday.

Friday worship, the *salat al-jum'ah*, is congregational and observed at noon, or soon after, at the major mosques (the *Jam'a Masjid*) of a city. If a man misses worship on Friday without a valid reason, he is considered to be out of Islam. For women, this is not obligatory, but they may attend it if they wish and find it convenient (as is more common in western countries), otherwise they engage in the noon prayer at home as usual.

Friday worship consists first of a sermon (*khutba*), delivered by the *imam* who is leading the prayer. This sermon is part of the worship and consists of two parts divided by a short interval. A sermon should begin and end with praise to God, blessings on the Prophet Mohammed and his Companions, and a supplication for all Muslims. The subject of these sermons consists of any matter related to Islam or the life of Muslims: be it current affairs, problems of Muslims, which may be local or worldwide. Also there is some commentary on Qur'anic passages or some explanation of religious practices. Friday sermons are designed to be a means of teaching Muslims concerning their responsibilities and obligations, and of keeping them abreast with current affairs, and of strengthening the spiritual bond (*ummah*) between the believers. The sermon is followed by two *rak'ahs* of *salat*.

Friday is often taken as a weekend holiday in many Muslim countries, but as Allah did not need to take rest from his exertions in creating, so Muslims are not obliged to take it as a holiday. Many Muslims work and undertake business transactions as permitted before and after the time of the Friday prayer.

Whereas in Muslim countries, Friday prayer is always observed in mosques, in western countries, where there are not many mosques, any place where people can gather is suitable for this purpose. It is emphasized to any community of Muslims that it is their duty to make some permanent arrangement for the observance of *Jum'a* (Friday) prayer.[11]

Friday may seem to resemble the Saturday Sabbath for Jews or Sunday for Christians.

The similarity, however, is apparent rather than real. The basis of the Sabbath observances in these religions originated from the idea that as God the Creator 'rested' on the seventh day after six days of 'labour' at completing the creation of the heavens and the earth, so man should also rest. ... This idea is fundamentally contrary to the teachings of Islam, as the omnipotent God does not become weary and requires rest from His 'work'. There is no Sabbath in this sense in Islam. Muslims can carry on their usual activities and business before and after the Friday prayer. God says in Quran: 'O you who believe! When the call is proclaimed for prayer on Friday, hasten earnestly to the remembrance of God, and leave off business; that is best for you if you but knew. And when the prayer is finished, then you may disperse through the land and seek the bounty of God, and celebrate the praises of God often, that you may prosper' (Sura 62:9–10).[12]

The Christian understands that the Almighty, by definition, does not experience tiredness, but he 'blessed the seventh day and sanctified it'.[13] The Sabbath is not a commandment confined to Jews, but being based on a creation day, it is a *creation* ordinance binding on all mankind. This means

God set it apart for the entire human race, for their benefit. Jews and Christians are to keep the Sabbath day because of the example the Almighty gave.

For Christians the Sabbath is a day of rest, a day on which to worship God as his family. For Christians the Sabbath has changed from Saturday (rather, 6pm Friday to 6pm Saturday) to Sunday, because of the resurrection of Jesus. This is in direct contrast to Muslims worshipping Allah on Friday, both with respect to the day and the reasons for such worship.[14]

Among the many problems that may occur for Christians living in Muslim countries, the question of when to worship may be raised. Some Muslim countries observe a Friday holiday as the 'weekend'. This may cause problems for Christians wishing to meet on a Sunday, when they are expected to work as others do. One solution is to meet outside working hours, either before the start of business, or after business later in the day. Another solution that many Christians have found profitable is to worship on the Friday, as opportunity for a time of rest is given that day. It may be that some Christians would want to include both opportunities! The solution must ultimately be a matter of conscience, taking all circumstances into account. Christian, we are not in bondage as to when we may worship. Worshipping on a Friday may be a helpful witness to Muslims.

Notes

1 Sura 62:9–10.
2 **Muslim**: http://isgkc.org/Hadith/Muslim/smt_toc_detail.html *Hadith* Book 4, Number 1856.
3 *Ibid.,* Book 4, Number 1858.
4 *Ibid.,* Book 4, Number 1863.
5 Such is the type of inconsistent statement with which we have to contend! It seems that though at any time of day Allah will grant his blessing, yet 'worship' is confined to one hour—the 'short and narrow'.
6 **Imam Ibn ul Qayyim al Jawziyyah**, www.islaam.com/Article.aspx?id=216. Article: 'The Excellence of Friday'.
7 **Muslim:** http://isgkc.org/Hadith/Muslim/smt_toc_detail.html *Hadith.* Book 38, No. 6707.

8 Sura 2:35–38; 7:19–25; 20:117–123.

9 **al-Tabar**: *The History of al-Tabari, Volume 1—General Introduction and from the Creation to the Flood* (Franz Rosenthal, transl.) (Albany, NY: State University of New York Press, 1989), pp.187–193.

10 Ibn Abbas, cited by Answering Islam: http://answering-islam.org.uk/Responses/Shabir-Ally/science03.htm. Article: 'Science in the Quran', chapter 3, 'Avoiding the Mistakes of Genesis'.

11 Ottawa Muslim: www.ottawamuslim.net/Religious%20events/holidays.htm#friday. Article: 'Fridays'.

12 *Ibid.*, ¶4.

13 Genesis 2:3.

14 For a fuller treatment of the subject of the Christian Sabbath, see **Andy McIntosh,** *Genesis for Today* (Epsom: Day One Publications, 2nd edition 2001), chapter 6, pp.84–99.

Muslim paradise

As explained on pp.62, Paradise, or Heaven (*janna*), is spoken of as having seven levels. However, we are also told that there are eight doors to Heaven, which is recorded in one of the *hadith*.[1] These eight 'doors' are considered to be various levels, or even stages within Paradise. The Muslim Paradise is a place where every physical delight imaginable is available, comforts that were for many just dreams in this life. It is clearly a man-centred Paradise, though women are promised that it will be a delightful place for them, and they will receive 'precious stones and pearls', homes, protection, modesty—and every woman, whatever their marital status on earth, will be married in paradise and their relationships protected by Allah.

Janna (Paradise, Heaven) is called by eight names in the Qur'an (see following chart).

The following are some Qur'anic statements on the quality of life in Paradise. *Sura* 56 deals in depth with the Day of Judgement and the rewards that await those men who have led a good life.

When that which is coming comes—and no soul shall then deny its coming—some shall be abased and others exalted. ... you shall be divided into three multitudes: those on the right (blessed shall be those on the right!); those on the left (damned shall be those!); and those to the fore (foremost shall be those!). They shall recline on jewelled couches face to face, and there shall wait on them immortal youths with bowls and ewers and a cup of purest wine (that will neither pain their heads nor take away their reason); with fruits of their own choice and flesh of fowls that they relish.[2]

And theirs shall be dark-eyed *houris*, chaste as hidden pearls: a guerdon [reward] for their deeds. There they shall hear no idle talk, no sinful speech, but only the greeting, 'Peace, peace.'[3]

Those on the right hand—happy shall be those on the right hand! They shall recline on couches raised on high in the shade of thornless sidrahs and clusters of talh; amidst gushing waters and abundant fruits, unforbidden, never-ending.[4]

The reference to the 'right hand' signifies the place of blessing, the reward of righteousness obtained by obedience. The blessings consist of being able to rest in the shade of palms and vines laden with fruit and beautiful flowers, with fresh gushing water, and nothing ever being out of reach—the very opposite of life in the desert!

We created the *houris* and made them virgins, loving companions for those on the right hand; a multitude from the men of old, and a multitude from the later generations.[5]

Another 'more free' translation of the Qur'an indicates that wives of Muslims have a rightful place in heaven, and that they will be recreated as virgins, with much better temperaments, and therefore of greater attraction seemingly to their husbands, perhaps a demonstration of the tensions over this issue in Islam.

Contrary to the perception of many Muslims, the Qur'an itself does not promise large numbers of wives for the faithful men who achieve heaven; it is silent on this issue. It is in the *hadith* we find definitive statements about numbers, some suggesting two wives, others up to seventy-two![6] However, the *hadith* that claim higher numbers are not treated as authoritative by the majority of Muslims, who wish to play down the idea of seventy-two virgins for every believer in Paradise. More sober Muslim commentators consider this to be a sensational and spicy fantasy of some ancient writer. Limiting the number of wives to two, these will have supreme qualities that surpass the best women on earth, free of imperfections and of great beauty.

Another *hadith* of interest purports to describe how these *houris* live in Paradise:

In Paradise there is a pavilion made of a single hollow pearl sixty miles wide, in each corner of which there are wives who will not see those in the other corners; and the believers will visit and enjoy them. And there are two gardens, the utensils and contents of which are made of silver; and two other gardens, the utensils and contents of which are made of so-and-so (i.e. gold) and nothing will prevent the people staying in the Garden of Eden from seeing their Lord except the curtain of Majesty over His Face.[7]

Here we see an allusion to the great value that Muslims place on pearls, as an indicator of great wealth and comfort. And can this also be a reference to the problem of two wives living in one Muslim household, where jealousy disrupts the harmony of home? Note also how the gardens of Paradise are equated with the Garden of Eden.

Allah is not seen in Paradise and so there is no sense of sharing heaven with him (*tauhid* is maintained). He is represented as having a curtain of majesty over his face. Enjoyment in heaven is never focused on the holy, always on the sensual.

See the next page for the Names of Paradise in the Qur'an.

Notes

1 Mishkat book 2, chapter 1, cited at Answering Islam: http://answering-islam.org.uk/Index/P/paradise.html. Article: 'Paradise', ¶2.
2 Sura 56:1–26.
3 Sura 56:22–26.
4 Sura 56:27–35.
5 Sura 56:36–38. Other references to the *houri*: Sura 55:70,72,74,76.
6 **Al-Bukhari**, www.usc.edu/dept/MSA/fundamentals/hadithsunnah/bukhari/. *Hadith:* Book 54, Number 468–469; compare with ibn Waraq, cited at *Guardian Unlimited:* www.guardian.co.uk/saturday_review/story/0,3605,631332,00.html Article: 'Virgins? What Virgins?', Saturday 12 January 2002, ¶6.
7 **al-Bukhari**, www.usc.edu/dept/MSA/fundamentals/hadithsunnah/bukhari/. *Hadith:* Book 60, Number 402.

The Names of Paradise in the Qur'an

No.	Name	Reference	Translators of the Qur'an					
			Pickthall	Yusuf Ali	Shakir	Sher Ali	Rashad Khilafa
1	Jannatu al-Khuld	25:15	The Garden of Immortality	Eternal Garden	Abiding Garden	Garden of Eternity	Eternal Paradise
2	Darul as-Salam	6:127	The Abode of Peace	The Home of Peace	The Abode of Peace	The Abode of Peace	The Abode of Peace
3	Darul al-Qarar	40:42	The Garden	The Garden (of Bliss)	The Garden	The Garden	Paradise
4	Jannatu al-'Adn	9:72–73	The Gardens of Eden	The Gardens of Everlasting Bliss	The Gardens of Perpetual Abode	The Gardens of Eternity	The Gardens of Eden
5	Jannatu al-a'wa	32:19	The Gardens of Retreat	The Gardens of Hospitable homes	The Gardens of Abiding place	The Gardens of Eternal Abode	Eternal Paradise
6	Jannatu an-Na'im	5:70	Paradise	The Garden	The Garden	Heaven	Paradise
7	'Illiyin	83:18	'Illiyin	'Illiyin	'Illiyin	'Illiyin	'Elleyeen
8	Jannatu al-Firduaus	18:107	The Gardens of Paradise	The Gardens of Paradise	The Gardens of Paradise	The Gardens of Paradise	Blissful Paradise

The symbols of Islam

The Crescent and Star
The crescent moon and star is the internationally-recognized symbol of Islam. It is famous for being part of the official emblem for the International Red Cross and Red Crescent Societies. But is it really a symbol of Islam?

Historically the crescent moon and star pre-dates Islam by thousands of years. These symbols were used in the worship of the sun, moon and sky gods. There are reports of the crescent moon being used to represent the Carthaginian goddess Tanit and the Greek goddess Diana. Some Christians have even accused Muslims of adopting the moon god whose name is *Allah*. This is something that Muslims vehemently deny.[1]

The only function the moon has in Islam is that it determines the Islamic calendar. This is confirmed in the Qur'an. 'Do you not see how Allah causes the night to pass into the day and the day into night? He has forced the sun and the moon into His service, each running for an appointed term.'[2]

Any suggestion that Muslims worship a 'moon god' is highly repugnant to Muslims, for Allah is the creator of all the celestial bodies. The Qur'an forbids moon worship, and there is only one reference to the moon crescent (*hilal*). 'They question you about the phases of the moon. Say: 'They are seasons fixed for mankind and for the pilgrimage.'[3]

Some Muslim historians trace the use of the crescent in Islam back to the building of the Dome of the Rock (Qubbat al-Sakhrah) in Jerusalem around AD 675, when crescents were used as decorative symbols. The majority refer to the Ottoman Turks using it some 800 years after the birth of Islam. In the *Dictionary of Islam*, T.P. Hughes states that the crescent 'was a symbol of sovereignty in the city of Byzantium' [i.e. Constantinople, the capital city of eastern Christianity, now Istanbul]. It appears that the Ottomans adopted the symbol from the Byzantines after the fall of Constantinople in AD 1453. It was the Ottomans who made it a symbol of Islam across the Muslim world.

It is used on the dome of mosques. It is positioned to indicate the direction of Mecca, towards which Muslims must pray. Some Muslims see it as symbolic of the beginning of Islamic months,

It is difficult to claim that there is any true symbol of Islam other than this. Many Muslims actually reject the use of the crescent to indicate Islam, as they are very wary of any symbol having a religious meaning attached to it. Such things are forbidden by the Qur'an.

So there is a difference in concept between 'symbols of the Islamic faith' and 'symbols adopted by Muslims'. Officially, the symbols of the Islamic faith are only those that have been declared as symbols by the Qur'an or the *sunnah*. These include the Ka'aba, the five daily prayers, the *hajj*, and the animal sacrifice at *Eid ul-Azha*.

Thus the crescent and star are merely symbols adopted by Muslims. They hold no special significance in Islam. They do not represent Islam as Christians might use the cross to represent the Christian faith. Yet it is clear that Muslims associate the crescent moon with Islam, and use it to represent their way of life. There is tension between the moon being used as a *religious* symbol, which is denied, and the moon being used as a popular symbol of Islam.

With respect to the star, research has drawn nothing of particular note about its use, except there are many legends about it. It has been said by some Muslims that the five points of the star represent the Five Pillars of Islam, but that is probably a fanciful suggestion. Perhaps the star is only significant together with the crescent moon, as representative of all God has created.

The Colour Green

Green is synonymous with nature. But also green (*akhdar*) is the symbolic colour of Islam. Mohammed is believed to have worn a green turban (his favourite colour). Green was the colour of the banners used on the battlefield and said to be the colour of the first Islamic flag. In the Qur'an and the *hadith*, Paradise is described as being filled with green. It states that the people of Paradise 'will wear green garments of fine silk'.[4]

Islam also considers green significant because it is the colour of nature. The Arabs treasured the colour green as it was in direct contrast to the relentless yellow of the desert. The desert oasis was green, and therefore symbolized life, comfort and peace. So, for the Arabs green is the symbol of good luck, natural fertility, vegetation, and youth. In the Qur'an green becomes a very attractive colour. In heaven, '[Believers] shall recline on green cushions and rich carpets.'[5] Green is also symbolic of God's rich blessing.

The *hadith* witness to the importance and pleasantness of the colour green: 'The sight of green is agreeable to the eyes as the sight of a beautiful woman.' One commentator writes, 'Green is always connected with Paradise and positive, spiritual things, and those who are clad in green, the *sabzpush* of Persian writings, are angels or saints.'[6] In Egypt, Muslims put green material around tombstones: this is said to foreshadow Paradise. Therefore in Muslim thought the colour green and Islam are synonymous. Muslims often use the colour green to represent themselves.

Notes

1   See Sura 41:37 and **Mohd Elfie Nieshaem Juferi:**
    http://bismikaallahuma.org/Polemics/lunar.htm. Article: 'What is the Significance of the Crescent Moon in Islam?'
2   Sura 31:29.
3   Sura 2:189.
4   Sura 18:31.
5   Sura 55:76.
6   First Ismaili Electronic Library and Database:
    http://www.ismaili.net/Source/myflag/09green.html. citing Schimmal, Annemarie: *Deciphering the Signs of God* (Cambridge, 1994), p.16.

The Muslim calendar

Muslims follow a distinct calendar which was first introduced in AD 638 by the second Caliph Umar ibn al-Khattab, who had been a close companion of Mohammed. It appears that he wanted to rationalize the various (and conflicting) dating systems that were in use. Consulting with his advisors, they agreed that the most appropriate reference point for a distinctive Islamic calendar was the year of the *Hijra*.

The actual starting date of the Muslim Calendar was chosen to be the first day of the first month (1 *Muharram*) of the year of the *Hijra*. By counting backwards on the basis of lunar months, the estimated date of the *Hijra* thus corresponds to 16 July 622.[1] This is the 1st day of *Muharram*, 1 AH, the years of the Islamic Calendar designated by the Latin *Anno Hegirae*.

One significant feature of the Muslim Calendar, as already mentioned, is the fact that it follows lunar months. This makes the 12-month Muslim Calendar of 354 days, 11 days shorter than the Gregorian calendar. Through a cycle of 34 *hijra* years the Muslim Calendar will have returned to the same comparative dates with those of the Western Calendar.

Each new month of the Muslim Calendar is marked by the first appearance of the crescent moon (not the new moon), hence one of the reasons why the crescent moon is the popular symbol of Islam. There are different ideas about how the visibility of the crescent moon should be defined. This results in small differences in calendars around the Muslim world, differing from each other by about a day. It also means in practice that the number of days in any one month can vary. Because of this there is a consensus nowadays that the observations made in Cairo in respect of the start and end of *sawm* (the fast in the month of Ramadan) have become the norm for most other Muslim countries.

There is a mathematical formula for converting between the Gregorian year and the Muslim year:
—from *Hijri* to Gregorian: divide by 1.031, then add 622.
—from Gregorian to *Hijri*: subtract 622, then multiply by 1.031

Now, for Muslims, it is not simply a case that they follow a different calendar. The *Hijri* Calendar is not based on mere sentimentality. It holds far deeper significance, both historically and religiously.

All the events of Islamic history, especially those which took place during the life of the Holy Prophet and afterwards are quoted in the Hijra calendar era. But our calculations in the Gregorian calendar keep us away from those events and happenings, which are pregnant of [*sic*] admonitory lessons and guiding instructions. And this chronological study is possible only by adopting the Hijri calendar to indicate the year and the lunar month in line with our cherished traditions.[2]

The Muslim Year[3]

1 Muharram	7 Rajab
2 Safar	8 Sha'ban
3 Rabi' al-awwal	9 Ramadan
4 Rabi' al-Thani	10 Shawwal
5 Jumada al-awwal	11 Dhu al-Qi'da
6 Jumada al-Thani	12 Dhu al-Hijja

Important Dates

Muharram 1   Islamic New Year

Muharram 10   *Ashura*
    Shia's commemorate the martyrdom of Imam Husain at Karbala, often flagellating themselves.

Rajab 27   *Isra & Miraj*
    Night of journey of Mohammed from Mecca to Jerusalem, then his ascension into heaven (and back).

Rab al-awwal 12   *Mawlid al-Nabi*
    Commemoration of Mohammed's birthday and his life.

Sha'ban 15   *Nisfu Sha'ban*
    Muslim night of fasting and prayer of repentance for all harm done.

Ramadan 1   First day of the month of fasting.

Ramadan 20–29   *Laylatu'l-Qadr*
the Night of Destiny, occurs on one of these days, the night of the great opening of Heaven when the Qur'an was revealed to Mohammed, an auspicious night.

Shawwal 1–4   *Eid ul-Fitr*
celebrated on 1 Shawwal and the following days, and marks the end of Ramadan. A time of giving presents, and sharing feasts.

Dhu ul-Hijja 7   1st day of hajj. Praying in the Great Mosque at Mecca, performing umrah.

Dhu ul-Hijja 8   2nd day of hajj. In plain of Arafat.

Dhu ul-Hijja 9   3rd day of hajj. Standing in the plain of Arafat, two sermons fill the day; after sundown the running to Muzdalifa.

Dhu ul-Hijja 10   4th day of hajj. Sermon at Muzdalifa. Throw stones at 3 pillars at Mina. Goat sacrificed (Eid ul-Adha). Shaving of heads.

Dhu ul-Hijja 11–13   5th–7th days of hajj. Days spent in feast and throwing stones at the 3 pillars at Mina. On 12th last opportunity to perform umrah in Mecca. Following this many hajji go to Mohammed's tomb at Medina.

Notes

1   Or 622 CE (Common Era), as Muslims tend to designate our Calendar, not wishing to use the allusion to the birth of Jesus Christ.

2   **Waleed A. Muhanna,** http://fisher.osu.edu/~muhanna_1/hijri-intro.html. Article: 'A Brief Introduction to the Muslim (Hijri) Calendar'.

3   There are no equivalent months as the Muslim lunar year is two weeks shorter than a solar year.

The Barnabas connection

Many Muslims make great claims for a book known as 'The Gospel of Barnabas'. According to this manuscript, Muslims have proof that Islam is the superior religion. This book is amazing, as it 'proves' that Jesus is a Muslim.

You will find this book available in most Muslim bookshops, but not in Christian bookshops. Yet it is reported to be an authentic gospel that records the life of Jesus Christ. Most Christians have never heard of it. It claims:

The Gospel of Barnabas is the only known surviving gospel written by a disciple of Jesus, that is by a man who spent most of his time in the actual company of Jesus during the three years in which he was delivering his message. He therefore had direct experience and knowledge of Jesus's [sic] teaching, unlike all the authors of the four accepted Gospels. Since it foretells the coming of Muhammad, and denounces the crucification [sic], and Trinity, it was sentenced to be destroyed and hidden for centuries. Finally, one can get a copy of this Gospel and find out just exactly why it was hidden.[1]

This gospel is used by Muslims in defence of Islamic teaching. There are some 222 'chapters', many of which are very short. It is an extremely confused book. On one hand there are statements that contradict the Qur'an (which Muslims put forward as reasons why Christians should believe its authenticity), and on the other hand there are many statements that contradict the four Gospels of the New Testament Scriptures. With respect to the birth of Christ, the angel Gabriel tells Mary that she is to be the 'mother of a prophet' (chapter 1). Later it describes how Barnabas is supposed to have become involved.

The angel Gabriel presented to him as it were a shining mirror, a book, which descended into the heart of Jesus, in which he had knowledge of what God hath done and what God hath said and what God willeth insomuch that everything was laid bare and open to him; as he said unto me: 'Believe, Barnabas, that I know every prophet with every prophecy, insomuch that whatever I say the whole hath come forth from that book.'[2]

Barnabas is included among twelve disciples in Chapter 14. The 'true' character of God is taught by Jesus together with the impossibility of God having sons in Chapter 17. Chapter 95 is a description of a supposed sermon given by Jesus in which he teaches God's transcendent character, but does not refer to him as 'My Father.' Chapter 215 describes how four angels (Gabriel, Michael, Rafael and Uriel) are sent on God's instructions to 'take Jesus out of the world', and how Judas Iscariot was put to death in Jesus' place (Chapter 217, see also Sura 4:157). Adam's creation is detailed in Chapter 39.

Adam, having sprung upon his feet, saw in the air a writing that shone like the sun, which said: 'There is only one God, and Muhammad is the Messenger of God. ...'

Adam besought God, saying: 'Lord, grant me this writing upon the nails of the fingers of my hands.' Then God gave to the first man upon his thumbs that writing; upon the thumb-nail of the right hand it said: 'There is only one God,' and upon the thumb-nail of the left it said: 'Muhammad is Messenger of God.' Then with fatherly affection the first man kissed those words, and rubbed his eyes, and said: 'Blessed be that day when you shall come to the world.'[3]

There are prophecies of the Prophet Mohammed's coming in Chapters 45, 82, 96, and he is even mentioned by name in Chapters 44, 54, 97, 112 and 163. Jesus denounces the idea that he is the 'Messiah'. The final chapter, which is quoted in entirety, seeks to put the record straight.

After Jesus had departed, the disciples scattered through the different parts of Israel and of the world, and the truth, hated of Satan, was persecuted, as it always is, by falsehood. For certain evil men, pretending to be disciples, preached that Jesus died and rose not again. Others preached that he really died, but rose again. Others preached, and yet preach, that Jesus is the Son of God, among whom is Paul deceived. But we—as much as I have written—we preach to those who fear God, that they may be saved in the Last Day of God's Judgment. Amen.[4]

So it is not surprising that Muslims are excited about this 'gospel'. They claim that it is 'more authentic than the NIV or KJV'—and because it contradicts the Qur'an, this proves a Muslim could not have written it. They also claim that Christians have suppressed it, because it contradicts the New Testament accounts.

One Muslim, Ata ur-Rahim, claims that it is of ancient origin, that it is 'the only surviving gospel written by a disciple of Jesus', while he makes several unsubstantiated conjectures:

It is not known when he wrote down what he remembered of Jesus and his guidance, whether events and discourses were recorded as they happened, or whether he wrote it soon after Jesus had left the earth, fearing that otherwise some of his teaching might be changed or lost. It is possible that he did not write down anything until he had returned to Cyprus with John Mark. The two made this journey some time after Jesus had left the earth, after parting company with Paul of Tarsus, who had refused to make any further journeys with Barnabas on which Mark was also present. But no matter when it was written, and although it too, like the four accepted Gospels, has inevitably suffered from being translated and filtered through several languages it is, at least, an eye-witness account of Jesus's life.[5]

It is claimed to be the most authentic gospel in our possession, and that it was accepted as a canonical gospel in the churches of Alexandria until AD 325. Ata ur-Rahim also makes other astounding claims.

It is known that it was being circulated in the first and second centuries after the birth of Jesus from the writings of Iraneus (130–200 A.D.), who wrote in support of the Divine Unity. He opposed Paul whom he accused of being responsible for the assimilation of the pagan Roman religion and Platonic philosophy into the original teaching of Jesus. He quoted extensively from the Gospel of Barnabas in support of his views.[6]

Reputable biblical scholars have examined such claims and find that there is no basis for giving any authenticity to this manuscript. There are a number of important reasons. There are no early manuscript editions of this gospel. The earliest script is only available after the fifteenth century, an Italian manuscript that was purportedly discovered in the Vatican. No early church father has ever quoted from it, nor is it ever referred to until the fifteenth century, nor has there ever been any allusion to it in the heated debates among Christians and Muslims between the seventh and fifteenth centuries (but the canonical books of Scripture were often quoted).

The gospel of Barnabas appears to have been confused with the first-century *Epistle of [Pseudo] Barnabas* (circa AD 70–90), which is an entirely different book. It appears that Muslim scholars have assumed that the two were identical. Also some have mistakenly assumed that the Apocryphal Acts of Barnabas (written before AD 478) was the Gospel of Barnabas. There is a statement in the former concerning Barnabas which disproves they were the same: 'Barnabas, having unrolled the Gospel, *which we have received from Matthew his fellow-labourer*, began to teach the Jews.'[7] So the phrase in italics is deliberately omitted, which gives a different emphasis, then implies a gospel written by Barnabas.

The internal evidence of the gospel of Barnabas is also critical. Jesus says, 'I am not the Messiah' (Chapters 42, 48), but the Qur'an repeatedly refers to Jesus the 'Messiah'.[8] There are references to geography that are wholly inaccurate; for instance, Nazareth is not a fishing village, and Jesus could not have sailed there by boat (Chapters 20,21).

Reading through the gospel of Barnabas it is clear that if the author was not a Muslim he had strong Muslim sympathies. The expressions used in the gospel of Barnabas are very Qur'anic. Internal evidence (for example, other references to medieval culture) demonstrates a much later time of writing.

Also some Muslim scholars have actually cast doubt on the authenticity of the gospel:

As regards the 'Gospel of Barnabas' itself, there is no question that it is a medieval forgery … It contains anachronisms which can date only from the Middle Ages and not before, and shows a garbled comprehension of Islamic doctrines, calling the Prophet the 'Messiah', which Islam does not claim for him. Besides its farcical notion of sacred history, stylistically it is a mediocre parody of the Gospels, as the writings of Baha Allah are of the Koran.[9]

Another strange quirk of the gospel of Barnabas is that it also uses the text from the fourth-century Roman Catholic Vulgate translation of the Bible. It also includes exaggerations of the biblical accounts mentioning, for example, 144,000 prophets, and 10,000 prophets being slain 'by Jizebel'. These figures have particular significance in Islam. Other mistakes include the fact that this writing claims that Jesus was born when Pilate was governor, when he actually became governor in AD 26–27.

As stated earlier, the writing has the hallmark of the author having inside knowledge of Islam. In the gospel of Barnabas Jesus is said to have preached from the 'pinnacle' of the temple—hardly a comfortable place—but this is translated into Arabic by the word *dikka*, the platform used by the *imam* in mosques. Indeed, in all, some fourteen Islamic elements have been identified throughout the text. Jesus is represented as coming only for Israel, but Mohammed 'for the salvation of the whole world' (Chapter 11). The denial that Jesus is the 'Son of God' is thoroughly Qur'anic. Jesus' sermon is modelled after a Muslim *khutba* which begins with praising God and his holy Prophet (chapter 12).

The gospel of Barnabas is usually ignored by Christians, but its existence should be addressed because of the emphasis that many Muslims place on it. We can quite categorically say that this book is a medieval fabrication, possibly written by a Muslim convert. It is obviously a rewrite of the life of Jesus by someone who is basically acquainted with the Qur'an, who wanted to show that Jesus taught Islam and predicted the coming of Mohammed. The events of the cross are portrayed as in the Qur'an and other Muslim writings, in a vain attempt to discredit the historical truth of Jesus' death and resurrection.

There is also a book called *The Gospel According To Islam*, copyrighted by Dr Ahmad Shafaat in 1979, which does a similar thing.[10]

The gospel of Barnabas is simply a fabrication that is elevated to authoritative status by Muslims who see it as a means to justify their own Qur'anic teaching and to undermine the true Christian position on the person of Jesus Christ. It is an unashamed attack on Christian truth that comes out of the Muslim arena.

In our seeking to share the truth of the Lord Jesus Christ we must present the Word of God authoritatively. We must face up to the accusations and inferences made concerning the Lord Jesus Christ, and know how to answer what is untrue. Also, we must graciously and lovingly seek to bring those who hold on to error into the light of the true gospel.

Notes

1 The Light of Islam: www.fortunecity.com/marina/commodity/1089/id95.htm. Section: 'The Gospel of Barnabas': Introduction.

2 *Ibid.,* Chapter 10.

3 *Ibid.,* Chapter 38.

4 *Ibid.,* Chapter 222.

5 **Muhammad Ata ur-Rahim:** http://admin.muslimsonline.com/babri/barnabas.htm. Article: 'The History of the Gospel of Barnabas', ¶1. (An Internet article that is an extract by courtesy from his book entitled *Jesus: A Prophet of Islam* (MWH London Publishers, 1983)).

6 *Ibid.,* ¶2.

7 Answering Islam: http://answering-islam.org.uk/Barnabas/saleeb.html. Article: 'The Gospel of Barnabas', ¶11. Citing **J. Slomp,** *The Gospel Dispute, Islamochristiana* (Rome: Pontifico Institute Di Studi Arabi e d'Islamistica, 1978), p.110.

8 Sura 5:19, 75.

9 Answering Islam: http://answering-islam.org.uk/Barnabas/. Article: 'The Different Arabic Versions of the Qur'an', ¶1. Citing **Cyril Glassé**, *The Concise Encyclopedia of Islam* (San Francisco: Harper & Row, 1989), p.65.

10 **Dr Ahmed Shafaat**: www.islamicperspectives.com/GospalAccordingToIslamCh1–3.htm. Article: 'The Gospel According to Islam'. ¶7.

Comparison of Muslim and Christian world views

The following is a representation of the differing viewpoints between Muslims and western Christians. A certain amount of difference has arisen because of the contrasting cultural backgrounds represented by 'East' and 'West'. But the differences are not merely cultural: the various doctrines have made a significant impact on both societies. As varied as the Muslim countries are, there is quite significant correspondence between them through the influence of Islamic doctrine.

Concept	Muslim	Western Christian
1. Unity	Basic to every aspect of life.	Considered important only if it appears reasonable.
2. Time	Great respect for the past and tradition. Generally regarded in indefinite terms: the event is more important.	Emphasis towards the future. Past is out-dated: the future is considered a challenge.
3. Family	Solidarity of the extended family. Family responsibility is considered a major priority.	Emphasis placed more on the rights of the individual in society. (However, biblical Christianity teaches solidarity of the family unit and responsibility of relationship.)
4. Peace	Idea of harmony, health and integration = Total way of life. Look for both subjective and external objective expression.	Idea of harmony and contentment = one aspect of life. Emphasis on subjective quality; often a more spiritual ideal.
5. Honour	All-important consideration. Maintaining family honour is a major priority.	Has importance for an individual; emphasis on being an honourable person.

Comparison of Muslim and Christian world views

6. Status in Society	Associated with birth, wealth, family name, and age (often over-riding educational considerations).	Usually through some achievement, accomplished through personal hard work.
7. Individualism	Considered much less important than the group opinion, esp. in matters of welfare and decisions to be made.	Independent thinking is considered beneficial; strong personal decisions valued.
8. Secularism	A totally unacceptable trend within society; upholding the principle of theocracy is vital. Islamic law is linked to national pride.	A largely acceptable trend; belief must be seen to be relevant to life. Often considered to co-exist with spiritual expression of life (yet spiritually unhealthy!).
9. Change	Undesirable; causes identity crisis in community.	Usually valued and considered desirable; looked on as synonymous with progress.
10. Equality	A highly valued but theoretical ideal of brotherhood of man which is rarely practised consistently.	Valued ideal, with practical breakdowns, and inconsistencies.
11. Organization	Very little concern shown for structured planning and method.	Considered an imperative for successful society and fulfilling life.

Comparison of religious terminology

Concept	Muslim	Western Christian
1. Allah/God	Sovereign.	Sovereign.
	Almighty.	Almighty.
	(Holy).	Holy.
	Merciful.	Loving & Merciful.
	Unpredictable.	Unchangeable.
	Unknowable.	Concerned.
	Indifferent.	Just.
	Distant.	Personal.
2. Jesus	Prophet.	God.
	Sinless.	Perfect Man.
3. Trinity	God, Mary, Jesus	Father, Son, Holy Spirit
	(in terms of human relations).	(in terms of spiritual relationship).
4. Bible	Revelation from God.	Final and complete revelation.
	Changed, corrupted.	Fully inspired and totally infallible.
5. Word of God	Qur'an.	Holy Bible.
	Arabic—untranslatable.	Hebrew & Greek—translatable.
6. Faith	Obedience to God's law.	Expressed in works.
	Object of: God, as revealed in the Qur'an	Exercised as gift of God.
	(through Mohammed).	In Jesus as God.
		Demonstrated through works.
7. Sin	Shame, embarrassment.	Rebellion, disobedience.
	—feels guilt when caught out!	—guilt is constant reality.

8. Salvation

Requirement: faith by works.
Provider: Allah.
No assurance.

Requirement: repentance/faith, not
works. Provider: God in Christ.
Assurance granted.

9. Sanctification

Emphasis on obedience and ritual.
A conforming to the will of God by
works.

A continuing work of the Holy Spirit in
the life of a believer.
A gradual conforming to 'be like Christ'.

10. Works

Obedience to the laws of God seeking to
win his favour.
To obtain merit that will earn acceptance
with and approval of God.

The grateful response to grace.
The evidence of a changed life as
thankful obedience for having received
mercy and forgiveness.
Not to win approval of God.

11. Love

No concept of a God of love.
(N.B. the 47th name, 'The All-loving' is
not identical as 'being Love' (1 John
4:8)—it is more akin to the lower level
of 'affection').
In human relationships, it is considered
as the bond that unites the extended
family.
Expressed as loyalty.

Motivating factor of the character of
God, his nature, to grant mercy and
forgiveness.
A vital concept of love to God primarily,
in response to his love, the motivating
principle of life.
To be extended in all human relationships.
Epitomized in Christian fellowship.
Love in the family is modelled on Christ's
love for his people.

12. Supernatural

Belief in the spirit world.
Belief in angels.
Superstition maintains animistic fears.

Belief based on biblical revelation.
Belief in angels who do God's will.
Spiritual relationships to be kept within a
biblical framework.
Love for God dispels all fear.

13. Grace

Inadequate concept.
It is understood that divine favour must
be merited.
No hope apart from works.

The free, underserved unmerited favour,
goodness and mercy of the just and holy
God toward sinners.
Basis of any meaningful relationship with
God.

Glossary of Islamic words

AH	*Anno Hegirae* (Latin)—the year of Hijra.
Al-Dajjal	Antichrist.
al-kafirun	Unbelievers.
al-mu'minun	Believers.
adhan	Muslim call to prayer.
ahadith	The Hadith, or sayings of Mohammed.
alim	Presiding 'scholar' at the madrasa, who ensures the Qur'anic traditions and ritual.
Allah	Arabic word for Almighty God, but also it includes all Muslim teaching and content.
Allahu akbar	'God is great.'
aqal	Rationality.
Ashura	Commemoration of the Massacre of Karbala, on the 10th day of Muharram.
awal	Gnostic-psychological state (Sufi Islam).
awrat	'Things to be ashamed of'; those parts of the body that could elicit sexual stimulation if seen (which in the case of women are all their bodies except face and hands), exposure of which would be shameful.
aya	Verse of the Qur'an.
baraka	Blessings, giftings.
bismillah	Alternative name for shahada, the first word of the Muslim creed.
burqa	Black veil that covers head; also called niqab
Cehennam	Gehenna, i.e., Hell.
chador	Black veil that covers head to toe, sometimes just head covering.
dakka	The platform in the mosque on which the meuzzin imitates the prayer stance of the imam leading prayers (in a large mosque).
Dar al Harb	Domain of War, a territory ruled by unbelievers (infidels).
Dar al Islam	House of Islam, a state under Muslim rule.
dhimmi	Muslim regime under which Christians are tolerated, taxed, and enjoy a protected status.
Dhul Hijjah	8th Month in Muslim lunar calendar. The month of pilgrimage (hajj).
din	The religious observances of Islam.
du'a	Personal prayer.
Eid	Celebration. Name given to a special festival.
Eid ul Azha	The major festival of Islam, beginning on the tenth day of the last month of

	the calendar, lasting for four days, characterized by the sacrificing of a sheep, in memory of the ransom of Ishmael with a ram.
Eid ul Fitr	Feast of breaking the fast, celebrated at the end of the fasting month Ramadan.
fatwa	Islamic legal opinion, usually proposed by a group of leaders/lawyers (ulama).
fiqh	Islamic jurisprudence.
gusl	Complete body wash.
hadith	The tradition of Mohammed, recorded by his Companions; sayings of the prophet Mohammed.
hajj	The pilgrimage of the holy places in Mecca.
hajji	Person who has completed the hajj.
Hajr al Aswad	The Black Stone set in the Ka'aba at Mecca.
hakim	Theology of the Druze.
halal	Meat that has been slaughtered by Muslim ritual.
haram	Prohibited area.
hazam	The belt that holds the cover of the Ka'aba in place.
hijab	Muslim women's dress, head covering; dress code; used interchangeably with purdah.
Hijra	The 'flight' from Mecca on 24 September AD 622; becoming known as the year that Mohammed and his followers 'emigrated' from Mecca to Medina; the year AH 1 of the Muslim Calendar.
houri	Fair maidens (virgins) in Paradise.
ibadah	Worship, devotion.
Iblis	Alternative name for Satan (Shaitan).
ihram	The seamless white sheets worn by those doing the hajj.
ijtihad	Exercising a judgement (fatwa).
ijma	Consensus of the Muslim community.
ilah	Deity, god.
imam	The leader in a mosque (Sunni Islam); the Caliph (Shi'a Islam).
iman	Faith.
injil	Gospel, good news.
islam	Submission.
jahada	To struggle.
Jahanam	Hell.

Glossary of Islamic words

jama'at	A Muslim society, 'congregation'.
Janna	Paradise.
jihad	Holy war, fight against infidels and infidel countries.
jinn	Invisible beings in an almost parallel world.
jizya	The tax Christians must pay to Islam for their defence under Islamic rule.
jum'a	Friday; the communal prayer at the mosque, midday on Fridays.
kalima	Statement of faith.
kafir	Infidel.
Ka'aba	The cube that contains the Black Stone in the mosque in Mecca (Makkah), Saudi Arabia.
kalimah	Declaration of faith, word.
khalifa	Caliph, or Muslim leader. Literally: someone who replaces someone who died. Hence the caliph, the recognized leader, replacing Mohammed when he died.
khilafa	The government of a Muslim State.
khatib	The orator at the mosque, who gives the Friday sermon.
khutba	Friday sermon at the mosque.
kiswa	The black cover over the Ka'aba.
kursi	The lectern in the mosque on which the Qur'an is placed from which it is publicly read.
madrasa	The Muslim school connected to the mosque, giving religious instruction.
Mahdi	'The divinely guided one.' The anticipated Muslim Messiah, some say 'the son of Mary', others deny this. His coming will unite all Muslims and heralds the Day of Judgement.
maqamat	Stages of piety (Sufi Islam).
masjid	Mosque.
mawali	Non-Arab converts to Islam.
mihrab	The niche in the mosque wall that indicates the direction of the qibla.
minaret	The tower at the mosque from which the muezzin recites the adhan.
minbar	The mosque pulpit.
miraj	Mohammed's ascension into Heaven.
moulvi	A Muslim lawyer/'priest' (word used in Asia).
muezzin	The one who calls to prayer.
Muharram	First month of Muslim year.
munafiqeen	Hypocrites.

murid	Students of pirs.
mufti	A Muslim lawyer.
muslim	Adjective of the noun Islam.
musallah	An uncovered place reserved for worship. A prayer rug.
muttah	Fixed-term marriage (Shi'a Islam).
muwahhidun	Monotheists.
nabi	Anyone who is inspired by Allah, a prophet.
nafs	Passion.
namaz	Prayer, worship (same as salat).
nazir	Administrator at the mosque.
nur	Light, especially of divine inspiration; divine light.
pir	Sufi leader; a learned, spiritual guide (sheikh).
purdah	Veil, curtain. Indicating the separation of women within a household.
qadi	Judge of Muslim law (shari'ah).
qibla	The direction for prayer, the direction of Mecca.
qira'at	'Readings', portions/statements of the Qur'an handed down.
qiyas	An analogy in Muslim law.
Qur'an	The Muslim holy book, attributed to having been received by vision to Mohammed.
qurra'	'Readers', those through whom the Qur'anic passages were transmitted.
Ramadan	Ninth month of the Muslim lunar calendar, the month of fasting.
rabb	Lord, Master, Sustainer.
rak'ah	Prayer cycle.
rasul	Distinguished prophet, entrusted with a special message.
rawi, pl. ruwah	'Transmitters', in connection with formulating the Qur'an.
ruh	Spirit.
rukn al yamani	The southern corner of the Ka'aba.
sa'i	Ceremony running between the hills of Safaa and Marwa (2nd day of *hajj*).
sahih	Means sound, with respect to an authentic *hadith*.
salat	Ritual prayer.
sawm	Fasting.
shahada	The Muslim confession of faith.
Shaitan	Satan (iblis).
shari'ah	Islamic law system inspired by the Qur'an and the *sunnah*.
sheikh	A spiritual leader, also known as a *pir*.

Glossary of Islamic words

Shi'a	The followers of the Caliphate of Ali, in opposition to the Sunni choice of caliph, Abu Bakr.
sunnah	Like the *ahadith*, they are the tradition of Mohammed, specifically depicting events in the life of Mohammed, as offering examples for ethics and way of life.
Sunni	The followers of the *sunnah*, *hadith* (usually considered to be the 'orthodox' Muslims).
Sufi	A more mystical group of Muslims who come from either Sunni or Shi'a backgrounds.
sura	Chapter of the Qur'an.
syrat	The thread to be walked on the very brink of hell.
talaq	Divorce.
tariqa	Path, order, group.
tauhid	Essential oneness.
Taurat	*Torah*, the Pentateuch.
tasawwuf	The belief (science) of Sufi Islam.
taziya	Shi'a passion plays.
Ulu al 'Azam	Possessors of Power.
ulema	A recognized group of Muslim leaders of the *ummah* community of Muslims, identifies the totality of Muslims.
ummah	Muslim community.
umrah	Doing circuits around the *Ka'aba* (often referred to as the little *hajj* when performed independently of the *hajj*).
waqf	A mosque endowment.
wahdat al-wujud	The unity of being (Sufi Islam).
wudu	Ritual washing before prayer, for spiritual purity.
yaum al-din	Day of Judgement.
Zabur	Book of Psalms.
zakat	Almsgiving.

The following is a further selection of books and internet sites that would give the reader a wider view of Islam than this book is able to give. The theological stance of authors is not necessarily endorsed, and their books have to be read with discernment. This does not mean that they are not worthy of our attention. These references present valuable information on important questions. Read them with an open Bible, and with spiritual perceptiveness. Sift out those ideas and propositions that are not helpful to a faithful presentation of the gospel of sovereign grace to people of Islamic persuasion.

Jack Budd, *Islam Teach in: How to Witness to Muslims* (Red Sea Mission Team, n.d.).

Jack Budd, *Studies on Islam: A Simple Outline of the Islamic Faith* (Red Sea Mission Team, 1973).

Jens Christensen, *The Practical Approach to Muslims* (The North Africa Mission, 1977).

J. Elder, *The Biblical Approach to the Muslim* (Leadership Instruction and Training International, n.d.).

Dr Norman Geisler, 'Is There a Gospel of Barnabas?' in *The Baker Encyclopedia of Christian Apologetics* (Grand Rapids: Baker Book House, 1999). (Internet pdf format edition: www.ankerberg.com/Articles/_PDFArchives/theological-dictionary/TD3W0102.pdf) Also found in the author's *Answering Islam,* appendix 3.

Dr Norman Geisler & Abdul Saleeb, *Answering Islam* (Grand Rapids: Baker Book House, 1993).

Alfred Guillaume, *Islam* (Harmondsworth: Penguin Books, 1977, 1954).

Abdiyah A. A. Haqq, *Sharing Your Faith with a Muslim* (Bethany Fellowship, 1980).

G. K. Harris, *How To Lead Moslems To Christ* (China Inland Mission, 1957).

Bassam Madamy, M., *Sharing God's Word With A Muslim* (The Back to God Hour Publications, 1981).

C. R. Marsh, *Share Your Faith With A Muslim* (Chicago: Moody Press, 1975).

Don M. McCurry, ed., *The Gospel and Islam* (MARC, 1979).

Mohammad Muslehuddin, *Sociology and Islam* (Lahore: Islamic Publications, 1977).

Geoffrey Parrinder, *Jesus in the Qur'an* (Faber and Faber, 1965).

Phil Parshall, *Beyond the Mosque* (Grand Rapids: Baker Book House, 1985).

Phil Parshall, *Bridges to Islam* (Grand Rapids: Baker Book House, 1983).

Phil Parshall, *Understanding Muslim Teaching and Traditions* (Grand Rapids: Baker Book House, 2002).

Phil Parshall, *New Paths in Muslim Evangelism* (Grand Rapids: Baker Book House, 1980).

Phil Parshall, *The Fortress and the Fire* (Bombay: Gospel Literature Service, 1976).

Phil and Julie Parshall, *Lifting The Veil* (Gabriel Resources, 2003).

Tony Payne, *Islam In Our Backyard* (Matthias Media, 2002).

Qur'an: The only authoritative edition is considered to be the Arabic, according to the Muslim. The following English renderings have been quoted in this book. Quotations have been taken from Dawood unless otherwise stated.

A. J. Arberry, *The Koran Interpreted* (Macmillan, 1955).

N. J. Dawood, *The Koran* (Harmondsworth: Penguin Books, 1956).

Mohammed M. Pickthall, *The Meaning of the Glorious Koran* (Mentor Books, New American Library, Inc., n.d.).

Dr Rashad Khalifa, *Authorized English Translation of Qur'an,* software version: http://www.submission.org/quran.html.

Reaching Muslims Today (North Africa Mission, 1976).

Maxime Rodinson, *Mohammed* (Harmondsworth: Penguin Books, 1976, 1972).

Dr Anis A Shorosh, *Islam Revealed* (Nashville: Nelson, 1988).

H. Spencer, *Islam and the Gospel of God* (Delhi: ISPCK, 1956).

W. St. Clair-Tisdall, *The Sources of Islam* (Edinburgh: T. & T. Clark, reprinted by Birmingham Bible Institute Press, n.d.).

Vivienne Stacey, *Practical Lessons for Evangelism Among Muslims* (Wiesbaden: Orientdienst eV., n.d.).

H.U. Weitbrecht Stanton, *The Teaching of the Qur'an* (SPCK, 1969).

Ahmad Zaky Tuffaha, *Al-Mar'ah Wal- Islam* (Beirut: Dar al-Kitab al-Lubnani, first edition, 1985).

S.M. Zwemer, *Translations of the Koran,* Muslim World, V, (1915).

Internet sites

The Internet is a valuable source of information and the following are chosen for their value in being resources of Islamic thinking and responses. The sites recorded here are those that the author has accessed between April 2003 and August 2004. The site list is by no means exhaustive. If a link does not work, take a key phrase or name and search for it in your internet browser.

Humayun Ansari, www.fieri.it/convegni/giu2003/ansary.pdf. *The Legal Status of Muslims in the UK,* June 2003.

Abdullah al Araby, www.islamreview.com/articles/godvsallah.shtml. Article: 'God of Christianity vs. Allah of Islam'.

Answering-Islam: http://answering-islam.org. This Christian site has many interesting papers on Islam.

al-Bayyinah.com: http://www.al-bayyinah.com/articles.asp. *On the Authenticity of the Qur'an*, by Abdur-Raheem Green, in *Muslim Answers*.

Lucy Berrington, *Why British Women Are Turning to Islam,* report by *The Times* newspaper, dated Tuesday 9th November 1993: www.afi.org.uk/,iscon/w/BRITISH.HTM.

Nick Compton, 'The New Face of Islam', article in *The Evening Standard,* 15th March, 2002, published on website: www.thetruereligion.org/newface.htm.

Ghadir Khumm, http://www.al-islam.org/ghadir/. Comprehensive source of *hadith*.

Dr Alan Godlas (University of Georgia): www.uga.edu/islam/Sufism.html. Article: 'Sufi's Many Paths'.

Samuel Green, http://answering-islam.org/Green/barnabas.htm. Article: 'The Gospel of Barnabas'.

Dr Muhammad Ali al-Hashimi, *The Ideal Muslim Woman*, published on the web: http://www.usc.edu/dept/MSA/humanrelations/womeninislam/idealmuslimah/Jamiatul Ulama (Council of Muslim Theologians).

A source of *Hadith*: www.jamiat.org.za.

Into The Light. http://islam.itl.org.uk/barnabas/. Article: 'The Gospel of Barnabas'.

Introduction to Islam: www.barghouti.com/islam: Compiled by Dr Mohamed Ibrahim Elmasry.

Muslim Hope: www.muslimhope.com. Christian site with detailed Muslim information.

Ottawa Muslim Network: www.ottawamuslim.net. Shows how Muslims cope in a western country.

Qur'an and Sunnah Society, Canada: www.qss.org/.

Submission, www.submission.org. An Islamic site claiming 'Best source of Islam on the internet.'

Ummah: www.ummah.net; or www.ummah.org.uk. An Arabic community site.

ibn Waraq, 'Virgins? What Virgins?' *Guardian Unlimited,* Saturday January 12, 2002, *Guardian* Newspaper Report www.guardian.co.uk/saturday_review/story/0,3605,631332,00.html.

Index

A

Index